Assessing Intelligence

Assessing Intelligence

The Bildungsroman and the Politics of
Human Potential in England, 1860–1910

Sara Lyons

EDINBURGH
University Press

Edinburgh University Press is one of the leading university presses in the UK. We publish academic books and journals in our selected subject areas across the humanities and social sciences, combining cutting-edge scholarship with high editorial and production values to produce academic works of lasting importance. For more information visit our website: edinburghuniversitypress.com

Edinburgh University Press Ltd
The Tun – Holyrood Road
12(2f) Jackson's Entry
Edinburgh EH8 8PJ

Typeset in 11/13pt Sabon
by Cheshire Typesetting Ltd, Cuddington, Cheshire, and
printed and bound in Great Britain

A CIP record for this book is available from the British Library

ISBN 978 1 4744 9766 4 (hardback)
ISBN 978 1 4744 9768 8 (webready PDF)
ISBN 978 1 4744 9769 5 (epub)

Contents

Acknowledgements

The research for this book was funded by an Arts and Humanities Research Council (AHRC) Early Career Research Grant entitled Literary Culture, Meritocracy, and the Assessment of Intelligence in Britain and the United States, 1880–1920. I am incredibly grateful to my collaborator, Dr Michael Collins, whose friendship and enthusiasm for the project sustained me throughout. I am also indebted to Natasha Periyan, who joined the project late but quickly became indispensable to it. Michael's work on meritocracy and the intelligence concept in American literature and Natasha's complementary work on English modernism have informed and enriched this book immeasurably. Their conversation and camaraderie helped make this unwritable book writable after all.

This book was also enriched by the questions and comments offered by participants and audiences at many conferences, seminars, and public events over the past six years. I especially wish to thank the participants at the Literature, Education, and the Sciences of the Mind conference held at the University of Kent in 2018 and the audiences at the University of Oxford Nineteenth Century Research Seminar, the Eighteenth/Nineteenth Century Studies Seminar at the University of Sussex, and the Nineteenth Century Graduate Seminar at the University of Cambridge. Special thanks are due to Cathy Waters and Michael Davis, for offering insightful feedback on various chapters. I wish to thank the anonymous reviewers at Edinburgh University Press, whose warm reader's reports rekindled my faith in the project in the darkest days of lockdown. Thanks also go to my colleagues in the School of English at the University of Kent for their solidarity in difficult times.

Sections of this book have appeared in print before. I am grateful to publishers for allowing me to reproduce sections from '"You Must be as Clever as We Think You": Assessing Intelligence in Henry James's *The Tragic Muse*', *Modern Philology* 115.1 (2017), pp. 105–30; 'Thomas Hardy and the Value of Brains', *Victorian Literature and Culture* 48.2 (2020), pp. 327–59; and 'Recent Work in Victorian Studies and the Bildungsroman', *Literature Compass* 15.4 (2018).

I want to thank Kate and Andre van Schaik for their heroic stint in Canterbury and for providing childcare just when I needed to finish the manuscript. As always, my greatest debt is to Noah Moxham, whose patience and love make everything possible. This book is for Ada, whose education has just begun.

Series Preface

Nineteenth-Century and Neo-Victorian Cultures
Series Editors: Ruth Heholt and Joanne Ella Parsons

This interdisciplinary series provides space for full and detailed scholarly discussions on nineteenth-century and Neo-Victorian cultures. Drawing on radical and cutting-edge research, volumes explore and challenge existing discourses, as well as providing an engaging reassessment of the time period. The series encourages debates about decolonising nineteenth-century cultures, histories, and scholarship, as well as raising questions about diversities. Encompassing art, literature, history, performance, theatre studies, film and TV studies, medical and the wider humanities, *Nineteenth Century and Neo-Victorian Cultures* is dedicated to publishing pioneering research that focuses on the Victorian era in its broadest and most diverse sense.

Introduction

> Equality? So far from being the 'holy law of nature', as Marat was
> wont to affirm, it is flat blasphemy against that law. Inequality
> is everywhere her rule and is the primary condition of progress.
> Man is nothing but the product of vast inequalities, of successive
> variations of previous animal types . . .
>
> — W. S. Lilly[1]

Toward the close of the nineteenth century in England, a chorus
of scientists and intellectuals proclaimed that modern understandings of human evolution and heredity had disproven once and for
all the American and French revolutionary doctrine of 'natural
equality'. Full democracy and universal education, however noble
as ideals, were essentially against nature, a denial of the 'vast
inequalities' which stratify the human species. For these belated
polemicists against American and French revolutionary ideals, the
problem with natural *in*equality — and the reason it still needed to
be defended against latter-day 'Rousseauists' – is that it manifests
itself most profoundly in an elusive essence: intelligence.[2]

The first practical intelligence test and the concept of IQ were
still some years away: it was not until 1905 that the French psychologists Alfred Binet and Théodore Simon would publish their
famous intelligence test and, in Simon's words, 'secure the idea of
human inequality on a basis other than that of a vague impression'.[3] By that time, English scientists and psychologists had been
dreaming about a viable test of intelligence for half a century, and
the components of the concept of IQ were familiar to the public
even if there was no easy shorthand for how they fit together.
Over the course of the nineteenth century, a new scientific model

I

of the human mind had emerged. 'Intelligence' named the continuity between human and animal minds as well the mind's capacity to function like a machine. This animal-like and machine-like capacity was the product of evolutionary adaptations, and largely – perhaps overwhelmingly – determined by heredity. It was a measurable entity in the brain (even if no entirely satisfactory measure had yet been found). Intelligence also came to be understood as homogenous 'general ability' which varies in quantity but not in kind among people and is thus open to comparison and ranking. By extension, intelligence can also be conceptualised in statistical terms, as something which organises itself around an average or a norm in a population: everyone can be said to possess above, below, or average intelligence. And lastly, these propositions can be demonstrated through the most ordinary type of scientific test: written examinations of the kind sat by school and university students. These claims about intelligence were associated without being inexorably linked; it was, of course, possible to endorse one or some of them without endorsing others. They are nonetheless the main components of the modern IQ notion of intelligence, and their high ideological stakes were obvious even if their scientific basis remained uncertain.

Catherine Malabou observes that 'intelligence' assumed the philosophical pride of place in the nineteenth century that 'reason' had occupied during the Enlightenment. However, nineteenth-century 'intelligence' was also a rebuke to the universalist scope of Enlightenment reason:

> The reign of intelligence was accompanied by an entire set of vocabulary for measurement, scales, and tests, all which presented so many enemies to [the Enlightenment] notion of the universal [. . .] Quantification necessarily implies inequality.[4]

For many of the architects and partisans of the new scientific model of intelligence in England, this implicit inequality was its virtue: it promised to make social judgements about mental differences and relative mental worth objective. It also promised to make the 'natural' basis of social inequality both provable and calculable, though whether to explain the existing social order or to create a new one was often unclear. A science of intelligence might enable a new meritocracy: a more rational world where social positions corresponded to mental capacities. It might even become possible to breed for intelligence and engineer a eugenic utopia. Yet 'intelligence' still had the status of a 'brashly modern notion', as Lorraine Daston writes.[5] And as the fin de siècle polemics against Enlightenment philosophers suggest, the exponents of the new paradigm were conscious that intelligence remained the '*unfounded* foundation of the origin of inequality among us all', to borrow Malabou's words (my italics).[6] Although science seemed to have settled the question, Grant Allen, Benjamin Kidd, Havelock Ellis, T. H. Huxley, Francis Galton, Henry Maudsley, H. G. Wells, and many other lesser luminaries still felt it necessary to denounce the stupidity of the doctrine of natural equality, which clearly had a persistent cultural vitality: indeed, Huxley was motivated to attack it because he was convinced it was working 'sad mischief' in the present (he was thinking primarily of the socialist movement).[7] And it was also necessary to appeal to the common sense and folk wisdom to argue the case for scientific intelligence. Huxley tried to distil it into a proverb: 'proclaim human equality as loudly as you like, Witless will serve his brother'.[8]

The biologisation of the mind accomplished by Victorian scientists and psychologists destabilised ancient and religious distinctions between mind and body, reason and instinct, and human and animal.[9] The new conception of intelligence which emerged from those destabilisations might be understood as an attempt to re-establish a rational ordering principle and a traditional hierarchy of value from within what could seem a relativistic morass. It might also be understood as an attempt to salvage a sense of individual distinction or a humanist soul-concept from the disenchantments of evolutionary science and biological psychology (often known in the period as 'physiological psychology'). Daston suggests that there was relative 'apathy' concerning individual mental differences in the early modern period, since these were 'dwarfed, according to the theologians, by the differences between humans and animals. This latter distinction completely overshadowed the minor distinctions among human minds.'[10] But when intelligence is recast as a materialist and evolutionary phenomenon in the second half of the nineteenth century, the reverse logic obtains: the erosion of the distinction between human and animal means that intellectual differences between humans come to matter intensely. The new cultural obsession with establishing the different degrees of intelligence possessed by individuals and groups and with articulating how these differences related to hierarchies of gender, class, and race served to 'sancti[fy] chasms between different types of humans', in Kurt Danziger's words.[11] This logic is certainly discernible in Charles Darwin's *The Descent of Man and Selection in Relation to Sex* (1871). The fact that human and animal 'mental powers' are separated not by any ontological gap but simply by 'numberless gradations' paradoxically both weakens and sharpens the significance of such distinctions within the exclusively human realm, which likewise must be understood as both subtle in their nature and profound in their cumulative effects.[12] As so often in Victorian scientific discussions of intelligence, archetypes of English genius – Shakespeare and Newton – must be called upon to ease the vertigo of lost distinctions:

> Man bears in his bodily structure clear traces of his descent from some lower form; but it may be urged that, as man differs greatly in his mental power from all other animals, there must be some error in this conclusion. No doubt the difference in this respect is enormous, even if we compare the mind of one of the lowest savages, who has no words to express any number higher than four, and one who uses hardly any abstract terms for common objects, with that of the most highly organised ape. The difference would, no doubt, still remain immense [. . .] The Fuegians rank amongst the lowest barbarians; but I was continually struck with surprise how closely the three natives on board H. M. S. 'Beagle' [. . .] resembled us [. . .] in most of our mental faculties [. . .]
>
> If no organic being excepting man had possessed any mental power, or if his powers had been of a wholly different nature from those of the lower animals, then we should never have been able to convince ourselves that our highest faculties had been gradually developed. But it can be shewn there is no fundamental difference of this kind. We must admit that there is a much wider interval in mental power between one of the lowest fishes, a lamprey or lancelet, and one of the higher apes, than between an ape and a man; yet this interval is filled up by numberless gradations [. . .] Nor is the difference slight in intellect, between a savage who uses hardly an abstract term, and a Newton and a Shakespeare. Differences of this kind between the highest men of the highest races and the lowest races, are connected by the finest gradations.[13]

Although the Victorian scientific understanding of intelligence would come to hinge upon Darwin's work, its three original architects in England were Alexander Bain, Herbert Spencer, and Darwin's cousin, Galton. As I explain below, the IQ concept began incubating in their works in the 1850s and 1860s as part of their varying efforts to come to terms with the fact that phrenology – the first effort to develop a materialist science of mental differences – had lost its credibility. The roots of the intelligence test and the concept of IQ in nineteenth-century eugenics and Social Darwinism, particularly in the work of Galton and Spencer, are generally acknowledged in histories of these phenomena, if often only in passing.[14] However, the extent to which intelligence became a biopolitical concern in Victorian England is not widely recognised. In Michel Foucault's work, 'biopolitics' refers to a transformation of political power which took place in the nineteenth century as states attempted to harness the insights of the life sciences and thereby take control of the biological. In place of the old sovereign right 'to take life and let live', states now assumed the prerogative to 'make live and to let die': that is, to nurture and regulate the health of the social body.[15] Foucault suggests that biopower emerges both through and alongside the forms of disciplinary power which he analysed in *Discipline and Punish* (1975). Where disciplinary power aims to render individual bodies useful and docile through techniques such as training and surveillance, biopower 'deals with the population as a political problem, as a problem that is at once scientific and political'.[16] It is characterised by efforts to measure and intervene in processes such as birth, death, reproduction, and disease as they play out at the level of the collective. The population is turned into a calculable, governable object through methods such as demography and statistics, and the individual is subsumed under the abstract imperatives of the 'species', or biological health in the aggregate.[17] Foucault closely identifies biopolitics with state racism, which he characterises as an impulse to fragment and stratify the human species into superior and inferior 'races', or 'healthy' and 'degenerate' bodies – a logic which he suggests reached its twentieth-century apogee in Nazi eugenics.[18] However, he also emphasises the more subtle and morally ambiguous manifestations of biopower in capitalist processes and state welfare systems, and claims that its characteristic *modus operandi* is not through laws or violent force but through the pressure of norms.[19] A biopolitical society is a 'normalising society', one in which institutions and social discourses 'measure, appraise, and hierarchise' around norms and which incites people to internalise and perpetuate norms for themselves.[20]

Although Foucault remarks in passing that biopolitics is concerned with optimising the 'aptitudes' of the population, he does not really address the fact that intelligence had been transformed into a measurable, biological entity in the nineteenth century.[21] Ansgar Allen has recently suggested how Foucault's notion of biopower illuminates the assumptions about intellectual ability circulating within the state education system which evolved in England following the Education Act of 1870. In particular, Allen highlights the continuities between Galton's eugenicist model of intelligence and the rationality and practices of the state school system, especially in its reliance on examinations.[22] Over the course of the nineteenth century, the formal written exam and procedures of grading, ranking, and prizes pioneered at Oxford and Cambridge universities in the eighteenth century came to dominate academic life at those institutions while also migrating to other contexts, most notably the Civil Service and the expanding mass education system and its 'scholarship ladder'.[23] As Gillian Sutherland, Simon Szreter, and Adrian Wooldridge have shown, Victorian examination culture generated a desire to distinguish between natural ability and acquired knowledge, and this in turn helped to crystallise the IQ concept: that is, the notion of intelligence as a general, innate quality which can be objectively captured by exams.[24]

This book explores how novelists engaged with the new scientific conception of intelligence and the meritocratic ideal entangled with it. In particular, it considers how novelists used the *Bildungsroman*, or the novel of education and personal development, to explore whether, and how, mental worth may be justly evaluated. The five writers considered in the book – George Eliot, Thomas Hardy, Henry James, H. G. Wells, and Virginia Woolf – have been chosen because they were all unusually well informed about contemporary psychology and (with the possible exception of James) deeply invested in the politics of education. As the book will demonstrate, all five novelists confronted the implications of the emerging IQ version of intelligence and used the *Bildungsroman* form to think through their ambivalence toward it. These *Bildungsromane* turn away – often regretfully – from the Romantic ideals of creativity and talent that once underpinned the form, and instead valorise mediocrity and failure. This Introduction explains how intelligence became a biopolitical concept and the crux of debates about social inequality and human potential in the second half of the nineteenth century in England. It then turns to the work of Jacques Rancière to theorise how Victorian and Edwardian *Bildungsromane* articulate egalitarian principles despite their apparent focus upon a 'gifted' individual.

The emergence of the intelligence concept in Victorian psychology

Mid-Victorian scientists and psychologists inherited the dream of measurable intelligence from the science of phrenology. Phrenology was not only an influential 'science of man' but a popular social movement in England between the 1820s and the 1850s.[25] The possibility that a person's innate characteristics and aptitudes might be divined from the formation of his or her skull helped to popularise the still controversial idea that the mind is a material entity and, as such, open to empirical investigation. It also diffused the idea that the mind's capacities may be scored on a scale and compared to population averages (and thereby kindled the popular desire to score better than those imagined averages).[26] As is often remarked, phrenology's focus on innate, measurable faculties did not produce an entirely deterministic view of the mind or of human potential. In England, phrenology was associated with optimistic ideals of education and social mobility. It appealed to ambitious, often marginalised members of the middle and lower classes and could seem to promise a new social hierarchy based upon natural talents.[27] However, by the 1850s, the scientific credibility of phrenology was on the wane. The various efforts of Bain, Spencer, and Galton both to preserve and overhaul the phrenological paradigm led them toward an IQ model of human intelligence.

The Scottish psychologist Bain was especially keen to emphasise the continuity between phrenology and his own theory of mental differences. Bain wanted to vindicate two aspects of phrenology: first, its wholly materialist model of the mind; and second, its effort to produce an ethology, or a science of character.[28] Bain tends to be overlooked in histories of intelligence testing and the notion of IQ, but he is nevertheless a significant figure in the nineteenth-century effort to develop a scientific model of intelligence.[29] Bain began to develop a theory of intelligence in his first major work of psychology, *The Senses and the Intellect* (1855), though it receives its first succinct formulation in his *On the Study of Character: Including an Estimate of Phrenology* (1861) and is then recapitulated faithfully in subsequent works.[30] According to Bain, intelligence has three basic components. First, it is the power of discrimination – drawing accurate distinctions.[31] Second, it is a good memory – 'the power of retentiveness'.[32] Third, it is the 'identifying power': accurate perception of similarity.[33] In this, Bain was trying to translate basic precepts of associationist psychology – that is, empiricist psychology – into a new kind of differential psychology: that is, he was trying to theorise not just how minds work, but why some minds work better than others.[34] Like Galton after him, Bain was particularly interested in theorising the underlying principles that give rise to 'intellectual ability of a higher order' and to varieties of genius.[35] Classifying individual differences had been central to phrenology too, but phrenology proposed a pluralistic model of intelligence: each person is a cluster of diverse traits and capacities. The novelty of Bain's project lay in his attempt to theorise the 'pure essentials of intelligence' or 'intellect in general': what would come to be known as g, or general intelligence, in twentieth-century psychology.[36]

Unlike Spencer or Galton, Bain did not grapple very fully with the evolutionary dimensions of human intelligence, nor with the question of heredity. He nevertheless understood differences in intelligence to have biological origins and attempted to articulate what would come to be known as a 'hard' hereditarian position. He believed that differences in intelligence were heritable by-products of constitution and brain size, and that parents bequeathed this biological ability to their offspring without passing on any characteristics that they had acquired during their lifetimes.[37] Probably under the influence of Galton, Bain speculated that an intelligence-based eugenics programme might be possible, though he seems to venture this idea for rhetorical effect rather than as a serious proposition: he was attempting to clarify how his own 'hard' hereditarian conception of intelligence differed from the then influential 'soft' or Lamarckian conception.[38] Bain's interest in developing a science of intellectual differences lay in its meritocratic rather than its eugenic possibilities. Bain believed that a science of 'aptitudes' would enable men to be allocated to appropriate careers and social positions:

> There is nothing more certain, than that the discriminating knowledge of individual character is a primary condition of much of the social

improvement that the present age is panting for. The getting the right man into the right place is mainly a problem of the judgment of character; the mere wish to promote the fitting person is nugatory in the absence of the discrimination.[39]

Like Bain's, Spencer's theory of intelligence grew partly out of his desire to vindicate the premises of phrenology: that people vary in their mental characteristics, and that these variations are biological in origin. For Spencer, one of basic questions of psychology is, 'Whence arise the different degrees of power possessed by different races of organisms, and different individuals of the same race?'[40] However, also like Bain, Spencer became dissatisfied with phrenology's division of the mind into separate faculties.[41] In his first major work of psychology, *Principles of Psychology* (1855), he uses 'intelligence' as an umbrella term for all mental operations, from the simplest to the most sophisticated.[42] Spencer was the first English-language writer to adopt 'intelligence' as a scientific term, and he uses it to undermine traditional distinctions between human and animal, mind and body, instinct and intellect.[43] In his *Principles of Psychology*, the rhetorical force of the term 'intelligence' is thus to level familiar hierarchies: Spencer aims to relativise human reason and place it on a continuum with animal instinct. In this sense, intelligence has no special moral or humanist significance for Spencer; it is simply the mechanism by which organisms adapt more or less successfully to their environments.[44]

Spencer's 'law of intelligence' is synonymous with his theory of evolution.[45] In his account, evolution is a process wherein simple, incoherent forms develop into heterogeneous ones with coordinated parts. This entails a division of labour: organisms become internally differentiated, with structures specialising in particular functions.[46] The ultimate *telos* of Spencerian evolution is equilibrium, or, in human terms, 'perfection and complete happiness': all organisms strive to adjust themselves ever more subtly to their environments.[47] The more subtle the correspondence between an organism and its environment, the more intelligence it possesses. These are for Spencer universal laws, accounting equally well for the development of organisms and the physics of the universe as for the nature of human consciousness and the history of civilisation.[48]

The fact that Spencer treats 'intelligence' as a law of biology gives the term an aura of scientific neutrality in his work. Yet for

Spencer 'intelligence' is also the concept which justifies understanding evolution as a moral, teleological process and arranging the human species into a natural hierarchy. Those who flourish in the struggle for existence prove the superiority of their intelligence – that is, their greater capacity for adaptation.[49] However, this does not mean that Spencer equated high intelligence with brute physical strength or success in war. He was a pacifist, and he claimed that societies became more peaceful and rational as evolution progressed. Spencer's ideal man is an altruistic intellectual whose capacities and sentiments are calibrated to the 'bloodless competition' of modern industrial capitalism.[50] It is in this sense that evolution – and, by extension, intelligence – acquires a heavy axiological burden in his analysis. His conception of intelligence is, in many respects, a recognisably puritanical moral code: the Protestant work ethic reified into biological law. He claims that industrial societies which promote freedom and individualism and have complex divisions of labour, with intellectual and physical forms of work clearly demarcated, are more advanced in evolutionary terms.[51] Men who prosper in such societies, and particularly those who perform the most intellectually specialised work within them, are the most fit or evolved.[52] This is because the skills and virtues that favour success – self-discipline, independence, rational cooperation – are organic traits, attesting to a person's underlying biological quality. Those who fail to thrive are 'unworthy' in both moral and biological terms.[53] Spencer also believed that intellectual ability was negatively correlated with sexual libido: libidinous men dissipated their mental vitality.[54] By a similar though more essentialist logic, women's intellects were congenitally impaired by the complexity of the female reproductive system.[55] The evolutionary scale is thus an intellectual and moral great chain of being, and an individual's place within it can be broadly assessed according to the indices of race, gender, sexuality, and class. The 'cultivated European', particularly the European scientific genius, is at the pinnacle of the scale, and women, non-European races and cultures, and the poor and labouring classes are all examples of more primitive development.[56]

The fact that Spencer identified intelligence with the capacity for adaptation and evolutionary progress would seem to imply that he emphasised human plasticity and rejected any notion of a fixed mental endowment. Indeed, his repudiation of phrenology was partly due to his difficulty with the fact that it treated mental characteristics as immutable, and therefore could not explain the phenomenon of evolutionary change.[57] By the time he wrote *Principles of Psychology*, he had adopted an associationist theory of the mind, but he jettisoned a cardinal tenet of associationist tradition: that the mind is a blank slate at birth, and that individuals are therefore malleable.[58] Spencer agreed with the associationist tradition that the mind is the product of experiences and has no innate ideas in a metaphysical sense. However, he interpreted 'experience' in evolutionary terms, not individual ones. His understanding of evolution hinges on a Lamarckian model of use-inheritance; over generations, habits 'become organic' and harden into innate traits.[59] Evolutionary progress thus occurs meaningfully at the level of the species, not within the individual; the slow pace of evolution means that the individual has minimal agency over his or her own character and fate, even though he or she may hope to contribute to the advancement of the species. This logic meant that Spencer believed in the importance of education, especially scientific education, to the progress of society, but thought that individuals could do little to improve their inborn characteristics, including their intellectual aptitude.[60] Spencer's evolutionary theory reserves all of its sense of dynamism for the human species as a whole; the individual is largely locked in place by the habits of his or her ancestors. 'Inherited constitution must ever be the chief factor in determining character,' he wrote in his autobiography.[61]

Spencer combined his faith in the overarching beneficence and rationality of evolution with a concept of natural selection. This partly accounts for the jarring shifts between his hopes for a utopia of altruists and his notorious emphasis upon the necessity of 'purifying' society of the 'essentially faulty', though such shifts were present in his work prior to the publication of Darwin's *On the Origin of Species* (1859).[62] In *Social Statics* (1851), he asserted that nature wisely culls the intellectually unfit just as surely as it does the physically weak:

Nature just as much insists on fitness between mental character and circumstances, as between physical character and circumstance [. . .] He on whom his own stupidity, or vice, or idleness, entails loss of life, must, in the generalisations of philosophy, be classed with the victims of weak viscera or unformed limbs [. . .] Beings thus imperfect are nature's failures, and are recalled by her laws when found to be such. Along with the rest they are put upon trial [. . .] If they are not sufficiently complete to live, they die, and it is best that they should die.[63]

In proclaiming 'nature' the ultimate arbiter of intellectual fitness, Spencer was renouncing his original project of rendering mental abilities measurable. When he was an enthusiastic phrenologist, he had designed a 'cephalograph' – an instrument for making skull measurements more accurate.[64] But by the time he wrote *Social Statics* in 1851, he had come to the conclusion that there was no objective means of determining 'relative merits' and 'degrees of [intellectual] ability', and for that reason, the political equality of all – including women – must be affirmed.[65] Spencer's belief in the natural inequality of human beings is paradoxically the grounds of his belief in political equality. He maintains that the state must remain agnostic on the question of the individual's mental capacities, and merely grant sufficient freedom for each to develop those capacities as far as he or she is capable.[66] He took this position to a libertarian extreme: the state must not presume to evaluate or shape the capacities of the individual in any way, including through education.[67] Spencer is thus a contradictory figure in relation to the emergence of a biopolitics of intelligence. As Danziger writes, Spencer popularises an 'image of the world as an arena in which living beings [are] constantly being tested' and graded on the basis of their intelligence.[68] Yet he was extremely hostile to the idea that intelligence and merit are open to objective measurement, and to the idea that educational institutions – especially state-run schools – have a right to adjudicate upon the question of a person's mental capacities.

Galton is often called the 'father of eugenics'. He is also commonly identified as the father of the modern IQ notion of intelligence. These two claims to fame, or to notoriety, are closely related: for Galton, eugenics and the effort to formulate a scientific theory of intelligence were the same consuming project. Galton both coined the term 'eugenics' (literally, 'good birth') and made intelligence the master concept of the eugenics movement in England. Like Spencer and Bain, Galton had an early interest in phrenology, and in fact consulted a phrenologist when attempting to settle upon a career for himself.[69] When he was a schoolboy at King Edward's School, a Cambridge examiner had measured Galton's head and those of his classmates and attempted to correlate their phrenological measurements with their exam results:

a method for measuring intelligence that Galton himself would often replicate, though he employed craniometry (the measurement of skull size) rather than phrenological techniques.[70]

Galton's efforts to demonstrate the fundamentally heritable nature of intelligence first reached the public in the form of an essay, 'Hereditary Talent and Character' in 1865, and were later elaborated in his book *Hereditary Genius: An Inquiry into its Laws and Consequences* (1869). In the Preface to the 1892 edition of the book, Galton clarifies that the 'idea of investigating the subject of hereditary genius occurred to me during the course of a purely ethnological enquiry into the mental peculiarities of different races'.[71] Galton had spent two years in Southern Africa and detailed his travels in a memoir for the Royal Geographical Society and a popular book published in 1853. As Raymond Fancher has shown, Galton's comparative evaluations of the different African groups he encountered are virulent in their racism even by mid-Victorian standards.[72] *Hereditary Genius* is an attempt to turn that ethnological gaze back on England and to analyse intellectual differences in the same way as he had analysed racial differences: as innate, empirically observable characteristics that can be used to make judgements of inferiority and superiority and construct a graded hierarchy of human worth.

Hereditary Genius received considerable attention in the popular press upon its first publication, though it met with hostility as well as more respectful critique at the hands of reviewers.[73] On the other hand, it was granted legitimacy by notable members of the scientific community: it was favourably reviewed by Alfred Russel Wallace, for example.[74] Most crucially, Galton changed Darwin's mind about intelligence. Prior to reading *Hereditary Genius*, Darwin professed a liberal, mid-Victorian faith in the rough equality of human capacity and in the gospel of work. Afterwards, Darwin wrote to his cousin: 'You have made a convert of an opponent in one sense, for I have always maintained that, excepting fools, men did not differ much in intellect, only in zeal and hard work.'[75] Galton's riposte alchemises hard work into proof of biological destiny: 'Character, including the aptitude for hard work, is heritable like every other faculty.'[76] In the *Descent of Man*, Darwin treats Galton's theory of intelligence as established science: 'we now know, through the admirable labours of Mr. Galton, that genius tends to be inherited'.[77] In his autobiography, Darwin wrote, 'I am inclined to agree with Galton in believing that education and environment produce only a small effect on the mind of anyone, and that most of our qualities are innate.'[78]

Galton's assimilation of effort into the category of predetermined biological inheritance captures the totalising logic of his work on intellectual ability. Galton sought to prove the fundamentally heritable nature of intelligence by charting genealogies of 'eminent men' and generating statistics from that data. Galton's science depended on the premise that English society was in the 1860s and always had been essentially (if somewhat imperfectly) meritocratic: 'social hindrances cannot impede men of high ability from becoming eminent'.[79] He goes on:

> High reputation is a pretty accurate test of high ability [. . .] I look upon social and professional life as a continuous examination. All are candidates for the good opinions of others, and for success in their several professions, and they achieve success in proportion as the general estimate is large of their aggregate merits. In ordinary scholastic examinations marks are allotted in stated proportions to various specified subjects [. . .] The world, in the same way, but almost unconsciously, allots marks to men [. . .] The metaphor of an examination may be stretched much further. As there are alternative groups in any one of which a candidate may obtain honours, so it is with reputations.[80]

The 'metaphor' of the examination expands imperiously in Galton's work. He loses sight of the fact that it is a metaphor and becomes absorbed in mathematising social reputation – 'eminence' – and proclaiming that the results disclose the truth of biological essence.

Hereditary Genius works by the same logic as the famous guides to the titled aristocracy, Debrett's and Burke's, but with a new meritocratic claim to legitimacy: entry is, at least ostensibly, not an accident of birth but a matter of proven intellectual ability.[81] Yet Galton's hard hereditarian understanding of biology renders intellectual ability itself an accident of birth. Although he uses the term 'genius' in his title, Galton's project is to divest that word of its quasi-mystical Romantic status and the clouds of sublimity and spirituality it trailed in its wake.[82] Romantic sentimentality about mad, eccentric, or marginalised geniuses also has no place in his model of intelligence: because his calculations rely on reputation – itself taken to be a self-evident social fact – his version of genius essentially abides by social norms and rises to public standards of intelligibility. More radically, Galton divests genius of its Romantic associations with individual creativity and originality. Exam performance and professional status displace the work of art, the invention, and the discovery as the proper measures of intellectual greatness. And genius matters to Galton primarily as population data: it does not truly belong to individuals or even to the families through which it circulates, but to the future of the 'race' and of the species. As Robin Durnford emphasises in her brilliant study of Galton, Galton's interest in genealogy is futurological rather than antiquarian: his 'eminent families' are significant only in aggregate and as 'eugenic data' which could allow the intelligence of the human species to be controlled and optimised.[83] For this reason, the nature or quality of intellectual achievements is a matter of indifference: the accomplishments of statesmen, military men, literary men, men of science, and divines are commensurable forms of data. (Although Galton does speculate about the contribution of the female line to the production of male geniuses, he decides it is secondary because women are essentially 'noisy' data: their general lack of public achievement makes their intelligence difficult to 'ferret out'.[84]) Nonetheless, and despite this apparent scientific neutrality toward the varieties of intellectual achievement, Galton's model of intelligence obviously privileges mathematical logic insofar as it presumes that intelligence itself is quantifiable. And indeed, a key inspiration for Galton's desire to quantify intelligence was the mathematics Tripos at Cambridge – an examination that induced such anxiety in him that he suffered a nervous breakdown before sitting it.[85] The Cambridge mathematics Tripos features prominently in *Hereditary Genius* and is clearly Galton's Platonic ideal of human intelligence: circularly, mathematical ability is the quintessence of human intelligence because it can be tested mathematically.[86] (I discuss the implications of Galton's essentially mathematical ideal of genius as well his erasure of female intelligence in relation to Woolf's 1919 novel *Night and Day* in the Coda of this book.)

Galton's fascination with the capacity of exams to sort and rank people on a mass scale directly led to his efforts to construe intelligence in statistical terms.[87] Galton was enchanted by the work of the Belgian mathematician Adolphe Quetelet, whose work seemed to him to demonstrate the 'marvellous' statistical orderliness underlying human diversity.[88] In particular, Quetelet had demonstrated that human height within a population obeys the law of 'the normal distribution' and can be plotted to yield the familiar bell-shaped curve on a graph. Galton's wager was that human intelligence is an attribute just like human height, and is therefore a phenomenon where the proper scientific question is: how high? Or, perhaps, how much? From Quetelet, Galton extrapolated the idea that nature bestows intellectual gifts in a reliable pattern: it predictably yields a preponderance of mediocrities, a relatively small intellectual elite, and a relatively small class of 'idiots and imbeciles'.[89] However, where the law of normal distribution had led Quetelet to celebrate the 'average' as a moral ideal, Galton is dissatisfied with the intellectual average – mere 'mediocrity' – and enshrines exceptional intelligence as the ideal toward which humanity as a whole ought to aspire: a logical contradiction that only eugenics can resolve into coherence.[90]

Galton was largely responsible for popularising the notion of intelligence as a unitary, heritable trait, largely impervious to environmental influences. He ventured an early theory of what we now call the genome (what he called the 'stirp', or root) and this constituted an 'epistemic rupture', as Maurizio Meloni puts it: it meant that heredity could be conceptualised as an autonomous package, transmitted across generations but sealed off from environmental effects.[91] Galton also fatefully introduced the phrase 'nature and nurture' into the language as means of clarifying his conviction of the primacy of hereditary factors in determining a person's character and life chances.[92] In pursuit of this thesis, he pioneered a remarkable range of experimental and statistical methods for investigating heredity and embarked on an ambitious anthropometric programme. (I discuss Galton's anthropometry in relation to the rise of intelligence testing later in this Introduction.) Galton was certainly the most zealous hard hereditarian of the Victorian age, but as we have seen, his conviction that intelligence is overwhelmingly determined by heredity was shared by the Lamarckian Spencer. And Lamarckian or 'soft' hereditarian thinkers like the psychiatrist Henry Maudsley could be as vehement as Galton in their insistence upon the supremacy of heredity in determining intelligence:

Perhaps of all the erroneous notions concerning mind which metaphysics had engendered or abetted, there is none more false than that which tacitly assumes or explicitly declares that men are born with equal original mental capacity, opportunities and education determining the differences of subsequent development. The opinion is as cruel as it is false. What man can by taking thought add one cubit either to his mental or to his bodily stature? Multitudes of human beings come into the world weighted with destiny against which they have neither the will nor the power to contend: they are the step-children of Nature, and groan under the worst of all tyrannies – the tyranny of a bad organisation.[93]

When he published *Hereditary Genius*, Galton believed that blank-slate theories of human nature prevailed in English culture.[94] Some of his contemporaries disputed this: for example, the political economist Herman Merivale claimed in his review of *Hereditary Genius* that Galton exaggerated the power of heredity in order to attack a straw-man environmentalist consensus, when, in fact, the importance of both hereditary and environmental influences was generally acknowledged.[95] Nonetheless, Galton had grounds for thinking his book iconoclastic, and not only in relation to Christian piety (the book was reviled in the religious press).[96] A liberal faith in the 'almost boundless' power of education and individual agency was at its cultural peak in the mid-Victorian decades.[97] Such faith was closely associated with the thinking of John Stuart Mill and had underwritten optimistic cultural narratives of progress, self-improvement, and upward mobility in the 1850s and 1860s (it was also associated with the work of Samuel Smiles – discussed in more detail later in this Introduction).[98] It was this Millian and Smilesian emphasis upon the plasticity and perfectibility of the individual that Galton sought to chasten.

If *Hereditary Genius* was iconoclastic in 1869, it would come to seem much less so as the century wore on. Reissued with a new Preface in 1892, the book was widely celebrated in the press and Galton acclaimed for the prescience of his insights. The reviewer in *The Nation* wrote: 'nature limits the powers of the mind as definitely as those of the body. On [this] point, among thinkers everywhere, [Galton] has prevailed.'[99]

The intellectual aristocracy, the Civil Service, and the meritocratic ideal

The meritocratic ideal and the concept of IQ are entangled and have common Victorian origins.[100] They both emerged from what the historian Noel Annan famously called 'the intellectual aristocracy': a cluster of Evangelical and Quaker families who formed close kinship and professional ties in the early nineteenth century. This web of intermarrying families – the Arnolds, Darwins, Haldanes, Huxleys, Keyneses, Macaulays, and Wedgwoods (to cite only some of the more famous names) – produced a remarkable number of Galtonian 'eminent men': writers, scholars, scientists, mathematicians, civil servants, colonial administrators, headmasters, and journalists. Annan writes:

> [These families] gradually spread over the length and breadth of English intellectual life, criticising the assumptions of the ruling class above them and forming the opinions of the upper middle class to which they belonged. They were leaders of the new intelligentsia. Stability is not a quality usually associated with an intelligentsia, a term which [. . .] suggests the [. . .] members of revolutionary or literary cliques who have cut themselves adrift from the moorings of family. Yet the English intelligentsia, wedded to gradual reform of accepted institutions and able to move between the realms of speculation and government, was stable.[101]

Darwin and Galton were descendants of this original network of influential families and self-conscious members of the intellectual aristocracy (as was Woolf – a subject that I discuss in more detail in the Coda). This network was largely responsible for embedding the meritocratic ideal in English society: it was instrumental in rendering the Civil Service and the universities 'open to talent' and making competitive examinations the test of that talent. Its objective was to ensure that 'no formal obstacle [could] prevent the man of brains from becoming a gentleman', as Annan writes.[102] The intellectual aristocracy's investment in accruing professional power and prestige was wedded to an ideal of active public service, itself born of the fervent religious convictions of its founding families. This gave the intellectual aristocracy's campaign to render Victorian society 'open to talent' a moral and religious zeal. It also endowed the Victorian intellectual aristocracy with a religious faith in its own distinction and entitlement to cultural and political power: a faith that is often potent even among its more apparently secular latter generations.[103]

The Whig politician and historian Thomas Babington Macaulay (1800–59), one of the sons of the intellectual aristocracy, is often identified as the original theorist and architect of Victorian meritocracy. He is also often credited with being the first to theorise general intelligence and posit it as a phenomenon open to objective testing and ranking.[104] Macaulay's twin ideological concepts of merit and general intelligence underpinned his campaign to reform the Indian Civil Service throughout the 1840s and 1850s. Macaulay wanted the Indian Civil Service to dismantle its patronage culture and create a new system of recruitment through open, competitive examinations – a blueprint that was implemented in 1854. Macaulay believed that his meritocratic system would not only improve the calibre of the Indian Civil Service but inject a salutary spirit of open competition into English culture at large. His other objective was to delay the entry of Indians into the Indian Civil Service and make superlative acculturation to British values – in the form of demonstrating the 'cultivation of English literature' expected of English (and preferably Oxbridge-educated) candidates – the prerequisite for their eventual admission.[105] Macaulay's ideal of meritocratic intelligence is thus a colonial ideal not only insofar as it attempted to enshrine colonial administration as a covetable prize for exceptional intellectual ability but insofar as it was designed to produce a class of Indian administrators inculcated with British cultural values.

In Macaulay's vision, the new Civil Service examinations would test 'not only the acquirements, but also the mental powers and resources of the competitors'.[106] As Simon Szreter points out, Macaulay's paradigm of general, testable intelligence formed the chrysalis of Galton's eugenics and the notion of IQ.[107] Thanks to his familiarity with Quetelet's work, Macaulay even anticipated the statistical logic of Galton's model of intelligence.[108] In his efforts to persuade parliament to adopt his meritocratic ideal of the Civil Service, Macaulay invoked Quetelet's normal distribution and suggested that it applied to the spread of intellectual ability in the English population:

> Among any 800 gentleman whom you might select at random, there would be a certain number of men of very superior powers; the great majority might be not very much above, nor very much below, the average ability; but there must necessarily be, in every body of 800 men, not selected by some test of ability, a considerable number – say tenth, or, if you please, a twentieth – who fall decidedly below the average of ability.[109]

Like Galton and like the IQ testers after him, Macaulay also attributed prophetic powers to formal examinations. His Civil Service exam would not simply identify young men who had undertaken serious study but also would be able to predict their future distinction: 'Those men who distinguish themselves most in academical competition when they are young, are the men who, in after life, distinguish themselves most in the competition of the world.'[110] Macaulay reasoned that, since middle- and upper-class Englishmen generally aspired to excellence in Greek and Latin, tests in those languages could serve as objective standards of intellectual capacity.[111] And also like Galton's, Macaulay's ideal of meritocratic intellectual ability is really an attempt to universalise the Cambridge competitive examination system – though in Macaulay's case, he wanted to extend its logic of ranking not to the study of human heredity but to the administration of the state and the empire.[112]

Macaulay's notion of meritocracy was nevertheless not simply a matter of innate, assessable intellectual ability, but a moral ideal. He contended that academic examinations tested not only the intelligence but the moral worth of candidates, since the application required to succeed attested to a man's 'character':

> Superiority in science and literature generally indicates the existence of some qualities which are securities against vice – industry, self-denial, a taste for pleasures not sensual [. . .] We therefore believe that the intellectual test which is about to be established will be found to be also the best moral test that can be devised.[113]

Although Macaulay was an essentially secular thinker, it is possible to discern the influence of his Evangelical upbringing in his puritanical ideal of the public servant (Macaulay's father, Zachary Macaulay, was a member of the Clapham Sect, a famous anti-slavery activist, and a founder of the Society for the Suppression of Vice.) As Szreter observes, 'Macaulay's "merit" strongly bore the moral charge of his Evangelical pedigree and remained an essentially transcendent concept.'[114]

Macaulay's desire to wreathe intelligence with the moral and spiritual halo of 'merit' is intimately connected to the imperial context of his thinking on the subject. Macaulay claimed that meritocratic reforms to the Civil Service were a matter of justice to the Indian subjects under British rule:

There is plenty of routine business to be done [in the home Civil Service] which a man of no great ability can transact [. . .] But the case is different in the Indian service. You have there 800 men charged with the happiness of 120,000,000 people [. . .] It is utterly impossible that one-tenth part or one twentieth-part of that service can consist of incapable men without causing great suffering.[115]

In other words, Macaulay's meritocratic ideal is a means of shoring up the moral legitimacy of the empire: only a rigorously selected moral and intellectual elite can rationalise the hubris of 800 Englishmen being 'charged with the happiness' of millions of Indians and enable Britain to justify itself to itself.

Macaulay's ideal of meritocratic intelligence was further consolidated within the British state and British culture more generally through the work of his civil servant brother-in-law, Sir Charles Trevelyan, and William Gladstone's private secretary, Sir Stafford Northcote, who recommended the introduction of equivalent meritocratic reforms to the home Civil Service. At first glance, the Indian and home Civil Service reforms can appear progressive and even radical in their spirit: in his recent book *The Aristocracy of Talent*, Adrian Wooldridge certainly acclaims them as such (though he is thinking primarily of their long-term effects in the twentieth century and beyond).[116] Hardy captures the egalitarian promise of Civil Service reform his 1874 short story 'Destiny and a Blue Cloak', where a poor but ambitious young man exults: 'Thanks to Macaulay, [. . .] I have as good a chance as the best of them! [. . .] What a great thing competitive examination is; it will put good men in good places, and make inferior men move lower down.'[117] And certainly the liberal rhetoric surrounding the reforms could sound stirringly egalitarian. Whig MP Sir Charles Wood proclaimed in parliament in 1864:

Our object is to go into the world to get well educated young men wherever they are to be found, no matter where or in what manner their education has been acquired. We wish to obtain the best cultivated young men [. . .] without requiring that that knowledge should have been imparted at a commercial school, or a university, or any other particular establishment.[118]

Sir Charles's private views were another matter, however. Behind the scenes, he was urging Trevelyan to increase the weighting of the marks for Greek and Latin in the exams in order to ensure that only 'University men who are gentleman' – rather than 'youths from Irish universities or the Commercial Schools' – would stand a chance of success.[119] Sir Charles's machinations were unnecessary, since the exams were already carefully constructed to favour young men from the ancient public schools and universities, and thereby ensure the class background of the candidate.[120] The weight given to 'English language, literature, and history' and to the history and languages of Ancient Greece and Rome in the marking system was intended to privilege Oxbridge candidates and very particularly those who had studied *Literae Humaniores*, or Greats, at Oxford: an effect of the decisive influence of Benjamin Jowett, Classics Professor at Balliol College, Oxford, upon the reform schemes.[121]

Szreter argues that the fact that the meritocratic ideal of intelligence was really an aristocratic ideal of gentlemanly education in lightly modernised attire reflects the fact that Victorian meritocracy was, in essence, a liberal compromise with the interests of the traditional landed aristocracy. Meritocratic reform was designed to keep the 'extant status hierarchy' essentially intact by opening competition up only to those already in possession of an elite education and the social refinements of a gentleman.[122] As Heather Ellis has recently argued, it is equally possible to understand the mid-Victorian shift toward meritocracy as a liberal effort to deflect the democratic demands of an increasingly assertive and potentially revolutionary working class. Ellis notes that Trevelyan confessed that the 1848 wave of revolutionary unrest across Europe was a motivating force behind the reforms.[123] Ellis also quotes D. B. Eaton, the American lawyer and Civil Service reformer who corresponded with Trevelyan and wrote a study of the English experiment in meritocracy. According to Eaton, the English Civil Service reforms were 'in intention, and in broad effect, a conservative force in government – a barrier against republicanism [. . .] an antidote against revolutions'.[124]

Meritocratic reform of the Civil Service was nonetheless controversial and provoked conservative anxieties about a brave new world dominated by brainy but unscrupulous upstarts and a culture of cut-throat 'place-hunt[ing]'.[125] Anthony Trollope feared that it marked the beginning of classless society:

> There are places in life which can hardly be filled except by 'Gentlemen'
> [. . .] Gates of one class should be open to the other; but neither to one

class or to the other can good be done by declaring that there are no gates, no barrier, no difference. The system of competitive examination is, I think, based on a supposition that there is no difference.[126]

Such anxieties were unwarranted: the actual effects of the reform in the latter half of the Victorian period were complex, but they certainly did not abolish class barriers. Thanks to the deliberate bias toward those who had received a gentlemanly education, entry into the Civil Service actually became more closely correlated with public school education in the decades following the meritocratic reforms.[127] However, the exams failed to attract Oxbridge graduates in the desired numbers, and the service had to accept many who had not attended university; those educated at the London, Irish, and Scottish universities also formed a significant minority of the successful candidates.[128] In 1863, Satyendranath Tagore became the first Indian candidate to win entry, and his success provoked consternation in England and more concerted efforts to exclude Indian candidates (which, in turn, galvanised an Indian political movement for fair admission into the Civil Service).[129]

Civil Service reform also sparked a cultural debate about the legitimacy and effects of 'cram': that is, intensive preparation for exams, typically involving rote-learning.[130] The reforms created a market in cram coaches and tutors who specialised in preparing students for the exams.[131] Like the 11 plus exam, which continues to select 'bright' students for entry to grammar schools in some parts of contemporary England, the vaunted capacity of the Civil Service exam to test the innate ability of the candidate incentivised students (or their families) to pay for tutoring – tutoring that was soon discovered to be effective in obtaining the desired proof of ability.[132] As Jennifer Ruth has shown, the mid-Victorian debate over cram is threaded through with anxiety that examinable intelligence might turn out to be mere mechanical intelligence, and that meritocratic competition will produce 'a race of mechanically driven examinees', in the words of one alarmed commentator.[133] Ruth notes that the caricature of the machine-like, lower-class crammer who was eager to commodify his own brains was conventionally contrasted with the aristocratic ideal of the 'disinterested' gentleman with a range of interests and talents. She also notes that it is possible to see an IQ definition of intelligence as an immutable, bedrock property of the self, something one simply has or is rather than does or labours for, being wielded on both sides of this debate. As we have seen, liberal advocates of Civil Service reform argued that competitive examinations could identify not only learning but innate 'general ability'. But conservative opponents complained that the examination would glorify crammers: lower-class men who merely possessed extreme capacities for mechanical labour. Genuine innate intelligence – the disinterested play of a gentleman's intellect – could never be objectified and commodified by an examination result.[134]

It was in the context of these debates that Galton published his thesis about the hereditary nature of genius. Galton sought to annul the distinction between labour and innate ability that structured the debate over the Civil Service reforms and cram, insisting that the propensity to work hard was itself heritable and proof of intellectual capacity. Like Macaulay's, Galton's model of 'merit' (or, to use Galton's own pet word, 'eminence') was a potent hybridisation of the aristocratic belief in innate superiority and the bourgeois values of self-discipline and hard work. Michael Young, who famously coined the term 'meritocracy' in 1958 as part of an effort to demystify its ideological power, suggested it could be rendered as an equation: intelligence + effort = merit.[135] While Young's use of an equation neatly skewers the mathematising bent of the work of Galton and his followers, it obscures the fact that the terms are all interchangeable: there are no real distinctions between intelligence, effort, and merit in Galton's worldview.

Galton's deterministic understanding of intellectual effort was not unique to him. As we shall see, a person's capacity for education and for intellectual work are increasingly understood in terms of a biologically fixed quantity of energy in late Victorian culture. This model of the body was an extrapolation from physics: the first law of thermodynamics, which holds that energy within a system cannot be created or destroyed, only transferred or converted. The translation of the conservation of energy principle from physics to biology gave rise to the idea that the brain–body system is an engine that requires careful management; intense brainwork can drain the body of vital energy and result in nervous collapse.[136] Most importantly, the risks posed by brainwork and education vary among people: some brain–body engines are better made and more efficient than others; some brains draw upon greater reserves of vital energy. This idea received one of its most influential expositions in Spencer's *Education: Intellectual, Moral and Physical* (1860):

Vigour of *physique* [is] needful to make intellectual training available in the struggle of life. Those who, in eagerness to cultivate their pupil's minds, are reckless of their bodies, do not remember that success in the world depends more on energy than information [. . .] The strong will and untiring activity due to abundant animal vigour, go far to compensate even great defects of education; and when joined with that quite adequate education which may be obtained without sacrificing health, they ensure an easy victory over competitors enfeebled by excessive study [. . .] A comparatively small and ill-made engine, worked at high pressure, will do more than a large and well-finished one worked at low pressure. What folly it is, then, while finishing the engine, so to damage the boiler that it will not generate steam![137]

As this passage suggests, Spencer was an early and vociferous critic of cram and warned of the baleful effects of what he variously called educational 'forcing', 'over-pressure', or 'over-education' – modern evils he claimed were especially injurious to women.[138] Spencer's insistence that intellectual capacity is a mechanical production system that can be tested to destruction by education circulated widely through Victorian culture via debates about cram, competitive examinations, and over-pressure – a Spencerian concept that became a catch-all term for the stresses of modern life, especially in relation to education and professional work.[139] Spencerian over-pressure popularised the idea that biology laid iron constraints upon the pursuit of education – and that those constraints weighed more heavily on some minds than others.

Oxbridge meritocracy and the scholarship ladder

The Civil Service reforms were both inspired by and inspired similar meritocratic reforms instituted at Oxford and Cambridge universities in the mid-Victorian period.[140] From the 1850s onwards, the universities began to establish public entry examinations that were intended to improve educational standards throughout the country and foster a spirit of competitive industry in the young.[141] The examinations were also designed to render Oxbridge more open to middle-class men of merit.[142] Meritocratic competition simultaneously became both more strenuous and more central to academic life within Oxford and Cambridge and a 'gospel of success' began to dominate undergraduate life.[143]

A richly melodramatic cultural mythology developed around the ritual of university examinations. As William Clark writes,

> [university] examinations functioned less as a certification of pragmatic or expert ability, and more as trials to ascertain charismatic leaders – as though Cambridge sought to ascertain a true genius and son of Newton annually. Such exams also served to rank students as an end in itself.[144]

Along with the Civil Service exams, Oxbridge examinations inspired critiques of cram, examination mania, and over-pressure.[145] However, it is important to distinguish between discourses of over-pressure and cram as they applied to young male Oxbridge students and those which surrounded the Civil Service exams (as well as those which pertained to lower-class elementary school-children, female students, and aspirants to the scholarship ladder – all of which I discuss below). As we have seen, the open Civil Service exams inspired anxieties about the class-levelling potential of meritocracy. The discourses of over-pressure and cram in relation to male Oxbridge students had different implications.

Meritocratic competition at Victorian Oxbridge inspired voluminous polemics, memoirs, and literary representations, as well as confessions of anxiety, illness, and anguish from both students and their families.[146] Of the Cambridge tripos, Clark writes, 'motifs of sickness, metaphorical death and rebirth went from cliché to archetype'.[147] The often impassioned protests raised against the examination systems can resonate as presciently modern critiques of the psychic costs of meritocracy. Yet as with contemporary critiques of meritocracy which dwell tenderly upon the 'wounded winners' or the psychic burdens borne by an elite, critique can be hard to distinguish from glorification: the suffering endured by participants sanctifies the competition and affirms the profundity of success and failure alike.[148] Clarke says that the gruelling nature of the examinations helped to generate 'a myth and cult of the hero, a ritual to recognise and celebrate academic charisma'.[149] Similarly, Paul R. Deslandes suggests that the Oxbridge discourse of examination distress enhanced the prestige of the competition and entrenched it as a glamorous rite of passage for young men as they assumed the mantle of middle- and upper-class masculinity. Deslandes also notes that the ritual of the examinations was frequently imagined as a fitting induction into imperial masculinity: the mental and physical rigours of the exams were compared to the challenges of colonial rule, while the high standards and competitive ethos embodied in them could be taken to ratify the superior intellectual fitness of the Anglo-Saxon race.[150]

The 1860s saw a series of Royal Commissions into the school system which led to the development of the fabled Victorian 'scholarship ladder', which served to popularise Oxbridge meritocracy as a fantasy if not as an accessible reality. The Taunton Commission of 1864–7 recommended the establishment of scholarships for the grammar schools 'open to merit, and merit only' – by which they meant open to wealthy and poor boys alike – and which would thereby enable 'boys of exceptional talent to rise to the highest education which the country could supply'.[151] (As with the Civil Service exams, 'merit' was here a modern euphemism for gentlemanly education: the Taunton Commissioners wanted to enshrine proficiency in Latin as the primary metric of 'exceptional talent'.[152]) The phrase 'the scholarship ladder' is often attributed to Huxley, who, in 1871, told the London School Board that he thought that:

> No educational system in the country would be worthy of the name [. . .] unless it was one which established a great educational ladder, the bottom of which would be in the gutter and the top in the University and by which every child who had the strength to climb might, by using that strength, reach the place intended for him.[153]

Tellingly, Huxley casts the scholarship boy's intellect as a form of physical strength and his meritocratic progress as proof of a natural fitness. In invoking a ladder of ascent, Huxley was surely thinking, however unconsciously, of the phylogenetic ladders that preoccupied him as an evolutionary biologist. Huxley's submerged suggestion of a link between meritocratic and evolutionary fitness perhaps accounts for the underlying circularity of his vision of the scholarship ladder: he imagines this ladder being thrown down as an enlightened corrective to an unjust social system, but also assumes the ladder must itself embody the hierarchical severity of that system in order to test the fitness of the boy who would ascend it. There is a further circularity in Huxley's suggestion that the scholarship boy has a place 'intended' for him. 'Intended' gestures at a natural hierarchy of brains, but surely it is only the scholarship ladder itself which 'intends' an elevated social position for the boy: without it, he will remain in the 'gutter'.

The notion that competitive examinations test not just one's intellect but one's biological fitness often surfaces in discussions of education and social mobility in the second half of the nineteenth century. For example, the Taunton Commissioners sought to create a scholarship competition that would identify 'those who can profit by education higher than the rudiments' by 'natural selection', as if exam performance were a proxy for evolutionary fitness.[154] And as Sutherland has noted, the 1895 Bryce Commission, another inquiry into secondary schooling, drew upon the logic of Social Darwinism when outlining its ideal of the scholarship ladder. The Bryce Commissioners posited the existence of a 'cultured class' who are 'naturally' destined for university and the professions, though they may originate from any social class; they characterised the scholarship competition as a means of 'recruiting the best blood and brains from all classes of society'.[155] Galton's efforts to prove that competitive scholastic examinations tell the truth about the 'stern examination board of nature', Darwinian natural selection, was thus not peculiar to him but an early articulation of what would become a cultural commonplace.[156]

The apparent idealism of the Victorian scholarship ladder contained a hard core of pessimism about the mental capacities of the masses. While the scholarship ladder could seem like a democratic extension of educational opportunity, its narrowness conveyed the idea that intellectual ability is rare among the lower middle and working classes. The brilliant scholarship boy – and his even rarer sister, the brilliant scholarship girl – are exceptions that only go to prove the prevailing dullness of the masses.[157] The Taunton Commissioners were concerned to provide scholarships for the 'exceptional boys' who attended the lowest grade of secondary schools – that is, lower middle-class boys – who *now and then* come up to the surface above their fellows' (my italics).[158] The Bryce Commissioners recommended that scholarships be awarded to impoverished boys 'of rare capacity'.[159] Such insults to the general intelligence of the masses did not need to be an expression of any strong ideological position: they could always be defended as a regrettable side effect of the fact that the state could not commandeer significant money for the scholarship ladder because to do so would be to violate the rule of laissez-faire which remained potent in English debates over education even after the 1870 Education Act. As Szreter has shown, the principle of laissez-faire serves to justify and naturalise the class-bound educational hierarchy in both the Taunton and the Bryce Commissions. The Taunton Commissioners did not intend the scholarship ladder to generate significant social mobility: they endorsed as a fixed and natural state of affairs that the English school system consisted of three hierarchically graded types of secondary school and these three grades corresponded to different grades of social class (and also the fact that this hierarchy excluded the vast majority of people, who did not attend secondary school at all).[160] As Sutherland remarks in relation to the Taunton Commission, 'The English version of meritocracy was both a weak and an unashamedly socially elitist one.'[161] Nearly thirty years later, little had changed: the 1895 Bryce Commission accepted the same class-bound hierarchy of educational opportunity. As Szreter remarks, the scholarship ladder was 'an almost spectral tokenism': in 1900, fewer than one in a thousand elementary schoolchildren were given assistance to attend the higher-grade schools which could make university entry feasible.[162] Both the Civil Service exams and the scholarship ladder are thus spectacular examples of the 'unexamined exclusion' that Pierre Bourdieu and Jean-Paul Passeron claim is one of the primary ideological functions of meritocratic examinations. The meritocratic 'truth' produced by the examination – the distinction between successful and unsuccessful candidates, or those who pass and those who fail – is designed to obscure the vast numbers whom the system has already 'excluded from the ranks of the candidates'.[163]

The inadequacy of the scholarship ladder – and the fact that its rungs were unevenly accessible in different parts of England – was often acknowledged by late Victorian and Edwardian writers on education.[164] The headmaster of Manchester Grammar School, John Lewis Paton, wrote in 1909:

[The] educational ladder [. . .] is a cant phrase [. . .] It suggests the picture of a few favoured spirits, who climb up into a faraway and solitary Paradise, and for the most part scorn the base degrees by which they did ascend. It is, at bottom, a selfish and individualist ideal [. . .] In the battle of life, which is based on the principle of each for himself and the devil take the hindmost, we fight each for our own hand, and grow into hardened individuals.[165]

Novels like Hardy's *Jude the Obscure* (1895) and Wells's *Love and Mr. Lewisham* (1900) nonetheless attest to the power of such fugitive meritocratic opportunity to possess the imagination. The spectrality of the scholarship ladder was, of course, the essence of its glamour.

Meritocratic providentialism

In his 1859 work *Self-Help*, Samuel Smiles created a powerful alternative to the elitist and scholarly paradigm of meritocracy which emerged from the Civil Service and university reforms of the mid-Victorian decades. *Self-Help* is a paean to the powers of hard work and to the capacity of the lower classes to achieve upward mobility under industrial capitalism, particularly through science and entrepreneurship. Originally a Chartist, Smiles had grown disillusioned with politics and reinvested his progressive ideals in a doctrine of individual self-empowerment. Smiles argues that the truly impressive men of modern English history sprang from humble origins, and he offers inspiring profiles of businessmen, inventors, artists, and scientists to illustrate his case. According to Smiles, such men achieved greatness not despite but because of their disadvantages: poverty and obscurity are spurs to self-reliance and thus 'blessings' in disguise.[166] *Self-Help* is an attempt to vindicate the talents of the nation's labouring classes and to insist upon the essentially plebeian character of English genius. But the book is also a polemic against the concept of genius:

> Men who have most moved the world, have not been men of genius [but] men of intense mediocre abilities, untiring workers, preserving, self-reliant, and indefatigable; not so often the gifted, of naturally bright and shining qualities, as those who have applied themselves diligently to their work.[167]

In its valorisation of hard work and depreciation of both inborn talent and inherited privilege, *Self-Help* can seem like the antithesis of Galton's *Hereditary Genius*. And indeed, Smiles's contention that 'what some men are, all without difficulty might be' was surely one of the popular egalitarian narratives Galton aimed to explode.[168] Yet Smiles's and Galton's books share an underlying shared assumption which meant they were more compatible than they appear at first sight: both Galton and Smiles held that meritocracy was the secret social law of nineteenth-century England. Like Smiles, Galton highlighted examples of men who rose to eminence from humble backgrounds as evidence that genuine individual superiority – in his construal, biological intelligence – will triumph over 'inferiority of social rank'.[169] In this, both Galton and Smiles's work is suggestive of the often remarked capacity of the meritocratic ideal to falsify sociological realities.[170] Certainly their shared vision of humble men rising irrepressibly to eminence – whether by dint of brains or through hard work – is not borne out by studies of Victorian social mobility.[171] Galton and Smiles's shared belief that meritocracy was not merely an ideal but an already extant, if inadequately understood, social reality also reflects the often remarked slipperiness of the concept of meritocracy: it tends to slide between a political ideal and a sociological description, or between *ought* and *is*.[172]

The underlying affinity between *Self-Help* and *Hereditary Genius* reveals the extent to which the Victorian vision of meritocracy was a secularised Christian providentialism: men of merit prosper and receive their due rewards in wealth and social status, while the idle or unfit are punished by poverty and abjection. This meritocratic providentialism can be more precisely understood as a secularised Calvinism.[173] Max Weber famously identified the ironic effect of the Calvinist doctrine of predestination when it is secularised by the forces of modern capitalism: it produces not fatalism about one's lot in life so much as an anxious will to prove to oneself and others that one is saved, and this proof is sought through an intense work ethic and found in material prosperity.[174] It is often noted that Smiles's secular self-help doctrine is clearly the product of his Scottish Calvinist upbringing and readily lends itself to a harsh and quasi-theological distinction between the industrious (the saved) and the feckless (the damned), or between the deserving and undeserving poor.[175] It has also been suggested that Galtonian meritocracy and the IQ concept have theological roots. John White argues that Galton's conception of intelligence as predetermined, innate 'eminence' is a secularised version of Calvinist predestination and its distinction between elect and non-elect souls (though this is not explicable by Galton's Quaker upbringing: Quakers reject the doctrine of predestination).[176] And as with Weber's secularised Calvinists, faith in the fixed and inborn nature of intelligence can inspire not the resignation which would seem logically to follow from it but an anxious work ethic. Wooldridge makes this point in relation to the psychology of twentieth-century intelligence testers in England: '[meritocratic] election was predetermined by innate intelligence but constantly had to be proved by work and educational effort'.[177] And because both Galtonian and Smilesian models of meritocracy treat a strenuous work ethic as proof of inner merit, they easily shaded into one another in late Victorian culture.

Recently, the philosopher Michael J. Sandel has characterised contemporary meritocracy as 'providentialism without God' and indicted both the moral narcissism this logic inspires in the successful – what he calls 'meritocratic hubris' – and the moral stigma it attaches to failure.[178] Sandal calls for a revival of a more tragic understanding of life which acknowledges the role of contingency in a person's social destiny. The novelists explored in this book are often sharp critics of the providentialist logic at play in both Galtonian and Smilesian versions of meritocracy and attempt to anatomise the often confusing forms of hubris and abjection they inspire. This is especially true of Eliot and Hardy, who both draw upon the genre of tragedy to offer a moral critique of meritocratic providentialism. Hardy and Wells are also sharp critics of the puritanism of Victorian meritocratic thinking, which is viscerally felt by the protagonists of Hardy's *Jude the Obscure* and Wells's *Love and Mr. Lewisham*. However, most of my chosen novelists – Eliot, Wells, James, and Woolf – also turn to comedy to deflate the moral pretensions of meritocracy and to critique its fetishisation of innate intelligence.

Ineducable children and mental deficiency

England was, by comparison to other major European countries, late to implement a mass state education system. The delay was primarily due to sectarian religious disputes over the denominational character of any proposed state education system and to the sway of laissez-faire liberal arguments in the mid-Victorian decades, which held that education was best supplied through private and voluntary initiatives. In 1870, England finally laid the groundwork for a network of state elementary schools. The new schools were known as 'board schools' and they plugged the gaps in the inadequate network of religious 'voluntary' schools, which were already subsidised by the state. The new board schools were secular and free for those who could not afford to pay (and became free to all after 1890).[179] However, it was after 1880, when attendance at elementary school became mandatory and thus near-universal, that the mental and physical condition of lower-class children began to be fully assayed and grasped in relation to a new biopolitical norm of educability.

Some commentators suggest that the rise of intelligence testing and the modern IQ concept of intelligence are essentially artefacts of mass education systems and the administrative exigencies they create. There is truth in Ian Hunter's remark that 'what counts as intelligence [. . .] has been determined by the milieu of the school'.[180] Yet as we have seen, the scientific and ideological foundations of the IQ concept had been laid in the decades prior to the 1870 Education Act and took their primary inspiration from the elite milieu of Oxbridge and from the exigencies of managing an empire, not from a mass education system. As we have also seen, the impetus to conceptualise examinations as tests not simply of learning but of underlying 'ability' began to make its presence felt from the 1850s onwards. It is nevertheless true that the development of a state education system decisively transformed intelligence into a biopolitical question: the spread of intellectual ability in the population became a pressing social and biological concern. This also entailed a shift in focus. Thanks to the university and Civil Service reforms, and to Galton's *Hereditary Genius*, Victorian debates about innate intellectual ability were initially focused on high intellectual ability and on the question of meritocratic justice: in effect, on the often glamourised figure of the ambitious young man and his performance in competitive examinations. After the advent of state elementary education, the discourse of innate intelligence settles on the figure of the lower-class child. In particular, it fixates on the problem of so-called 'slow', 'dull', or 'backward' children within the state school system.

After the roll-out of compulsory elementary education, school-teachers, managers, and inspectors were forced to reckon with the wretched physical conditions of vast numbers of children, many of whom were plainly too badly nourished to be educated. They were also confronted with the challenges of delivering standardised education to many children with untreated illnesses or with physical or intellectual disabilities.[181] The new board schools were subject to a system of payment-by-results: the pay and promotion of teachers was linked to the number of students who passed standardised examinations in reading, writing, and arithmetic at the annual visit of the school inspector. Originally introduced to the government-subsidised 'voluntary' religious schools in 1862, payment-by-results – also known as the Revised Code – was a measure intended to keep education cheap and efficient for the state and to guarantee basic standards. For obvious reasons, it was extremely unpopular with teachers and often decried as an example of the utilitarian tyranny of examinations and their tendency to incentivise rote learning.[182] When payment-by-results was carried over into the new system of board schools after 1870, it made the problem of the so-called 'ineducable' children stark. Payment-by-results effectively enforced a standard of educational normalcy that many children in receipt of state education could not be made to meet, no matter the drilling and cramming techniques of their teachers. The figure of the ineducable child posed epistemological as well as administrative problems: the discourse of 'ineducability' tended to elide physical and intellectual disabilities while eliding both kinds of disability with the effects of poverty. Doctors, teachers, scientists, social investigators, and charity workers became preoccupied with disentangling the varieties and causes of ineducability in schoolchildren and with finding ways to classify such children more precisely and objectively.[183]

Binet and Simon's invention of their famous intelligence test in 1905 was intended to address analogous problems in the public school system in France. Binet and Simon were tasked by the French state with devising a procedure for identifying children with intellectual disabilities so that they could be assigned to a special school.[184] Intelligence tests, albeit cruder ones, had already begun in appear in English schools in the 1880s. The first systematic intelligence tests in English schools were conducted by Dr Francis Warner, a doctor at the East London Children's Hospital. Warner's tests were essentially medical examinations that rested on the assumption that 'the body [is] the mirror of the mind', in Wooldridge's words.[185] Warner was an expert in the relationship between the brain and motor development, and his primary method for assessing 'brain power' was to ask children to perform a series of simple movements while he noted any obvious abnormalities in their gait, posture, and appearance, especially their facial expressions.[186] Warner also employed craniometry and sometimes conducted simple interviews to assess the children's speech and social competence, but he essentially hoped to prove that the 'character of every mind is written in the features, gestures, gait and carriage of the body, and will be read there, when, if ever, the extremely difficult language is fully and accurately learnt'.[187] In 1888, the British Medical Association resolved to appoint a committee to 'conduct an investigation as to the average development and condition of brain function among the children in primary schools', and Warner's intelligence tests were deployed on a mass scale.[188] Some 100,000 students were assessed using his methods between 1888 and 1894. The committee sought to identify and provide statistical estimates for the numbers of 'dull' and 'exceptional' children in English schools, though it relied upon teacher's reports rather than medical examinations for this purpose.[189] In the final report, both 'dull' and 'exceptional' intelligence appear as medical categories alongside rickets, malnutrition, eye defects, and abnormal bodily movements.[190] In the 1924 Hadow Report on 'Psychological Tests of Educable Capacity and their Possible Use in the Public System of Education', the psychologist Cyril Burt hailed Warner as a pioneer: 'whatever may nowadays be thought of Dr Warner's reliance upon physical criteria [. . .] his surveys did much to draw attention in this country to the question of inborn differences of intelligence and to the problem of the subnormal child'.[191]

Warner's findings about the prevalence of illness, physical disabilities, and 'dullness' among state elementary schoolchildren caused a furore when they were published in 1891.[192] This was in part because the public was already primed to be alarmed about the conditions of state schoolchildren in the wake of another over-pressure controversy. As we have seen, concerns about the damaging effects of academic pressure in schools and universities had been raised in relation to examination culture since the 1850s, but from the 1870s, they clustered around the new context of the state education system. In 1875, Frederick MacCabe, the Resident Physician at the State Criminal Asylum in County Down, Ireland, raised his concern that the extension of education was tempting the labouring classes into unnatural forms of intellectual exertion:

The general spread of education [. . .] has, it is to be feared, somewhat fostered an unhealthy contempt for manual and mechanical labour. It has been intensified by the adoption of a system of competitive mental tests of competency. With the extension of compulsory education and the increasing overcrowding in the professions this struggle for existence by brain-work would appear likely to become more severe. It is true that in this contest for [. . .] professional pre-eminence the 'survival of the fittest' may possibly result; but the struggle itself is, I believe, attended with [. . .] serious risk to the mental integrity of the competitors [. . .].[193]

It is telling that MacCabe conflates the 'extension of compulsory education' – that is, state-run elementary education – with the competitive examinations associated with the universities, the Civil Service, and scholarships to secondary schools, especially public schools. Although it was notoriously difficult for anyone to pass out of the state elementary education system into higher levels of education and a profession, MacCabe nevertheless imagines labourers swelling the ranks of the professional class and producing a Darwinian meritocracy in which only the fittest brainworkers can survive. Like meritocratic aspirations, meritocratic anxieties can run wildly ahead of sociological realities.

In 1883, the psychiatrist Dr (later 'Sir') James Crichton-Browne published a sensational report upon the degenerative effects of the state education system. Crichton-Browne argued that the education system, particularly its focus on examinations and payment-by-results, was producing an epidemic of physical and mental illness. He suggested that pushing the minds of children beyond their biological limits resulted in a profusion of mental and physical illnesses: headaches, diabetes, insomnia, neurological disorders, hydrocephalus, lunacy, and suicide, as well as a general loss of physical vigour. He warned that the elementary school system, which he likened to a child-eating giant, threatened to transmit 'degeneration and disease' to future generations and degrade the national stock.[194] Crichton-Browne highlighted that starvation and malnutrition were rife in the elementary school system.[195] He also laid emphasis upon the heightened risks that education posed to girls, whom he supposed more sensitive to 'mental strain'.[196] William Gladstone's Liberal government attempted to squelch the report and commissioned a counter-report by J. G. Fitch, Her Majesty's Chief Inspector of Schools, who debunked Crichton-Browne's claims. Nevertheless, Crichton-Browne succeeded in igniting a far-reaching public debate about over-pressure, examination culture, and the educational capacities of the masses.[197]

Crichton-Browne's Gothic account of the education system lent itself to conflicting political agendas: some took it as proof of the intrinsic evils of state-run education, while others used it to argue for more generous state provision for the poor or for more child-centred approaches to education.[198] It was open to these contradictory appropriations because of a basic ambiguity in the report. Dr Crichton-Browne characterises the state education system as reckless meddling with the laws of nature, which place strict limits on the educability of children and will have their revenge for any 'contraven[tion]'.[199] Much of Crichton-Browne's critique rests upon general claims about child development, but since the report focuses on the children within the state education system, the dangers of over-education seem to pertain with trenchant force to the minds and bodies of poor children. Central to Crichton Browne's case was his belief that between 20 and 30 per cent of state schoolchildren were backward or ineducable, and that forcing such children to conform to the demands of the education system risked brain damage.[200] He exhorted the government to make education 'proportionate to the capacities of the child, to its age, circumstances, and prospects in life'.[201] Although couched in a language of paternalistic concern for the welfare of children, Crichton-Browne's report was readily compatible with Galton's contention that intellectual ability is a fixed biological quality that is spread thinly among the lower classes.[202]

The over-pressure controversy of the 1880s clearly linked education with biological degeneration at the fin de siècle and lent the era's meritocratic imaginary a distinctly morbid cast. The over-pressure controversy focused primarily upon state-educated elementary schoolchildren but it also permeated debates about the scholarship ladder and women's access to higher education and the professions. The figure of the New Woman – the cultural stereotype of the 'advanced', intellectual woman that emerged in the 1890s – was often imagined as exhausted and neurotic because of her biologically perverse determination to study.[203] In popular and literary representations, the New Woman is frequently an 'exam girl': one who has sacrificed her romantic prospects and fertility to cramming and scholarship-chasing.[204] The development of the scholarship ladder also provoked alarm that poor young men were jeopardising their mental and physical health in pursuit of educational opportunities:

> In the case of children of the less wealthy clergy and professional men [scholarships] are the only chance of obtaining [entry to a public school]. Such entrance scholarships being open to all, the candidates

are many, the prizes are few, the competition is severe, and the poor little brain is driven to work [. . .] under the pressure of competitive strain . . . if the successful boy takes a high place in the school, two or three years in advance of the average boys, and continues to rise – unless, indeed, Nature, resenting the strain, reasserts her authority, and the boy becomes dull and idle [. . .] I am constantly hearing [. . .] of the most painful collapse of health and vigour at the end of a scholastic career of early promise [. . .] Have we not heard a note of warning from India, that intense competition for its Civil Service appointments, the parent and model of modern competition, is telling its tale and bearing its natural fruit in premature failure of health, exhausted faculties, and shattered nervous systems?[205]

[To obtain a scholarship] infinite labour and pressure is needed. The young brain is being constantly forced to things not natural to it [. . .] Here and there, an exceptionally gifted boy is able to do with a light heart all the work required of him to get his scholarship and to rise rapidly [. . .] But such cases are rare [. . .] If we leave out of consideration those brilliant boys whom no system could spoil, the chances seem to be tolerably even whether a boy will, or will not, recover mentally and physically from the strain necessary to gain a scholarship.[206]

The explicit targets of these critiques are the homogenising, excessively competitive, and commercially driven nature of the education system. They nevertheless illustrate how biological determinism about intelligence emerges from the interstices of over-pressure discourses: both writers conceive of intelligence as a biologically fixed reservoir of energy that education may exhaust beyond renewal. The conservative potential of such discourses is obvious even when it is not clearly intended: meritocratic social mobility must be easeful, or else it is a dangerous transgression against the 'laws of physiology'.[207] I have already quoted Young's meritocratic formula: intelligence + effort = merit. In the final decades of the nineteenth century, the shadow of pathology falls over the second half of this formula. In a direct inversion of the mid-Victorian, Smilesian exaltation of hard work, mental striving is often constructed as a self-destructive attempt to defy the dictates of biology.

In these last few decades of the nineteenth century, England's faith in its own economic and imperial supremacy began to falter. The National Efficiency movement attracted thinkers from across the political spectrum in a drive to make England fitter and more productive, particularly in comparison to Germany. The protean cause of 'national efficiency' helped to shift political common sense away from laissez-faire liberalism and toward state interventionism, particularly in relation to the education system and the health of the population.[208] The discourse of national decline also provided a context in which eugenic arguments became more compelling. The boundaries between Social Darwinist and the eugenic discourses were porous, but it is nevertheless possible to understand the rise of Galtonian eugenics as a political movement as signifying the partial eclipse of Spencerian Social Darwinist thinking. As Maurizio Meloni points out, the persuasive force of Spencer's Social Darwinism relied upon the ascendancy of laissez-faire liberalism and the economic and imperial self-confidence of mid-Victorian England; Galton's eugenics movement spoke to the bleaker and more self-doubting national mood of the fin de siècle and the first decade of the twentieth century. Where Social Darwinism preached faith in the overarching rationality of the operation of evolutionary processes upon society, eugenicists preached the urgent necessity of intervention into those processes.[209] The sense of national self-doubt grew especially acute following England's humiliating defeats in the Boer War of 1899–1902, which deepened anxieties about national deterioration and the fitness of the national stock. The official membership of the eugenics movement in England was relatively small (at least as measured by membership of the Eugenics Education Society, which was formed in 1907 and never grew beyond around 1,700 members).[210] However, the eugenics movement rapidly gained cultural prestige and political influence from the 1890s onwards because it appealed to a significant fraction of England's intellectual elite and many of its most prominent advocates were biologists and medical experts who commanded scientific authority.[211]

In the 1890s and the first decade of the twentieth century, concern about the problem of 'ineducable' lower-class children became entangled in a wider cultural panic about the prevalence of mental 'defect' or mental deficiency: that is, intellectual disability. This cultural panic was transatlantic in scope and focused particularly upon the apparent prevalence of 'feeble-mindedness' in the English and American populations. I discuss the relationships between class, eugenics, and the concepts of educability and feeble-mindedness in depth in Chapter 4, particularly in relation to Wells's *Kipps* (1905). Here it is sufficient to note that the late Victorian and Edwardian preoccupation with the figure of the ineducable lower-class child both shaped and was shaped by the rise of the eugenics movement, as well as by more free-floating anxieties about degeneration and national efficiency.

As Paul Michael Privateer has pointed out, 'subnormal' intelligence attracts far more elaborate classificatory schemes and scales than normal or above normal intelligence in the late nineteenth and early twentieth centuries.[212] There is a proliferation of scientific terms to describe those of subnormal intelligence – imbecile, moron, feeble-minded, defective, degenerate – as well as efforts to give medical significance to terms that clearly originate in the everyday culture of the school – 'slow', 'dull', and 'backward'.[213] The concept of 'average' or 'normal' intelligence also becomes ubiquitous and idiomatic in this period, but normal intelligence generally passes untheorised and unclassified; as Stephen Byrne has shown, it often simply meant meeting the minimal requirements imposed by the state education system, though the concept simultaneously carried medical connotations of good health, or at least of a non-pathological mind.[214] Intellectual 'normalcy' was thus by turns a minimal and an optimal standard.[215] Paradoxically, however, 'normal' intelligence could also be imagined as dysgenic. As we have seen, Galton treated the intellectual 'average' or 'norm' not as an ideal or standard but as undesirable mediocrity. For him, mediocrity really means inferiority and, over time, degeneration:

> Enough is already known to make it certain that the productiveness of both the extreme classes, the best and the worst, falls short of the average of the nation as a whole. Therefore, the most prolific class necessarily lies between the two extremes, but at what intermediate point does it lie? Taken altogether, on any reasonable principle, are the natural gifts of the most prolific class, bodily, intellectual, and moral, above or below the line of national mediocrity? If above that line, then the existing conditions are favourable to the improvement of the race. If they are below that line, they must work towards its degradation.[216]

Intellectual ability, meanwhile, generally attracts a rhetoric of singularity and scarcity in this period – as we have seen, it is associated with the 'rare', 'uncommon', or 'exceptional' individuals, or 'the favoured few' who distinguish themselves from the masses. The association of intelligence with scarcity was partly due to the influence of the eugenics movement, which framed intelligence as a precious but dwindling national resource because of the failure of intellectually superior types – that is, the middle and upper classes – to reproduce at the same rate as the lower classes. As we have seen, it was also inscribed into the tenuousness of the scholarship ladder and the 'weak and socially elitist' nature of Victorian meritocracy, to repeat Sutherland's words. However, the exceptional status of intellectual ability also meant that it could be posited as a form of statistical deviation and therefore as biological deviance.[217] Despite eugenicist reverence for high intellectual ability, 'genius' was thus not safe from the pathologising embrace of fin de siècle discourses about intelligence. In 1891, Cesare Lombroso's *Man of Genius* was translated into English. Lombroso, an Italian criminologist, effectively revived the Romantic identification of genius with mental illness and social deviance, though under the new aegis of degeneration theory. For Lombroso, the fact that 'genius is a special morbid condition' goes to prove his larger thesis, which he condensed into an aphorism: 'education counts for little, heredity for much'.[218] Lombroso's paradigm was sufficiently influential to prompt Galton to regret that he had used the term 'genius' rather than 'ability' in *Hereditary Genius* and to acknowledge – albeit reluctantly – that there might be a connection between 'exceptionally able men' and mental illness.[219] Lombroso inspired the Scottish literary critic J. F. Nisbet to take up the same question in his *The Insanity of Genius and the General Inequality of Human Faculty Physiologically Considered* (1891). Nisbet argued that 'both genius and insanity are but different phases of a morbid susceptibility of, or want of balance in, the cerebro-spinal system'.[220] Nisbet asserted that the hereditary nexus between genius and madness made Galton's eugenic project untenable.[221] Nevertheless, as Nisbet's title spells out, his overall thesis affirmed Galton's view of intelligence as the biologically fixed basis of human inequality.

The overwhelming negativity of late Victorian and Edwardian discourses about intelligence may also be explained by the fact that the eugenics movement struggled to define its goals in positive terms. As Geoffrey Searle points out, eugenicists had trouble arriving at a clear eugenic ideal, and their rhetorical tendency to conflate intelligence with physical health, moral virtue, and all-round civic worth was easily critiqued by opponents and often not fully satisfactory to eugenicists themselves.[222] While the eugenic ideal remained hazily utopian, dysgenic types and groups – the feeble-minded, the unreproductive New Woman, the unemployed and pauperised (often known as the 'residuum') – seemed both more real and more susceptible to political intervention. Although eugenicists continued to debate the 'recipe for genius', in Grant Allen's phrase, the political campaigning of the eugenics movement was focused more intently on the menace of mental deficiency and the multiplication of the unfit.[223]

The problem of mental deficiency naturally became a crux in debates about the relative influences of heredity and environment in determining a person's character and fate. Due to the continuing influence of Lamarckian arguments, 'heredity' and 'environment' were not always understood in Galton's strictly oppositional terms in these debates.[224] However, as I have noted, Lamarckian thinkers such as Spencer and Maudsley were also often apt to emphasise the fixed and congenital nature of intelligence and contributed to the era's generalised scientific determinism about intellectual ability. The dissemination of the work of the German biologist August Weismann on the immutability of the 'germ plasm' in the late 1880s and the rediscovery of Gregor Mendel's work on plant heredity in 1900 both consolidated the authority of Galton's hard hereditarianism – now often referred to as the 'neo-Darwinian' position – and the scientific rationale of the eugenics movement.[225] After the turn of the century, a person's intellectual capacities were frequently imagined as intractable biological material – as Weismannian germ plasm or Mendelian character units – and this often inspired a self-consciously modern sense of pessimism about education. In 1900, the historian (and later Liberal MP) H. A. L. Fisher ironised this hereditarian zeitgeist and its consequences for the cultural status of education:

> The perfectibility of man by education is a doctrine calculated to increase the responsibility and dignity of the schoolmaster but in spite of the spread of National Schools, it ceases to command the respect of the philosophers. The optimism of [Enlightenment philosophers such as] Condorcet and Godwin was a pretty mirage, but we all now, with our Darwinian binoculars, fancy we can see through it. Everything is now apt to be explained by heredity [. . .] All our thoughts and feelings are physically transmitted to us from sources over which neither we nor our schoolmasters have the slightest possible control. Orbilius [that is, the flogging schoolmaster] may take his ease. The clever boys

will learn anyhow, and the stupid boys will learn nohow, birch he never so briskly.[226]

In 1908, F. H. Hayward, a schools inspector for London County Council, published a book entitled *Education and the Spectre of Heredity*. In it, he lamented that 'much educational thought [. . .] is tinged' with the hereditarian pessimism of Galton and his loyal lieutenant, the statistician Karl Pearson:[227]

The soul, from birth or from before birth, has its predestined form, its fixed potentialities; education can do little to shape the form, and nothing to increase the potentialities [. . .] For a brief moment we have dreamt that the educator may reach his pupil's will [. . .] We have fondly thought that the pupil may '*receive* the form that is right', not develop a form already predestined in the structure of the germ [. . .] Alas, Mr. Galton will tell us that culture, gentleness, fearlessness, truth-seeking, and intelligence have been, in large measure, weeded out from the human stock.[228]

Hayward condemned the widespread influence of such hereditarian pessimism upon education in Britain and urged his readers to recognise the 'plasticity, suggestibility, educability' of the human mind.[229] But the scientific quest to prove the essentially fixed and heritable nature of intelligence was already well under way.

Intelligence testing in England before Binet

In the decades following the publication of *Hereditary Genius*, Galton busied himself amassing anthropometric data that could be converted into statistics and used to substantiate his theories about intelligence and heredity. In 1884, he established an Anthropometric Laboratory as part of the International Health Exhibition in London's South Kensington Museum. Over 9,000 customers paid threepence each to be subjected to a battery of simple physical tests and measurements: their heights and weights were taken, and their eyesight, hearing, breathing, muscle strength, and response times to various stimuli measured. Although apparently measuring bodies, Galton was really attempting to anatomise the intangible substance he had traced through family trees in *Hereditary Genius*: the gift of intelligence. As Fancher has noted, the customers of the laboratory were participants in the first mass intelligence test.[230] Fancher suggests that Galton's customers were in this sense unwitting subjects, but Galton made no secret of the fact that measuring intellectual ability and proving the predominance of nature over nurture lay at the heart of his scientific enterprise. The late Victorian public also would have been readily familiar with the idea that the body and its measurements could be interpreted as indices of the mind: phrenology had been discredited but it lingered in the cultural imagination, and craniometry retained scientific authority. (Indeed, when the exhibition was over and the Anthropometric Laboratory moved to the Science Galleries of the Museum to continue its work, craniometry was included as part of the testing.) Galton also believed that the Anthropometric Laboratory had a salutary ideological effect insofar as it inured the public to the idea that all human characteristics – including moral and intellectual 'powers' – are measurable and rankable.[231] In any case, the real stakes of the Anthropometric Laboratory were clarified when Galton conducted the same tests on 1,450 Cambridge undergraduates the following year. Collaborating with the mathematician John Venn, Galton divided the undergraduates into three categories based upon the predictions of their tutors: first, a first-class man in the Tripos examinations; second, an 'honours' man, or passing man; and third, a 'poll' or 'plucked' man, who would not obtain a degree. Venn and Galton then sought – and failed – to correlate the predictions of the tutors with the student's physical characteristics and thereby discover an 'objective standard' for 'clever[ness]' within the 'upper professional class of Englishman'.[232]

As Galton's anthropometric labours and Warner's medical examinations of schoolchildren suggest, intelligence testing in the 1880s and 1890s was still partly wedded to the logic of phrenology and of the even older science of physiognomy (the art of reading character through facial features): it rested upon the assumption that the body can measure the mind. Galton inspired a cadre of other psychologists to pursue mental testing based upon this hypothesis. For example, in 1887, Joseph Jacobs measured the 'prehension' abilities (that is, the capacity to reproduce sounds accurately) of schoolboys at the Jews Free School in Bell Lane, London, hoping that this could serve as a yardstick of general mental capacity.[233] Galton thought Jacobs's work on prehension sufficiently promising as a measurement of intelligence that he conducted Jacobs's experiments upon the intellectually disabled at the

Earlswood Asylum with the assistance of Bain and at the Asylum for Idiots at Darenth with the assistance of James Sully in 1886.[234] Meanwhile, Galton's American protégé, James McKeen Cattell, embarked on large-scale studies of sensory acuity and response time that he called 'mental tests'.[235] McKeen Cattell conducted these tests first in the Cavendish Laboratory in Cambridge and then at the University of Pennsylvania and Columbia University, again attempting to correlate students' physical test scores with their academic records. Cattell inspired a flourishing mental testing movement in the United States until his work was successfully debunked by one of his own graduate students, Clark Wissler, in 1901.[236]

In the 1880s, Galton was also experimenting with ways of measuring more abstract mental processes. He invented the form of the psychological questionnaire and asked hundreds of diverse subjects detailed questions about the quality of their mental imagery (one of his subjects was Eliot, though Galton enlisted Sully to put the questions to her informally and she obliged).[237] Galton here sought to delineate the 'natural differences' between scientific and artistic minds, and he summarised his findings in his 1883 work, *Inquiries into Human Faculty and its Development*.[238] At Galton's suggestion, the Anglo-Irish psychologist Sophie Bryant conducted a study of the intellectual characteristics of a group of thirteen-year-old schoolchildren in 1886. Unlike most intelligence testers of the period, Bryant attempted to devise a direct test of her subjects' higher mental processes. Her test was essentially a creative writing task – she asked the students to describe a series of objects from memory – though the students' empirical accuracy was being assessed as well as their imaginative and 'emotional' tendencies (though, strikingly, not their linguistic skills, which Bryant omits from her analysis: the students' descriptions are taken as transparent records of the quality of their sense impressions rather than something mediated by language). Bryant hoped her test would identify 'mental defects' as well as 'mental excellencies' and occupational aptitudes.[239]

The quest to develop a viable intelligence test and transform intelligence into a quantifiable phenomenon gathered pace in England, France, and the United States in the 1890s and in the first decade of the twentieth century. Most of the prominent English and American 'intelligence men' – Cyril Burt, McKeen Cattell, Henry H. Goddard, Pearson, Charles Spearman, and Lewis

Terman – were self-conscious disciples of Galton and committed eugenicists.[240] In 1895, Pearson appealed to schoolteachers across England to supply him with data on the moral, intellectual, and physical characteristics of the nation's schoolchildren. Pearson hoped that he would be able to use the data on siblings to demonstrate the hereditary nature of 'mental characters'. He sent out 6,000 'schedules' for recording the data to schoolteachers, and received 4,000 completed schedules back from over 200 schools. He asked the teachers to classify their students according to his 'quantitative intelligence scale': (i) *Quick intelligent*, (ii) *Intelligent*, (iii) *Slow intelligent*, (iv) *Slow*, (v) *Slow Dull*, (vi) *Very Dull*, and (vii) *Inaccurate–Erratic*. Pearson had also asked teachers to report upon a range of other characteristics, but when analysing the data, it was the intelligence of the students which assumed overwhelming significance for him.[241] In his 1903 Huxley Lecture, he drew upon his research into schoolchildren to argue that education is overrated and England must turn instead to producing better 'raw material'. The lecture ends with a plea for eugenics as the only solution to the pressing problem of declining levels of intelligence within the population:

> The mentally better stock in the nation is not reproducing itself at the same rate as it did of old: the less able, and the less energetic, are more fertile than the better stocks ... The only remedy ... is to alter the relative fertility of the good and bad stocks in the community ... Intelligence can be aided and trained, but no training or education can *create* it. You must breed it.[242]

In 1904, Spearman – a retired British army officer and mathematician – published 'General Intelligence: Objectively Determined and Measured'.[243] While posted in Guernsey during the Boer War, Spearman had assessed and amassed data on the intellectual abilities of local children; he later collected the same data on children in a village school in Berkshire and an unnamed preparatory school (he used teachers' and classmates' reports and his own estimations of children's 'common sense').[244] By developing a statistical method now known as 'factor' analysis – a technique for reducing a series of statistical correlations to an underlying factor or factors – he claimed to have proven the existence of general intelligence, which was now construable as a mathematical value (g). The correlations between the various 'tests'

– really social judgements – he had gathered demonstrated that intelligence was homogeneous and 'monarchic': all abilities are expressions of the same underlying factor, general intelligence.[245] As Wooldridge observes, Spearman's 1904 article crystallised all of the major axioms that would underpin the rise of intelligence testing in the twentieth century: it sought to demonstrate that 'there is a central fund of mental energy, fixed by inheritance, common to all mental acts, varying from person to person, and open to objective, abstract and mathematical definition'.[246]

In 1909, the young psychologist Cyril Burt published 'Experimental Tests of General Intelligence'. Burt gave a variety of tests – motor and sensory discrimination tests as well as tests of memory, attention, and pattern recognition – to two groups of children: the first from a preparatory school catering to the sons of 'men of eminence in the intellectual world', and the second from a state elementary school where the parents were local tradesmen.[247] When the preparatory schoolboys scored better on his tests than their state school counterparts, Burt took this as decisive proof of 'the existence of class differences in native intelligence' since the tests themselves assumed little prior knowledge.[248] He further took it as a vindication of the eugenics movement.[249] Burt is exemplary of the drive to naturalise class differences that was central to English eugenics. In 1912, he denied that there were meaningful group variations in intelligence based upon gender or race; but proving that the social and economic hierarchy in England reflected differences in inborn intelligence became his abiding preoccupation.[250] When Burt discovered Binet's tests in 1913, he believed he had found an apparatus for vindicating Galton's hereditarian interpretation of intelligence and he soon adapted it for use in British classrooms.[251] In his initial role as educational psychologist for the London Education Authority and later as a prolific academic researcher and public intellectual, Burt was the most influential exponent of the IQ concept and intelligence testing in English culture up until his death in 1971. (Soon after Burt's death, allegations that he had fabricated his most important data began to surface, and the controversy over his legacy continues to this day.[252])

As often noted, it is ironic that the 'invention' of the IQ test is primarily associated with Binet, who did not believe that intellectual ability was fully amenable to testing and ranking, nor that it was reducible to a number.[253] He was also resistant to the idea that intelligence is fixed by heredity. In 1909, he remarked, some recent philosophers seem to have given their moral approval to these deplorable verdicts that affirm that the intelligence of an individual is a fixed quantity, a quantity that cannot be augmented. We must protest and react against this brutal pessimism; it is founded on nothing.[254]

In France, the intelligence test and the notion of IQ have only enjoyed a relatively modest cultural life.[255] It was in England and especially in the United States that the IQ notion of intelligence found fertile ideological soil and the technology of the intelligence test proliferated in educational settings and in psychology as a discipline (as well as in the military and in workplaces, prisons, and psychiatric hospitals). The history of the successful, if always controversial, career of the intelligence test and the IQ concept in England and in the United States has been told often and well.[256] This book focuses on the novelistic prehistory of IQ in England between 1860 and 1910. In this period, the IQ concept was thinkable – Macaulay was essentially capable of thinking it in 1853 – but still readily contestable because Binet had not created a technology that seemed to prove its reality. (Dr James Kerr, London's Medical Officer for Education, was in 1909 the first in England to draw attention the utility of Binet's tests, but they were not systematically employed in English classrooms until 1913.[257]) The provisional and essentially speculative character of the IQ concept in this period did not mean that its social and political implications remained entirely nebulous. As this Introduction has outlined, Galton and his followers ensured that both the meritocratic and eugenic possibilities of the IQ concept felt near at hand.

The *Bildungsroman* and the cruel optimism of meritocracy

The Victorian *Bildungsroman* has been described as the 'great literary vehicle for the meritocratic myth', or even as an 'essentially meritocratic' form.[258] This perception derives principally from Franco Moretti's highly influential account of the nineteenth-century European *Bildungsroman*, *The Way of the World* (1987). Moretti generally understands the *Bildungsroman* as a form of social compromise: it allegorises how 'the French Revolution could have been avoided' by charting how a quixotic youth comes to tailor his (and sometimes her) dreams to modern capitalism and by aligning the getting of wisdom with bourgeois getting on and getting ahead.[259] Moretti is scathing about the manipulative and childish way the English *Bildungsroman* in particular performs this allegorical work: the English *Bildungsroman* is merely a fairy-tale form where innocence is rewarded and the conflicts of modern life evaded.[260] In essence, Moretti objects to the strong current of Christian providentialism he discerns in the English *Bildungsroman*. As I have argued elsewhere, critics of the nineteenth-century English *Bildungsroman* have generally accepted Moretti's frameworks but used them as a standard against which to measure the critical force of a particular novel's departure from them.[261] This has led to a situation where the number of Victorian novels commonly praised as 'anti-*Bildungsromane*', 'critiques' of the *Bildungsroman*, *Bildungsromane* of 'non-fulfilment', or 'meta-*Bildungsromane*' far exceeds the number of novels which are taken to exemplify the form. Moretti's complaint that the English *Bildungsroman* is a fairy tale of bourgeois conformity rewarded rests on only a handful of novels: Charlotte Brontë's *Jane Eyre* (1847) and Charles Dickens's *David Copperfield* (1849) and *Great Expectations* (1861). By extension, the perception that the Victorian *Bildungsroman* is a form that celebrates the upward mobility of a humble but clever and morally deserving hero or heroine relies on the canonical centrality of Dickens and Brontë. However, as Isobel Armstrong has suggested, this reading of the *Bildungsroman* obscures the fact that many nineteenth-century novels are, in fact, narratives of 'dispossession and dereliction', not meritocratic triumph.[262] Indeed, many of the canonical Victorian examples of the *Bildungsroman* – and the novels I examine in this book – are novels about bad education, blighted potential, and failure.[263] It is true that these *Bildungsromane* are preoccupied with the promises of meritocracy, but they do not offer fairy-tale wish fulfilment: instead, they explore the psychic effects of the jarring discrepancies between meritocratic ideals and social realities. I argue that the Victorian *Bildungsroman* ought to be understood as a genre of what Lauren Berlant famously called 'cruel optimism': a fantasy of flourishing or of the good life which is at once sustaining and self-destructive, given the person's social conditions.[264] Berlant's coinage was designed to capture the often unbearable double-binds of contemporary American life under neoliberalism, but it also captures the predicaments of Victorian protagonists for whom a tenuous and socially elitist meritocracy is the primary source of hope for self-realisation.

The *Bildungsroman* form is bound up with Romantic ideals of education and individual development. The term *Bildung* itself conjures the expansive and optimistic notion of education embedded within German Romanticism; it gestures at the idea that the individual possesses diverse moral and intellectual capacities that he (or possibly she) must cultivate through a complex process of self-discovery and engagement with the world. As Gregory Castle has helpfully shown, the English literary tradition inherits two distinct traditions of *Bildung* from German Romanticism. The first, associated with Johann Wolfgang von Goethe, is more mystical, elitist, and invested in the arts as a touchstone for self-cultivation. The second, associated with Wilhelm von Humboldt, is more practical, democratically minded, and preoccupied with formal education as mechanism of personal development.[265] Castle then posits this as a further split: the nineteenth century rationalised and bureaucratised Romantic ideals of self-cultivation, and Victorian writers produce a 'socially pragmatic' *Bildung*, which essentially works to manufacture consent to bourgeois social norms. In Castle's account, this then sets the stage for modernist writers to rediscover the radical potential latent in the 'aesthetico-spiritual' or Goethean tradition: its ideals of creative autonomy and self-cultivation can be used to critique the narrowly pragmatic tradition of *Bildung* as getting ahead in the world, even if those ideals remain painfully out of reach.[266] Although Castle treats Hardy's *Jude* and Oscar Wilde's *A Picture of Dorian Gray* (1890) as honorary modernist texts, Victorian literature fares little better in Castle's account than it does in Moretti's: it is the dull bourgeois way station between the bohemian adventures of Romanticism and modernism. Nonetheless, it is possible to adopt Castle's useful taxonomy of the different varieties of *Bildung* without accepting his sense of a sharp Victorian/modernist divide.

Georg Lukács is one of the original sources of the notion of the *Bildungsroman* as an affirmative genre of bourgeois socialisation. In *The Theory of the Novel* (1916), he notes *Bildungsromane* typically make social conformity seductive precisely because they fully acknowledge its ambivalent character: they make it seem the 'fruit of a rich and enriching resignation, the crowning of a process of education; a maturity attained by struggle and effort'.[267] However, this ambivalence also means that the 'dividing line' between the *Bildungsroman* and another kind of novel – the 'novel of disillusionment' – is 'fluid'.[268] The novel of disillusionment dramatises 'a profound dissonance between behaviour and soul, between outward destiny and inner fate': such novels have a 'contemplative' rather than an 'active' protagonist and exhibit an 'over-intensified, over-determined desire for an ideal life as opposed to a real one, a desperate recognition of the fact that this desire to doomed to remain unsatisfied, a utopia based from the start on an uneasy conscience and the certainty of defeat'.[269] Lukács wrote *Theory of the Novel* prior to embracing Marxism, at a time when he still thought that a Hegelian ideal of synthetic wholeness was the supreme test of aesthetic value. He thus valorises the *Bildungsroman* and treats the novel of disillusionment as an inferior genre, one always on the verge of dissolving into incoherence, maudlin pessimism, and mere navel-gazing. Yet he nonetheless betrays an attraction to the kind of proto-modernist fragmentation and alienation embodied in the novel of disillusionment. He suggests that, at its finest, this type of novel finds profundity in failure:

> By a strange and melancholy paradox, the moment of failure is the moment of value; the comprehending and experiencing of life's refusals is a source from which the fullness of life seems to flow. What is depicted is the total absence of any fulfilment of meaning, yet the work attains the rich and rounded fullness of a true totality of life.[270]

This book obviously retains the term *Bildungsroman*, but in my usage, it does not necessarily designate a novel of successful social adjustment: it also encompasses what Lukács calls the 'novel of disillusionment'. I resist labelling these novels 'anti-*Bildungsroman*' or 'critiques' of the *Bildungsroman* form, since, like Castle, I understand the Romantic concept of *Bildung* as a vital critical resource rather than as the object of critique. The critical force of *Bildung* for Victorian and Edwardian novelists paradoxically lies in its vagueness and open-endedness: it supplies a wistful rhetoric of human 'potential' and 'possibilities' that require cultivation to come into fruition, and of thereby asserting that the individual might be – or, in a more tragic key, might have been – something more or other than his or her social position. The concept and rhetoric of *Bildung* thereby provides a means of critiquing the cruel optimism of Victorian meritocracy. It simultaneously provides a means of resisting the often oppressive determinisms of the emerging IQ concept of intelligence.

The Romantic ideal of *Bildung* was entangled in eighteenth-century scientific debates about human biology, particularly debates between preformationist and epigenist views of human development.[271] The preformationists argued that unborn organisms were fully formed in miniature in the eggs or sperm of their parents prior to conception; development of an organism is simply the unfolding of a predetermined structure. In contrast, epigenists argued that organisms develop form gradually from unstructured matter, and that development entails the emergence of real novelties. The epigenists gained cultural ascendancy in this debate in 1781, when Johann Blumenbach posited the existence of a *Bildungstrieb* or 'formative drive': all living organisms possess an intrinsic impulse to develop, preserve, and restore form.[272] As Daniel Aureliano Newman writes, the concept of *Bildungstrieb* 'reverberated throughout German culture' and gave wide cachet to the idea that 'identity [. . .] is not given but realised'.[273] The primary reverberation of the idea of *Bildungstrieb* within aesthetics is the literary form of the *Bildungsroman*. The eighteenth-century battle between the preformationists and epigenists was often invoked in nineteenth-century debates about evolution and heredity.[274] Even when Victorian and Edwardian novelists were not fully conscious of the *Bildungsroman*'s original affiliation with epigenist theory, its emphasis upon plasticity, education, and self-formation made it a natural vehicle for contesting nineteenth-century determinism about intellectual potential. However, it is important to emphasise that the novelists in this book have been chosen because they are not simply attempting to debiologise intelligence or retreat to a Romantic ideal of intelligence as an ineffable gift; in different ways, they each attempt to think seriously about the implications of the IQ concept.

My reading of Victorian and Edwardian *Bildungsromane* is inspired by Rancière's efforts to theorise intellectual equality and the politics of the nineteenth-century novel. Rancière's work celebrates and attempts to think through the extent to which democratic politics entail the 'mad presupposition that everyone is intelligent as anyone else'.[275] This is also the provocation at the core of his book *The Ignorant Schoolmaster* (1987), which recuperates the theories of the Romantic pedagogue Joseph Jacotot in order to critique the inequality at the core of modern ideas of intelligence and education. When Rancière recuperates the idea of the equality of intelligence from Jacotot, he constructs it not as a sober thesis for which he is going to supply evidence but as a kind of dare or wager, an invitation to an intellectual 'adventure' upon which we ought to 'gamble all [our] credibility'.[276] He writes:

> the problem isn't proving that all intelligence is equal. It's seeing what can be done under that supposition. And for this, it is enough that the opinion be possible – that is, that no opposing truth be proved.[277]

In other parts of his work, Rancière has made bold claims for the radically egalitarian character of the nineteenth-century novel. He defines the novel as a 'genre without genre' which shatters the hierarchical protocols of classical literature and takes for its subject anyone and anything at all.[278] In his view, the egalitarianism of the form is independent of the political beliefs of any given novelist and distinct from explicitly political campaigns for democracy or social emancipation. 'Literary democracy' inheres in the propensity of the novel to honour the capacity of 'anyone whomsoever [to] experience any emotion or passion whatsoever'.[279] He goes on:

> This new capacity of anyone at all to live any life at all ruins the model linking the organicity of the story to the separation between active and passive men, elite and vulgar souls. It produces this new real, [. . . which is] the interlacing of a multiplicity of individual experiences, the lived fabric of a world in which it is no longer possible to distinguish between the great souls who think, feel, dream and act and individuals locked in the repetition of bare life.[280]

The novels analysed in this book do not straightforwardly affirm 'the equality of all intelligences' or the 'capacity of anyone at all to live any life at all': in many ways, they attest to the fact that natural equality seemed like a 'pre-Darwinian figment' in the late Victorian and Edwardian years, in Grant Allen's words.[281] These novels also attest to the pervasiveness of the biopolitics of intelligence in the second half of the nineteenth century. However, I argue that these novels are, in various ways, invested in testing how far it is possible to think equality after science had seemed to make intelligence the key to all inequalities.

Most of the *Bildungsromane* explored in this book do not focus on a single individual but are double- or triple-plot *Bildungsromane* which ask the reader to compare the life chances and developmental trajectories of two or more primary characters, typically across divides of gender and class. This 'distribution of narrative attention', in Alex Woloch's terms, is designed to provoke questions about differences in social circumstances and problematise conventional social judgements about intelligence and potential.[282] As Woloch has argued, nineteenth-century novelists often put pressure on the distribution of narrative attention in order to 'register the competing pull of inequality and democracy within the nineteenth-century bourgeois imagination'.[283] In particular, he emphasises that although nineteenth-century novels are typically fascinated with the interiority and distinctiveness of a specific protagonist, they tend also to highlight the arbitrariness of the distinction between that protagonist and a cluster of minor characters who are not granted a full narrative or real psychological depth but who may have equally compelling claims to the status of protagonist or hero. In the novels under examination here, minor characters often embody a challenge to the nineteenth-century hierarchy of intelligence: they disrupt the presumed correlation between intellectual capacities and social identities and the biopolitical logic which made intelligence a scarce resource or the property of the few. At the same time, the protagonists of these *Bildungsromane* are defined by their unstable identifications – sometimes explicit, but often furtive and imaginative – with those generally dehumanised by the modern science of intelligence: the lower classes, racialised others, and the intellectually disabled. In their various efforts both to vindicate overlooked and stigmatised intelligence and to make the surplus intelligence of minor characters a problem, these novels enact, in Rancière's terms, a 'count of the uncounted': they 'spoil the fit between bodies and meanings' and thereby expose the contingency of what he calls the 'police distribution of the sensible'.[284]

Chapter 1 explores George Eliot's *Mill on the Floss* (1860) and *Daniel Deronda* (1876). Eliot's novels problematise the extent to which Victorian science and psychology had reformulated intelligence as an objective, morally neutral category, and demonstrate the morally fraught nature of judgements about intellectual superiority and inferiority. Eliot's novels also attempt to substantiate arguments that Eliot's partner, the psychologist George Henry Lewes, had made about the fundamentally social and emotional nature of intelligence, but they do so to different ends from Lewes's work: Eliot attempts to rehabilitate female intelligence. Chapter 2 focuses on Hardy's novels *The Woodlanders* (1887), *Tess of the d'Urbervilles* (1891), and *Jude the Obscure* (1895). Hardy's novels at once embrace the new biological model of intelligence and seek to resist the scientific reification of intellectual inequality. Chapter 3 reads Henry James's *The Tragic Muse* (1890) as an attempt to expose the extent to which aristocratic ideals haunt apparently modern conceptions of talent and merit. By extension, James calls attention to the extent to which intelligence is an unstable social performance. Chapter 4 reads three of Wells's comic *Bildungsromane*, *Love and Mr. Lewisham* (1900), *Kipps* (1905), and *The History of Mr. Polly* (1910), as Wells's interrogation of his own attraction to the IQ model of intelligence. The Coda examines Virginia Woolf's *Night and Day* (1919) as a melancholic reflection upon the legacy of Victorian conceptions of intelligence and merit.

Notes

1 W. S. Lilly, 'Darwinism and Democracy', *Fortnightly Review* (1886), 34–50, p. 42.
2 See, for example, Grant Allen, rev. of L. F. Ward's *Dynamic Sociology*, *Mind* 9 (1884), 305–31, p. 309; Francis Galton, *Hereditary Genius* (London: Macmillan, 1869), p. 14; T. H. Huxley, 'On the Natural Inequality of Men', *Nineteenth Century* 27 (1890), pp. 1–23; Benjamin Kidd, *Social Evolution* (London: Macmillan, 1894), p. 184; Lilly, p. 42; Henry Maudsley, *Body and Mind* (New York: D. Appleton & Co., 1871), p. 43; and H. G. Wells, *Anticipations of the Reaction of Mechanical and Scientific Progress upon Human Life and Thought* (London: Chapman & Hill, 1901), p. 291. See also Havelock Ellis's discussion of the untenability of Rousseauean natural equality after Darwin in *Little Essays on Love and Virtue*, although this was published in 1921. See Ellis, *Little Essays* (New York: George H. Doran Company, 1921), pp. 137–8. Contemporary thinkers also remarked upon the fact that it had become routine to invoke evolution or heredity in order to contest the principle of equality. See H. A. L. Fisher, 'Heredity and Imitation', *The Speaker* (28 July 1900), pp. 455–6; D. G. Ritchie, 'Equality', *Contemporary Review* 62 (1892), pp. 563–8; and Karl Pearson, 'Socialism and Natural Selection', *Fortnightly Review* 56 (1894), pp. 1–21.

3 Qtd in Catherine Malabou, *Morphing Intelligence: From IQ Measurement to Artificial Brains*, trans. Carolyn Shread (New York: Columbia University Press, 2019), p. 3.

4 Ibid., p. 1.

5 Lorraine Daston, 'The Naturalised Female Intellect', *Science in Context* 5.2 (1992), 209–35, p. 211.

6 Malabou, p. 3.

7 See Huxley, p. 4. See note 1 for other references.

8 Ibid., p. 10.

9 On the 'biologisation' of the mind and the emergence of psychology as a discipline in the nineteenth century, see Edwin Clarke and L. S. Jacyna, *The Nineteenth-Century Origins of Neuroscientific Concepts* (Berkeley: University of California Press, 1987); Robert J. Richards, *Darwin and the Emergence of Evolutionary Theories of Mind and Behaviour* (Chicago: Chicago University Press, 1987); Edward S. Reed, *From Soul to Mind: The Emergence of Psychology from Erasmus Darwin to William James* (New Haven, CT: Yale University Press, 1997); Rick Rylance, *Victorian Psychology and British Culture 1850–1880* (Oxford: Oxford University Press, 2000); and Robert M. Young, *Mind, Brain, and Adaptation: Cerebral Localisation and its Biological Context from Gall to Ferrier* (Oxford: Oxford University Press, 1990).

10 Daston, p. 214.

11 Kurt Danziger, *Naming the Mind: How Psychology Found its Language* (London: Sage, 1997), p. 70.

12 Ibid., p. 68.

13 Charles Darwin, *The Descent of Man and Selection in Related to Sex* (London: John Murray, 1871), pp. 33–4.

14 See John Carson, *The Measure of Merit: Talents, Intelligence, and Inequality in the French and American Republics, 1750–1940* (Princeton, NJ: Princeton University Press, 2007); Raymond Fancher, *The Intelligence Men: Makers of the IQ Controversy* (New York: W. W. Norton, 1985); Stephen Jay Gould, *The Mismeasure of Man, Revised and Expanded Edition* (New York: W. W. Norton & Company, 2006); Michael Paul Privateer, *Inventing Intelligence: A Social History of Smart* (Oxford: Blackwell, 2006); Gillian Sutherland, *Ability, Merit, and Measurement: Mental Testing and English Education, 1880–1940* (Oxford: Clarendon Press, 1984); Adrian Wooldridge, *Measuring the Mind: Education and Psychology in England c. 1860–1990* (Cambridge: Cambridge University Press, 2006); and Leila

Zenderland, *Measuring Minds: Henry Herbert Goddard and the Origins of American Intelligence Testing* (Cambridge: Cambridge University Press, 2001).

15 Michel Foucault, *The History of Sexuality, vol. 1: An Introduction*, trans. Robert Hurley (London: Penguin Books, 1976), pp. 135–6.

16 Michel Foucault, *Society Must be Defended: Lectures at the Collège de France, 1975–76*, trans. David Macey (London: Penguin, 1997), p. 245.

17 Ibid., 242.

18 Ibid., pp. 254–7.

19 Foucault, *History of Sexuality*, p. 141 and *Society Must be Defended*, pp. 250–1.

20 Foucault, *History of Sexuality*, p. 144.

21 Ibid., p. 141.

22 Ansgar Allen, *Benign Violence: Education In and Beyond the Age of Reason* (Basingstoke: Palgrave Macmillan, 2014), pp. 97–125 and pp. 136–250.

23 For a detailed history of the rise of examination culture, see John Roach, *Public Examinations in England 1850–1900* (Cambridge: Cambridge University Press, 1971).

24 Sutherland, *Ability, Merit, and Measurement*, pp. 97–163; Simon Szreter, *Fertility, Class, and Gender in Britain 1860–1940* (Cambridge: Cambridge University Press, 1996), pp. 160–73; and Wooldridge, *Measuring the Mind*, pp. 167–76.

25 John Van Wyhe, *Phrenology and the Origins of Victorian Scientific Naturalism* (London: Routledge, 2004), p. 5.

26 See Fenneke Sysling, 'Phrenology and the Average Person 1840–1940', *History of the Human Sciences* 34.2 (2021), pp. 27–45.

27 On the association of phrenology with self-improvement and meritocratic aspirations, see Roger Cooter, *The Cultural Meaning of a Popular Science: Phrenology and the Organisation of Consent in Nineteenth-Century Britain* (Cambridge: Cambridge University Press, 1984), p. 47 and p. 86; and Sally Shuttleworth, *Charlotte Brontë and Victorian Psychology* (Cambridge: Cambridge University Press, 1996), pp. 63–6.

28 Alexander Bain, *On the Study of Character: Including an Estimate of Phrenology* (London: Parker, Son & Bourn, 1861), pp. 1–17.

29 I was alerted to Bain's indirect role in the development of intelligence testing by Walter M. Humes, 'Alexander Bain and the Development of Educational Theory', in *The Meritocratic Intellect: Studies in the History of Educational Research*, ed. James V. Smith

and David Hamilton (Aberdeen: Aberdeen University Press, 1980), pp. 15–25, pp. 24–5.

30 See Alexander Bain, *Mental and Moral Science: Psychology and the History of Philosophy*, vol. 1 (London: Longmans Green, 1872), pp. 84–5; and Bain, *Mind and Body*, pp. 83–9.

31 Bain, *Study of Character*, pp. 254–5.

32 Ibid., pp. 260–6.

33 Ibid., pp. 268–71.

34 On Bain's attempt to develop a new differential psychology, see Laurent Clauzade, 'From the Science of the Mind to Character Study: Alexander Bain and the Psychology of Individual Differences', *Revue d'histoire des sciences* 60.2 (2007), pp. 281–301.

35 Ibid., pp. 320–44.

36 Bain, *Study of Character*, p. 271 and p. 254.

37 Alexander Bain, *Emotions and the Will*, 3rd edition (London: Longmans Green, 1880), pp. 49–53.

38 Ibid., pp. 50–1.

39 Bain, *Study of Character*, p. v.

40 Herbert Spencer, *The Principles of Psychology* (London: Longmans, 1855), p. 580.

41 Ibid., p. 609.

42 Ibid., pp. 491–533.

43 As Danziger explains, Spencer adopted 'intelligence' from French scientific discourse, where it was associated with Lamarckian thought and became a means of discussing the 'quasi-rational accomplishments' of animals without resorting to the idea of 'reason'. See Danziger, p. 69.

44 Spencer, *Principles of Psychology*, pp. 506–21.

45 Ibid., pp. 506.

46 Ibid., pp. 376–482.

47 Herbert Spencer, *First Principles* (London: Williams and Northgate, 1863), p. 486.

48 Ibid., p. 218.

49 Herbert Spencer, *The Study of Sociology* (New York: D. Appleton & Co., 1874), pp. 345–6.

50 Herbert Spencer, *The Principles of Psychology*, vol. 2 (New York: D. Appleton & Co., 1873), pp. 575–7, pp. 609–11.

51 Spencer, *First Principles*, pp. 159–62.

52 Spencer, *Study of Sociology*, pp. 333–6.

53 Ibid., p. 346 and p. 351.

54 Herbert Spencer, *A New Theory of Population, Deduced from the General Law of Animal Fertility* (London: John Chapman, 1852), p. 33 and p. 37.

55 Spencer, *Study of Sociology*, pp. 373–5.

56 Spencer, *Principles of Psychology*, pp. 573–7; *Study of Sociology*, pp. 373–5; and *Essays: Scientific Political and Speculative*, vol. 1 (London: Williams and Norgate, 1868), pp. 419–22.

57 Spencer, *Principles of Psychology*, p. 610.

58 Ibid., pp. 580–2.

59 Ibid., p. 527.

60 For Spencer's advocacy of scientific education, see his *Education: Intellectual, Moral, and Physical* (New York: D. Appleton & Co., 1896).

61 Herbert Spencer, *An Autobiography*, vol. 2 (London: Williams and Norgate, 1904), p. 18.

62 Herbert Spencer, *Social Statics, or the Conditions Essential to Human Happiness Specified* (London: John Chapman, 1851), p. 380.

63 Ibid.

64 Spencer, *An Autobiography*, vol. 1, appendix H, p. 634.

65 Spencer, *Social Statics*, pp. 91–2, pp. 107–8, and pp. 171–3.

66 Ibid., pp. 107–8.

67 Ibid., pp. 330–56.

68 Danziger, p. 70.

69 On Galton's early interest in phrenology, see Nicholas Wright Gilham, *A Life of Sir Francis Galton: From African Exploration to the Birth of Eugenics* (Oxford: Oxford University Press, 2001), p. 57.

70 Ibid.

71 Galton, *Hereditary Genius: An Inquiry into Its Laws and Consequences* (London: Macmillan & Co., 1892), 2nd edition with additional Preface, p. v.

72 Raymond Fancher, 'Francis Galton's African Ethnography and its Role in the Development of Psychology', *The British Journal for the History of Science* 16.1 (1983), pp. 67–79.

73 See Emel Aileen Gökyiğit, 'The Reception of Francis Galton's *Hereditary Genius* in the late Victorian Periodical Press', *Journal of the History of Biology* 27 (1994), pp. 215–40.

74 Alfred Russel Wallace, 'Hereditary Genius', *Nature* 1 (17 March 1870), pp. 501–3.

75 Charles Darwin to Francis Galton, 3 December 1869. Qtd in

Galton's autobiography, *Memories of My Life* (London: Methuen, 1908), p. 290.

76 Ibid.

77 Darwin, p. 111.

78 Qtd in Michael Bulmer, *Francis Galton: Pioneer of Heredity and Biometry* (Baltimore: Johns Hopkins University Press, 2003), p. 57.

79 Galton, *Hereditary Genius*, p. 41.

80 Ibid., p. 2.

81 Galton was conscious of this meritocratic revision of the idea of a peerage. In his unpublished utopian novel *Kantsaywhere*, a character reads a calendar akin to 'Burke's or Debrett's Peerages', except that entry is gained on the basis of examination results rather than by marriage or birth right. See Galton, *The Eugenic College of Kantsaywhere*, p. 40, University College London digital edition. Available at: <https://www.ucl.ac.uk/library/special-collections/ka ntsaywhere> (last accessed 21 March 2022).

82 For a useful account of the Romantic conception of genius, see Penelope Murray, 'Introduction', in *Genius: The History of an Idea*, ed. Penelope Murray (Oxford: Basil Blackwell, 1989), pp. 1–9.

83 Robin Durnford, 'Posthumanous Victorians: Francis Galton's Eugenics and Fin de Siècle Science Fictions', PhD thesis, University of Alberta, 2013, p. 115.

84 Galton, *Hereditary Genius*, p. 63.

85 Gilham, pp. 37–45.

86 Galton, *Hereditary Genius*, pp. 16–21.

87 Ibid., pp. 6–7 and pp. 19–35.

88 Ibid., pp. xi–xii and p. 30.

89 Ibid., pp. 26–32.

90 On the different valuations Quetelet and Galton gave to the concept of the 'average', see Ian Hacking, *The Taming of Chance* (Cambridge: Cambridge University Press, 1995), pp. 184–5.

91 Maurizio Meloni, *Political Biology: Science and Social Values in Human Heredity from Eugenics to Epigenetics* (Basingstoke: Palgrave Macmillan, 2016), p. 48.

92 The phrase 'nature versus nurture' was popularised by the subtitle to Galton's follow-up work to *Hereditary Genius*, which pursued the same thesis about natural talent in relation to notable scientists: it was entitled *English Men of Science: Their Nature and Nurture* (1874).

93 Maudsley, p. 43.

94 See Meloni, p. 46.

95 Herman Merivale, 'Galton on Hereditary Genius', *Edinburgh Review* 132 (1870), pp. 100–25.

96 See Gilham, p. 165.

97 John Stuart Mill wrote 'the power of education is almost boundless: there is not one natural inclination which it is not strong enough to coerce'. See Mill, *Three Essays on Religion* (New York: Henry Holt, 1874), p. 82.

98 See Diane Paul and Benjamin Day, 'John Stuart Mill, Innate Differences, and the Regulation of Reproduction', *Studies in History and Philosophy of Biological and Biomedical Sciences* 39 (2008), pp. 223–31; Angelique Richardson, *Love and Eugenics in the Late Nineteenth Century: Rational Reproduction and the New Woman* (Oxford: Oxford University Press, 2003), pp. 186–8; Meloni, pp. 45–6; and Paul White, 'Acquired Character: The Hereditary Material of the Self-Made Man', in *Heredity Produced: At the Crossroads of Biology, Politics and Culture 1500–1870*, ed. Staffan Müller-Wille and Hans-Jörg Rheinberger (Cambridge, MA: MIT Press, 2007), pp. 375–98.

99 Qtd in Gilham, p. 171.

100 For further analysis of the roots of the meritocratic ideal in the Victorian intellectual aristocracy, see Szreter, pp. 160–73.

101 Noel Annan, 'The Intellectual Aristocracy', in *Studies in Social History*, ed. J. H. Plumb (Longmans: London, 1955), 256–83, p. 244.

102 Annan, p. 247.

103 Vincent Pecora has analysed the Bloomsbury Group as an outgrowth of the Victorian intellectual aristocracy and both 'kinship groups' as secularised versions of Evangelical Christianity, particularly the Clapham Sect. See Pecora, *Secularisation and Cultural Criticism: Religion, Nation & Modernity* (Chicago: University of Chicago Press, 2006), pp. 165–9.

104 Sutherland, *Ability, Merit, and Measurement*, pp. 98–101.

105 House of Commons, *Hansard's Parliamentary Debates*: *The Government of India Bill* (24 June 1853 vol 128 cc734–78). Available at: <https://api.parliament.uk/historic-hansard/commons/1853/jun/24/government-of-india-bill-adjourned> (last accessed 11 November 2021).

106 *Macaulay Report on the Indian Civil Service*, November 1854. Reprinted in the Fulton Committee, *The Civil Service: Volume I: Report of the Committee 1966–69* (London: Her Majesty's Stationery Office, 1969), p. 122.

107 Szreter, pp. 159–60.

108 Ibid., p. 166.

109 House of Commons, *Hansard's Parliamentary Debates*: *The Government of India Bill*.

110 Ibid.

111 *Macaulay Report*, p. 123.

112 Ibid.

113 Ibid., p. 127.

114 Szreter, p. 161.

115 House of Commons, *Hansard's Parliamentary Debates*: *The Government of India Bill*.

116 Adrian Wooldridge, *The Aristocracy of Talent: How Meritocracy Made the Modern World* (London: Allen Lane, 2021), pp. 161–2.

117 Thomas Hardy, 'Destiny and a Blue Cloak', in *An Indiscretion in the Life of an Heiress and Other Stories*, ed. Pamela Dalziel, Oxford World's Classics (Oxford: Oxford University Press, 1999), p. 15.

118 Qtd in J. M. Compton, 'Open Competition and the Indian Civil Service, 1854–1876', *English Historical Review* 83.327 (1968), 265–84, p. 271.

119 Qtd in ibid., p. 271.

120 Ibid., pp. 268–70.

121 Szreter, pp. 153–4.

122 Ibid., p. 162.

123 Heather Ellis, 'Efficiency and Counter-revolution: Connecting University and Civil Service Reform in the 1850s', *History of Education* 42.1 (2013), 23–44, p. 24.

124 Qtd in Heather Ellis, p. 28.

125 Anonymous, 'Competitive Examination', *The Examiner* (5 April 1862), p. 211. See also Wooldridge, *Aristocracy of Talent*, p. 157.

126 Qtd in Cathy Shuman, *Pedagogical Economies* (Stanford, CA: Stanford University Press, 2000), p. 78. For an analysis of Trollope as a critic of the Civil Service reforms, see Shuman, pp. 170–212; and Jennifer Ruth, *Novel Professions: Interested Disinterest and the Making of the Professional in the Victorian Novel* (Columbus: Ohio State University Press, 2006), pp. 83–104.

127 J. M. Compton, 'Open Competition', pp. 279–80.

128 Ibid., pp. 277–8.

129 J. M. Compton, 'Indians and the Indian Civil Service, 1853–1879: A Study in National Agitation and Imperial Embarrassment',

Journal of the Asiatic Society of Great Britain and Ireland 3/4 (1967), 99–113, pp. 100–13.

130 See Ruth, pp. 71–89.

131 James Elwick, *Making a Grade: Victorian Examinations and the Rise of Standardised Testing* (Toronto: University of Toronto Press, 2021), pp. 153–4.

132 On the tutoring industry associated with the 11 plus examination, see Sally Weale, '"An Education Arms Race": Inside the Ultra-competitive World of Private Tutoring', *The Guardian*, 5 December 2018. Available at: <https://www.theguardian.com/education/20 18/dec/05/an-education-arms-race-inside-the-ultra-competitive-wo rld-of-private-tutoring> (last accessed 12 November 2021).

133 Qtd in Ruth, p. 87.

134 Ibid., pp. 86–90.

135 Michael Young, *The Rise of the Meritocracy* (Abingdon: Routledge, 1958), p. 84.

136 See Cynthia Eagle Russett, *Sexual Science: The Victorian Constitution of Womanhood* (Cambridge, MA: Harvard University Press, 1989), pp. 104–29.

137 Spencer, *Education: Intellectual, Moral, and Physical*, pp. 276–7.

138 Ibid., pp. 103, 226, and 280.

139 For a detailed analysis of the popular currency and uses of the over-pressure concept in Victorian culture, see Amelia Bonea, Melissa Dickson, Sally Shuttleworth, and Jennifer Wallis, *Anxious Times: Medicine and Modernity in Nineteenth-century Britain* (Pittsburgh: University of Pittsburgh Press, 2019), pp. 149–80.

140 Wooldridge, *Aristocracy of Talent*, pp. 158–62.

141 Wooldridge, *Measuring the Mind*, p. 172.

142 Ibid.

143 Sheldon Rothblatt, *Education's Abiding Moral Dilemma: Merit and Worth in the Cross-Atlantic Democracies* (Oxford: Symposium Books 2006), pp. 50–1.

144 William Clark, *Academic Charisma and the Origins of the Research University* (Chicago: University of Chicago Press, 2008), p. 117.

145 See Sheila Cordner, *Education in Nineteenth-century British Literature: Exclusion as Innovation* (London: Routledge, 2016), pp. 12–16.

146 See Paul R. Deslandes, 'Competitive Examinations and the Culture of Masculinity in Oxbridge Undergraduate Life, 1850–1920', *History of Education Quarterly* 42.4 (2002), pp. 544–78.

147 Clark, p. 134.

148 'Wounded winners' is Michael J. Sandel's phrase; see *The Tyranny of Merit: What's Become of the Common Good?* (New York: Farrar, Straus and Giroux, 2020), p. 177. However, I am not thinking of Sandel's work but of Daniel Markovitz's *The Meritocracy Trap*, which dwells upon the heavy workloads and anxiety that meritocracy inflicts upon elites in the contemporary United States. See *The Meritocracy Trap* (London: Penguin Random House, 2019).

149 Clark, p. 134.

150 Deslandes, pp. 564–5.

151 *Taunton Report: Report of the Schools Inquiry Commission* (London: George E. Eyre and William Spottiswoode, 1868), p. 96 and p. 27.

152 Ibid., p. 27.

153 Qtd in Sutherland, *Ability, Measurement, and Merit*, p. 107.

154 *Taunton Report*, p. 158.

155 Qtd in Sutherland, *Ability, Measurement, and Merit*, p. 109.

156 Galton, 'Hereditary Talent and Character', *Macmillan's Magazine* 12 (1865), 157–327, p. 323.

157 On girls' limited and often contested access to the late Victorian scholarship ladder, see Carol Dyson, *No Distinction of Sex? Women in British Universities 1870–1939* (London: UCL Press, 1995), pp. 25–35.

158 *Taunton Report*, p. 96.

159 *Bryce Report: Report on the Royal Commission of Secondary Education* (London: Eyre and Spottiswoode, 1895), p. 171.

160 Szreter, pp. 149–52.

161 Gillian Sutherland, 'Measuring Intelligence: English Local Education Authorities and Mental Testing, 1919–1939', in *The Meritocratic Intellect*, ed. James V. Smith and David Hamilton (Aberdeen: Aberdeen University Press, 1980), 79–95, p. 87.

162 Szreter, p. 165.

163 Pierre Bourdieu and Jean-Claude Passeron, *Reproduction, Education, Society, and Culture*, 2nd edition, trans. Richard Nice (Los Angeles: Sage, 2000), p. 159.

164 See also Hugh B. Philpott, 'The Educational Ladder', *The English Illustrated Magazine* (February 1904), pp. 513–22; and Frances Warwick, 'The Cause of the Children', *Nineteenth-Century and After* 50.293 (1901), pp. 67–76.

165 J. L. Paton, 'The Secondary Education of the Working Classes', in *The Higher Education of Boys in England*, ed. C. Norwood and A. H. Hope (London: John Murray, 1909), p. 553.

166 Samuel Smiles, *Self-Help with Illustrations of Character and Conduct* (London: John Murray 1859), p. 16.

167 Ibid., p. 50.

168 Ibid., p. 220.

169 Galton, *Hereditary Genius*, p. 43.

170 See Jo Littler, *Against Meritocracy: Culture, Power, and Myths of Mobility* (Abingdon: Routledge, 2018); and Sandel, *Tyranny of Merit*.

171 See Andrew Miles's *Social Mobility in Nineteenth- and Early Twentieth-century England* (Basingstoke: Macmillan, 1999).

172 See Sandel, pp. 78–80.

173 For an analysis of modern meritocracy as secularised Calvinism, see Sandel, pp. 37–50.

174 Max Weber, *The Protestant Work Ethic and the Spirit of Capitalism*, trans. Talcott Parsons (Oxford: Taylor and Francis, 2001), pp. 65–80.

175 See Tim Travers, *Samuel Smiles and the Victorian Work Ethic* (London: Routledge, 2017); and Theodore Koditschek, *Class Formation and Urban Industrial Society: Bradford, 1750–1850* (Cambridge: Cambridge University Press, 1990), pp. 183–4.

176 See John White, *Intelligence, Destiny and Education: The Ideological Roots of Intelligence Testing* (London: Routledge, 2006).

177 Wooldridge, *Measuring the Mind*, p. 215.

178 Ibid., p. 42, pp. 24–5, and pp. 143–50.

179 For a concise account of the emergence of a state education system in Britain, see Florence S. Boos, 'The Education Act of 1870: Before and After' (2015). Available at: <https://www.branchcollective.or g/?ps_articles=florence-s-boos-the-education-act-of-1870-before-and-after> (last accessed 20 November 2021).

180 Ian Hunter, *Rethinking the School: Subjectivity, Bureaucracy, Criticism* (Sydney: Allen and Unwin, 1994), p. 117. Hunter is drawing upon the work of Nikolas Rose. See Rose, *Inventing our Selves: Psychology, Power and Personhood* (Cambridge: Cambridge University Press, 1998), pp. 109–12.

181 For a full account of the advent of compulsory education and the ensuing concern about children with physical and intellectual disabilities within the state school system, see Stephen Byrne, 'Classification, Variation, and Education: The Making and Remaking of the Normal Child in England, c. 1880–1914', PhD thesis, Oxford Brookes University, 2013, pp. 86–158;

Mark Jackson, *Borderland of Imbecility: Medicine, Society and the Fabrication of the Feeble Mind in Late Victorian and Edwardian England* (Manchester: Manchester University Press), pp. 25–7; and Sutherland, *Ability, Measurement and Merit*, pp. 6–13.

182 Cordner, pp. 7–8.

183 See Sutherland, *Ability, Measurement and Merit*, pp. 6–13; and Byrne, pp. 86–158.

184 Carson, p. 139.

185 Wooldridge, *Measuring the Mind*, p. 409.

186 See Francis Warner, 'Mental and Physical Conditions among Fifty Thousand Children seen 1892–94 and the Methods of Studying Recorded Observations, with Special Reference to the Determination of the Causes of Mental Dullness and other Defects', *Journal of the Royal Statistical Society* 59.1 (1896), pp. 71–100.

187 Warner qtd in Wooldridge, *Measuring the Mind*, p. 32.

188 Ibid., p. 30.

189 Ibid., p. 32. The fact that Warner used craniometry and posed questions to judge speech and social competence is clear in his *Report on the Physical and Mental Condition of 50,000 Children Seen in 106 Schools in London* (London: Committee on the Mental and Physical Condition of Children, 1891). See page 1082.

190 Warner, 'Mental and Physical Conditions', p. 126.

191 Cyril Burt, 'Historical Sketch of the Development of Psychological Tests', *Hadow Report on Psychological Tests of Educable Capacity and their Possible Use in the Public System of Education* (London: Her Majesty's Stationery Office, 1924), p. 3, n.1.

192 Wooldridge, *Measuring the Mind*, p. 31.

193 Frederick MacCabe, 'On Mental Strain and Overwork', *Journal of Mental Science* 21 (October 1875), 388–403, p. 392.

194 *Report of Dr. Crichton-Browne to the Education Department upon the Alleged Over-pressure of Work in Public Elementary Schools* (London: Henry Hansard & Son, 1884), p. 7 and p. 55.

195 Ibid., p. 9.

196 Ibid., p. 24.

197 For analysis of the government and public reception of the report, see Sally Shuttleworth, *The Mind of the Child: Child Development in Literature, Science, and Medicine, 1840–1900* (Oxford: Oxford University Press), pp. 135–40.

198 See Shuttleworth, *Mind of the Child*, pp. 135–40; and Gretchen R. Galbraith, *Reading Lives: Reconstructing Childhood, Books, and*

Schools in Britain, 1870–1920 (Basingstoke: Macmillan, 1997), pp. 101–19.

199 *Report of Dr. Crichton Browne*, p. 4.

200 Ibid., p. 7.

201 Ibid., p. 4.

202 On the 'Galtonian' nature of Crichton-Browne's thinking on education, see Michael Neve and Trevor Turner, 'What the Doctor Thought and Did: Sir James Crichton-Browne (1840–1938)', *Medical History* 39 (1995), 399–432, p. 413.

203 Russett, pp. 116–29.

204 See William Greenslade, *Degeneration, Culture, and the Novel* (Oxford: Oxford University Press, 1994), pp. 135–7.

205 T. Pridgin Teale, 'Address on Health', *Transactions of the National Association for the Promotion of Social Science* (London: Longmans, Green, & Co., 1884), pp. 75–6.

206 Anonymous, 'Education à la Mode', *Journal of Education* (January–December 1883), 90–1, p. 91.

207 Teale, p. 81.

208 See Geoffrey Searle, *The Quest for National Efficiency: A Study in British Politics and Political Thought, 1889–1914* (London: The Ashfield Press, 1971).

209 Meloni, pp. 69–70.

210 Daniel J. Kevles, *In the Name of Eugenics: Genetics and the Uses of Human Heredity* (Berkeley: University of California Press, 1985), p. 59.

211 See Geoffrey Searle, *Eugenics and Politics in Britain 1900–1914* (Leyden: Noordhoff International Publishing, 1976), pp. 9–19; and Pauline Mazumdar, *Eugenics, Human Genetics, and Human Failings: The Eugenics Society, Its Sources and Its Critics in Britain* (London: Routledge, 1991), pp. 7–57.

212 Privateer, p. 167.

213 See Privateer, p. 167, and Danziger, p. 75.

214 Byrne, p. 156 and pp. 266–7.

215 Byrne, pp. 65–6 and 311–14.

216 Galton, *Hereditary Genius*, p. xxii.

217 See Anne Stiles, *Popular Fiction and Brain Science in the Late Nineteenth Century* (Cambridge: Cambridge University Press, 2011), p. 126.

218 Cesare Lombroso, *Man of Genius* (London: Walter Scott, 1891), p. v and p. 137.

219 Galton, *Hereditary Genius*, p. ix.

220 J. F. Nisbet, *The Insanity of Genius and the General Inequality of Human Faculty: Physiologically Considered*, 2nd edition (London: Ward & Downey, 1891), p. xv.

221 Ibid., p. 325.

222 Searle, *Eugenics and Politics*, pp. 74–91.

223 Grant Allen, 'The Recipe for Genius', *Cornhill Magazine* 5 (October 1885): 406–15.

224 On the persistence of Lamarckian and environmentalist interpretations in debates over degeneration and mental deficiency, see Mazumdar, pp. 146–9; and Jackson, pp. 110–11.

225 See Meloni, p. 36 and pp. 64–7.

226 Fisher, pp. 455–6.

227 F. H. Hayward, *Education and the Spectre of Heredity* (London: Watts & Company, 1908), p. 6.

228 Ibid., pp. 6–9.

229 Ibid., p. 14.

230 Fancher, *Intelligence Men*, p. 41.

231 Francis Galton, *Anthropometric Laboratory: Notes and Memoirs* (London: Richard Clay & Sons, 1890), p. 8.

232 John Venn, 'Cambridge Anthropometry', *Journal of the Anthropological Institute of Great Britain and Ireland* 18 (1889), p. 143 and p. 145.

233 Joseph Jacobs, 'Experiments on "Prehension"', *Mind* 45.1 (1887), pp. 75–19.

234 Karl Pearson, *The Life, Letters and Labours of Francis Galton* (Cambridge: Cambridge University Press, 2011), p. 272.

235 J. M. Cattell, 'Mental Tests and Measurements', *Mind* 15 (1890), pp. 373–80.

236 On Cattell's mental tests, see Carson, pp. 172–6.

237 Sully questioned Eliot about her 'visualising power' on Galton's behalf at some point in the 1870s. Sully's recollections are quoted in K. K. Collins, *George Eliot: Interviews and Recollections* (Basingstoke: Palgrave Macmillan, 2010), p. 197.

238 Galton, *Inquiries into Human Faculty and its Development* (London: Macmillan, 1883), pp. 57–64.

239 Sophie Bryant, 'Experiments in Testing the Character of School Children', *Journal of the Anthropological Institute of Great Britain and Ireland* 15 (1886), 338–51, p. 343.

240 'Intelligence men' is Fancher's term. He provides illuminating profiles of the key early intelligence testers in *Intelligence Men*.

241 Karl Pearson, 'On the Inheritance of the Mental and Moral

Characters in Man, and its Comparison with the Inheritance of Physical Characters', *Journal of the Anthropological Institute of Great Britain and Ireland* 33 (July–December 1903), 179–237, pp. 181–96.

242 Ibid., p. 207.

243 Charles Spearman, 'General Intelligence: Objectively Determined and Measured', 15.2 (1904), 201–92.

244 See Wooldridge, *Measuring the Mind*, p. 79; and Spearman, 'General Intelligence', p. 246, p. 248, and p. 251.

245 Charles Spearman, *The Abilities of Man: Their Nature and Measurement* (London: Macmillan, 1927), pp. 4–5.

246 Wooldridge, *Measuring the Mind*, p. 80.

247 Cyril Burt, 'Experimental Tests of General Intelligence', *British Journal of Psychology* 3.1–2 (1909), 94–117, p. 100.

248 Ibid., p. 169.

249 Ibid., p. 171.

250 See Kevles, p. 84; and Fancher, *Intelligence Men*, pp. 173–4.

251 Sutherland, *Ability, Merit, and Measurement*, p. 54.

252 See the edited collection, *Cyril Burt: Fraud or Framed?*, ed. N. J. Mackintosh (Oxford: Oxford University Press, 1995).

253 See, for example, Gould, pp. 181–5.

254 Qtd in ibid., pp. 183–4.

255 For a comparative analysis of the status of IQ testing in France and America in the twentieth century, see Carson, pp. 229–70.

256 See note 13.

257 Sutherland, *Ability, Merit, and Measurement*, p. 55 and p. 127.

258 Penny Boumelha, '"A Complicated Position for a Woman": *The Hand of Ethelberta*', in *The Sense of Sex: Feminist Perspectives on Hardy*, ed. Margaret R. Higonnet (Champaign: University of Illinois Press, 1993), 242–59, p. 243; and Mandy Treagus, *Empire Girls: The Colonial Heroine Comes of Age* (Adelaide: University of Adelaide Press, 2014), p. 3.

259 Franco Moretti, *The Way of the World: The Bildungsroman in European Culture* (London: Verso, 1987), p. 64.

260 Ibid., pp. 213–14.

261 Sara Lyons, 'Recent Work in Victorian Studies and the Bildungsroman', *Literature Compass* 15.4 (2018). Available at: <https://doi.org/10.1111/lic3.12460> (last accessed 25 March 2022).

262 Isobel Armstrong, *Novel Politics: Democratic Imaginations in Nineteenth Century Fiction* (Oxford: Oxford University Press, 2016), p. 91.

263 My own reading of the *Bildungsroman* is indebted to Jed Etsy's *Unseasonable Youth: Modernism, Colonialism and the Fiction of Development* (Oxford: Oxford University Press, 2011). Etsy emphasises that the modernist *Bildungsroman* tends to be a narrative of failure, blighted potential, and arrested development. However – and despite the fact that he offers brilliant readings of several Victorian novels – he treats this negativity as something alien to the *Bildungsroman* tradition and as a modernist innovation rather than as constitutive of the nineteenth-century *Bildungsroman*.

264 Lauren Berlant, *Cruel Optimism* (Durham, NC: Duke University Press, 2011), pp. 1–3.

265 Gregory Castle, *Reading the Modernist Bildungsroman* (Gainesville: University Press of Florida, 2006), pp. 34–47.

266 Ibid., pp. 47–62.

267 Georg Lukács, *Theory of the Novel* (London: Merlin Press, 1971), p. 133.

268 Ibid., p. 136.

269 Ibid., p. 116.

270 Ibid., p. 126.

271 See Denise Gigante, *Life: Organic Form and Romanticism* (New Haven, CT: Yale University Press, 2009), pp. 46–7.

272 Daniel Aureliano Newman, *Modernist Life Histories: Biological Theory and the Experimental Bildungsroman* (Edinburgh: Edinburgh University Press, 2019), p. 30.

273 Ibid.

274 August Weismann's hard hereditarianism was often characterised as a revival of preformationism. See Peter J. Bowler, *The Mendelian Revolution: The Emergence of Hereditarian Concepts in Modern Science and Society* (London: The Athlone Press, 1989), p. 75; and Meloni, pp. 50–1. Darwin's theory of evolution was also sometimes received as a decisive intervention in the contest between epigenist versus preformationist worldviews by informed commentators. See George Henry Lewes, 'Mr. Darwin's Hypothesis', *Fortnightly Review* 16 (1868), pp. 354–509.

275 Jacques Rancière, *Chronicles of Consensual Times*, trans. Stephen Corcoran (London: Continuum, 2010), p. 2.

276 Jacques Rancière, *The Ignorant Schoolmaster: Five Lessons in Intellectual Emancipation*, trans. Kristin Ross (Stanford, CA: Stanford University Press, 1991), p. 27 and p. 86.

277 Ibid., p. 46.

278 Jacques Rancière, *The Flesh of Words: The Politics of Writing*,

trans. Charlotte Mandell (Stanford, CA: Stanford University Press), p. 92.

279 Jacques Rancière, *The Lost Thread: The Democracy of Modern Fiction*, trans. Steven Corcoran (London: Bloomsbury, 2017), p. 14.

280 Ibid., p. 15.

281 Allen, Rev. of L. F. Ward's *Dynamic Sociology*, p. 309.

282 Alex Woloch, *The One Versus the Many: Minor Characters and the Space of the Protagonist in the Novel* (Princeton, NJ: Princeton University Press, 2009), pp. 40–2.

283 Ibid., p. 31.

284 Jacques Rancière, *The Politics of Literature*, trans. Julie Rose (Cambridge: Polity Press, 2011), p. 41. The 'police order' is Rancière's name for the hierarchical, totalising account of society which presumes that mental capacities are aligned with social identities and which attempts to predetermine what counts as intelligent thought, speech, and action. My use of Rancière here and my notion of 'surplus intelligence' are indebted to Emily Steinlight's ground-breaking reading of how the Victorian novel attempts to represent and often to question the biopolitical idea of demographic surplus by using 'excesses of figures and signs that throw representation into question'. My own reading suggests that when Victorian and Edwardian novels attempt to perform a 'count of the uncounted', it is the despised or discounted intelligence of the masses that is often at stake. See Steinlight, *Populating the Novel: Literary Form and the Politics of Surplus Life* (Ithaca, NY: Cornell University Press, 2018), p. 17 and p. 119.

George Eliot's Moral Intelligence

[A] system of moral tests might be as delusive as what ignorant people take to be tests of intellect and learning. If the scholar or *savant* cannot answer their haphazard questions on the shortest notice, their belief in his capacity is shaken. But the better-informed have given up the Johnsonian theory of mind as a pair of legs able to walk east or west according to choice. Intellect is no longer taken to be a ready-made dose of ability to attain eminence (or mediocrity) in all departments; it is even admitted that [. . .] an intellectual quality or special facility which is a furtherance in one medium of effort is a drag in another [. . .] It is not true that a man's intellectual power is like the strength of a timber beam, to be measured at its weakest point.[1]

The above passage is from *The Impressions of Theophrastus Such* (1879), George Eliot's final work. It is a collection of brief essays on diverse subjects, all purportedly from the pen of an embittered minor scholar. Theophrastus Such's critique of the impulse to measure 'intellectual power' clearly springs in part from personal failure, but it is nonetheless striking: like several other of his 'impressions', it has an untimeliness that can disorient the twenty-first-century reader.[2] Such writes as if he were living after the demise of the IQ test, rather than two decades before its rise; he dismisses the notion of a general, measurable intelligence as if it were a discredited fetish of the Enlightenment, rather than a brave new idea.[3] Eliot's implicit target is Galton, who first aired his theory of general, innate mental ability in 1865, and who treated social 'eminence' as a proxy measurement for it (Eliot's choice of Galton's keyword – 'eminence' – is surely barbed).[4] As noted in the

Introduction, Galton's 1869 book *Hereditary Genius* was initially met with widespread scepticism, and it is unsurprising that Eliot failed to predict the cultural authority that his theory would come to command in the late nineteenth and early twentieth centuries. She clearly felt confident that her own conception of intelligence as a protean, immeasurable phenomenon, inextricable from emotion and from social context, was aligned with the direction of modern science. And yet Eliot's lack of prescience about Galton also grants her genuine insight. In this chapter, I suggest that turning to Eliot's *Mill on the Floss* (1860) can enable us to imagine an alternative to the IQ model of intelligence that was beginning to crystallise when she wrote the novel in the late 1850s. In other words, it enables us to wonder: what if Eliot rather than Galton had won the cultural argument about the nature of intelligence?

Eliot was extraordinarily well informed about nineteenth-century evolutionary science and biological psychology. Her editorship of *The Westminster Review* between 1851 and 1854 meant she kept abreast of scientific developments and debates, and throughout her adult life she read widely and deeply across scientific disciplines. For my purposes here, it is most significant that she was very familiar with the works of major evolutionary scientists and biological psychologists: Bain, William Carpenter, Darwin, Huxley, Spencer, Maudsley, and, of course, those of her romantic partner, the polymathic George Henry Lewes. As Nancy Paxton has shown, Eliot's close friendship with Spencer – itself complicated by his romantic rejection of her – inspired a complex, often antagonistic engagement with his ideas in her fiction.[5] Lewes's work in the field of psychology was much more straightforwardly congenial to Eliot, and several scholars have traced the continuities between his scientific speculations and her fiction, particularly their shared emphasis upon 'the physical basis of mind' (the title of one of Lewes's works of psychology).[6] The depth of their intellectual kinship and collaboration is reflected in the fact that Eliot undertook the task of editing and completing the final two volumes of Lewes's five-volume *magnum opus*, *Problems of Life and Mind*, when he died in 1878. In order to understand Eliot's creative intervention in contemporary efforts to develop a scientific theory of human intelligence, it is first necessary to clarify Lewes's contributions to – and critiques of – that enterprise. This is not because Lewes's views can simply be assumed to be Eliot's, or that Eliot can be read as 'passive vessel into which the ideas of Darwin, Spencer, Comte, Bain and others were poured' – a practice that Paxton rightly counsels against.[7] However, outlining Lewes's ideas about intelligence helps to contextualise Eliot's at once moral and feminist critique of the emerging IQ concept and its relationship to the ideology of meritocracy.

Modern commentators often suggest that Lewes's most important achievement as a thinker was his innovative solution to the mind–body problem. As Rick Rylance observes, Lewes essentially treats the problem as a philosopher's illusion, or an 'analytical fiction'.[8] In its place, Lewes advocates a 'dual aspect' monism inspired in part by his reading of Baruch Spinoza. Lewes's theory is monistic and materialistic insofar as he regards body and mind as inseparable and constituted out of the same substance. However, he argues that mental and physical processes are different aspects of, or ways of apprehending, this same substance. In making this argument, Lewes was elaborating a non-reductive model of psychology, one in which the human mind could be understood in biological terms without being treated as entirely reducible to those terms. Lewes was also attempting to stake out a conciliatory middle position in the often rancorous Victorian debates over religion and science: while himself obviously aligned with the broadly secular and materialist assumptions of the new biological psychology, Lewes's dual-aspect monism helped him to sustain a humanist emphasis upon the irreducible complexity of the mind.[9]

Lewes broadly accepted the definitions of human intelligence proposed by Bain and Spencer. His own definition is clearly an attempt to reconcile theirs: echoing Spencer, he asserts that intelligence is a 'readiness in adapting actions to circumstances'; and echoing Bain, he asserts that intelligence consists of the capacity to recognise 'similarities and diversities'.[10] In his *Physiology of Common Life* (1859), Lewes also affirmed the heritability of mental characteristics, though – like Eliot in *Mill on the Floss* – he puzzles at length over the commonly observed discrepancies between the intellectual abilities of family members.[11] However, Spencer and Bain's shared interest in a theory of 'general intelligence' that could be the basis of hierarchies of human value and meritocratic competition – an interest also shared, of course, by Galton – is alien to Lewes's project in crucial ways. As Rylance observes, Lewes is unusual among Victorian scientific thinkers in his disinclination to construct graded hierarchies out of the phenomena he analysed (though, as we shall see, he does not abstain from this entirely).[12] More broadly, Lewes's dual-aspect monism also led him to think holistically and non-reductively about human intelligence: within his logic, intelligence cannot be reified as a stable, measurable trait, nor even securely located in the individual mind. In his *The Physiology of Common Life*, Lewes argues that the mind extends outward to the entirety of the body: '[Mind] includes all sensation, all volition, and all thought [. . .] this psychical life has no one special centre: it belongs to the whole and animates the whole.'[13] Lewes's commitment to the idea that sentience is diffused throughout the body made him suspicious of any scientific effort to measure or locate intelligence as an innate 'thing' in the head. He was sceptical of craniometry as a means of measuring intelligence, and hostile to the efforts of contemporary scientists such as Paul Broca and David Ferrier to identify the intellect with specific regions of the brain.[14]

Lewes's other distinctive contribution to Victorian psychology was his recognition of the role of society in determining the 'intellect and conscience'.[15] Following Auguste Comte, Lewes saw the mind as the confluence of biological and sociological factors, and his philosophical project is the effort to think biology and society in all their complexity at the same time. While Lewes was happy to recognise continuities between human and animal intelligence, he insisted that the complexity of human society 'interposed' a fundamental distinction between the two: 'the Social Medium – the collective accumulations of centuries, condensed in knowledge, beliefs, prejudices, institutions and tendencies' constitutes 'another kind of Psychoplasm to which the animal is a stranger'.[16] As Edward Reed points out, Lewes's effort to grasp the simultaneously biological and social determinants of the mind made him unique among his generation of biological psychologists.[17] Lewes's preoccupation with what he called the 'social factor' in human psychology also made him wary of imputing too much influence to the forces of heredity in the formation of the mind:

Some writers who are disposed to exaggerate the action of Heredity believe that certain specific experiences of social utility in the race become organized in descendants, and are thus transmitted as instincts. With the demonstrated wonders of heredity before us, it is rash to fix limits to the specific determinations it may include; but the evidence in this direction is obscured by the indubitable transmission through language and other social institutions.[18]

Lewes also stands out among Victorian evolutionary scientists and biological psychologists in his emphasis upon the inseparability of thought and feeling, reason and emotion (though, in keeping with his dual-aspect monism, he sometimes suggests that thought and feeling are different aspects of the same phenomenon).[19] In this, Lewes was partly building upon Spencer, who writes in his *Principles of Psychology*: 'All cognition implies emotion, and all emotion implies cognition.'[20] Lewes echoes Spencer's dictum twenty-four years later in his *Problems of Life and Mind, Third Series* (1879): 'There can be no Cognition which does not involve Feeling, no Feeling which does not involve the characteristic element of Cognition.'[21] Yet Lewes goes further than Spencer in insisting on the primacy of the emotions:

> The intellectual life is the outcome of the affective; it is only a mode of representation of the feelings, which afterwards becomes their substitute, and is thus a guide of actions: but it is a guide only as a torch which lights the way.[22]

Lewes's impulse is always to undercut the supreme status of the intellect within Western philosophy, to deny the intellect's purity, stability, and autonomy, and emphasise the messiness of its entanglement in the body and society. And while Lewes embraced elements of both Spencer's and Darwin's accounts of evolution and believed that the mind was the product of evolutionary adaptations, he nevertheless emphasised the role of individual experience in constituting the nature of intelligence.[23] He suggests that the intellect is best understood as a nexus for integrating and regulating the totality of our emotional experience:

> Intelligence or intellect is the personality which condenses the perceptions and conceptions that reproduce and represent sensible affections, and which regulates conduct. It is the supreme psychical centre to which all affections converge, from which all impulses are directed. It is the light of the soul; the spiritual person. We can no longer adopt the notion of the Intellect being an independent function, still less can we admit it to be an inherited product, which we bring with us full-statured on our entrance into the world. It is a product which is evolved in Experience – the summation of myriads of sentient states and varying with the experiences, so that the intelligence of the child is different from that of the adult, and the Intellect of a Goethe is dif-

ferent from that of a Kaffir on the one hand and of a Newton on the other.[24]

Here Lewes celebrates his model of the emotional intellect as an inspiring secular substitute for the religious notion of the soul or spirit. Lewes's argument is not simply about the nature of the mind, but an effort to suggest that a secularised model of subjectivity need not be coldly rationalistic or reductionist – a project he shares with Eliot. As so often in the writing of Victorian psychologists, Lewes's dismantling of one conventional hierarchy – in this case, the ascendancy of reason over the emotions – seems to inspire the anxious buttressing of another (here, the supremacy of the European man of genius over anonymous racialised others, though Lewes's emphasis is more on cognitive difference than on a clear hierarchy). Lewes appears to spy the risks of jettisoning the distinction between emotion and reason for the idea of Western intellectual superiority, and so summons Newton and Goethe in a bid to reassure his readers – or perhaps himself – that his argument does not entail this radical implication.

This chapter will argue that Eliot does pursue some of the more radical implications of Lewes's theory of emotional intelligence in her fiction. Affirming reason's ascendancy over emotion was crucial to how many Victorian scientists and psychologists delineated the differences between the sexes and posited the mental inferiority of women. Eliot's effort to bring Lewes's theory of emotional intelligence to life in fiction is at the same time an effort to redeem the much-disparaged 'feminine' intellect. In effect, Eliot read the mainstream of Victorian biological psychology against itself, using its destabilisation of the hierarchical dualisms of mind and body, reason and emotion, to challenge another dualism that generally remained precious to Victorian psychologists: the distinction between male and female minds. This was a distinction upheld even by Lewes: he claimed that the 'masculine mind is characterised by the predominance of the intellect, and the feminine by the predominance of the emotions' (and, by extension, that men were best suited to the field of philosophy and women to that of literature).[25]

Eliot's feminist credentials have often been found lacklustre, both in terms of her reluctance to engage with campaigns for women's rights, and in terms of the conservative plots in which she seems to entrap and even to punish her heroines. Yet as Kyriaki

Hadjiafxendi has remarked in passing, Eliot's most crucial contribution to Victorian feminism lies elsewhere: it is to be found in her effort to 'overcome the gendered dichotomy between reason and emotion' in her fiction.[26]

As Jill Matus has suggested, Eliot's model of the emotional intellect has affinities with Martha Nussbaum's efforts to theorise the intelligence of the emotions.[27] According to Nussbaum, emotions are *eudaimonistic*: that is, they are judgements about what will enable us to flourish. For this reason, 'emotions are not just the fuel that powers the psychological mechanism of a reasoning creature, they are parts, highly complex and messy parts, of this creature's reasoning itself'.[28] For Nussbaum, recognising that emotions are appraisals of value necessitates reconceptualising moral philosophy: morality cannot be conceived as a set of principles to be fathomed by a detached rationality, but as the complex work of emotional intelligence. In what follows, I trace how *The Mill on the Floss* and *Daniel Deronda* also compel us to understand morality in such terms.

The notion of 'emotional intelligence' was popularised in the late twentieth century as an antidote to the fixation on IQ testing among psychologists and culture at large, especially in North America. 'Emotional intelligence' has itself a powerful emotional appeal, seeming to offer a humane and holistic alternative to the IQ concept and its eugenicist taint. Yet as Merve Imre has recently argued, the popular notion of emotional intelligence – largely the product of psychologist Daniel Goleman's 1995 bestseller – has its own repressive politics: it is a self-help discipline that promises to enable the individual to adapt to the pressures of a neoliberal economy.[29] Goleman's model of emotional intelligence is actually remarkably Victorian in its emphasis upon self-control and the cultivation of will power.[30] Eliot's conception of emotional intelligence is not a self-help discipline, much less a strategy for social and professional success under capitalism. Quite the opposite: in Eliot's work, the fruits of emotional intelligence are often failure and self-abnegation, even self-destruction; like Hardy, Eliot suggests that the highest form of emotional intelligence may be tragic knowledge. In Eliot's work, the valorisation of emotional intelligence is joined to a critique of the ideology of meritocracy which, as discussed in the Introduction, began to flourish in the 1850s. As also discussed in the Introduction, the ideology of meritocracy can be understood as a secularised form of Christian providentialism, and Eliot's antipathy to it is of a piece with her more general rejection of providentialist logic in her fiction – that is, the logic which suggests that human fates are shaped by divine justice.[31] Eliot's critique of meritocratic logic is also a thread in her larger moral critique of laissez-faire capitalism, particularly its encouragement of an ethos of self-seeking, competitive individualism.[32]

Breeding stupid lads and 'cute wenches

The extent to which a person's level of intelligence is attributable to the workings of heredity is a question at the centre of the opening book of *The Mill on the Floss*. As Mary Jean Corbett observes, the novel 'enquires into the origins of character from the beginning' and invokes the 'language of family resemblances' and a 'discourse of breeding' in its effort to identify how the two protagonists, Maggie and Tom Tulliver, 'come to be who they are – or appear to be'.[33] And yet Corbett's framing of this part of the novel as an 'enquiry into character' makes the Tullivers' discussion about their children seem far more open-ended and humanist than it is. Mr Tulliver really has just one burning question about his children: why is Maggie cleverer than Tom? And, as Eliot makes plain, this preoccupation is not driven by curiosity about his children's inner lives or development. It is a coldly utilitarian calculus. A clever daughter is a much less valuable commodity than a clever son:

> 'It seems a bit of a pity though as the lad should take after the mother's side istead o' the little wench. That's the wost on't wi' the crossing o' breeds; you can never justly calkilate what'll come on't. The little un takes after my side, now; she's twice as 'cute as Tom. Too 'cute for a woman, I'm afraid [. . .] It's no mischief much while she's a little un, but an over 'cute woman's no better nor a long-tailed sheep. She'll fetch none of the bigger price for that.'[34]

Much of the comedy of the novel's early chapters arises from Mr Tulliver's crassly materialist evaluations of his children's mental capacities. It is not merely that he appraises his children as if they were livestock, but that he reifies intelligence as a fixed, fully exteriorised characteristic, as unmistakable (and phallic) as a long tail. His theory of intelligence clearly exposes the limitations of his own mind; like his son, he is presented as a literal-minded man who is easily flummoxed by complexity. As he himself puts it, 'Everything winds about so – the more straightforward you are, the more you're puzzled.'[35] At bottom, Mr Tulliver's theory of heredity is the narcissism of patriarchal reason: openly vain about his own 'brains', Mr Tulliver nevertheless chose his wife because he believed her not 'overly' intelligent and now laments that their union may 'go on breeding [. . .] stupid lads and 'cute wenches until the world has gone topsy turvy'.[36] Mr Tulliver's speculations about gender and heredity register as Eliot's sly joke on Victorian scientific writing on sexual roles and sexual differences, which often similarly relied on folk wisdom and '*ben trovato* conclusions', as Flavia Alaya observes.[37] And yet Mr Tulliver's perplexity about his children's aptitudes is not meant to register as simply benighted or foolish. His anxieties about his son resonate as distinctly modern – a symptom of an emergent ideal of meritocratic social mobility.

The Mill on the Floss is set among 'unfashionable families' – the yeoman Tulliver, Dodson, Glegg, and Pullet families – in the late 1820s or early 1830s in St Ogg's, a fictional Lincolnshire town.[38] However, Eliot's interest in the recent past – the era of her own childhood – is driven by her desire to provide genealogies of her mid-Victorian present. As Suzanne Graver has argued, a major part of Eliot's realist project is the effort to grasp the intersection of *Gesellschaft* and *Gemeinschaft* in early nineteenth-century England – that is, to trace how secular, capitalist, urban values of individualism and rational calculation began to emerge in rural communities and disrupt their attachments to kinship, localism, and the sacred.[39] Mr Tulliver's desire to 'calkilate' his children's mental qualities suggests that *Gesellschaft* ideas have begun to percolate in the apparently hidebound culture of St Ogg's. Although Mr Tulliver does not explicitly refer to physiognomy or phrenology, his appraisals of his children are suggestive of how those logics penetrated everyday life and encouraged a rhetoric of scientific objectivity in even the most intimate judgements about mental worth.

Mr Tulliver's fixation on cleverness, or ''cuteness', as he calls it, is itself a study in miniature of the collision of *Gesellschaft* and *Gemeinschaft* worldviews. Mr Tulliver's insecurity about his own lack of formal education and sense of disadvantage in his legal dispute with the lawyer Mr Wakem encourage him to identify the intellect with what seems to him the bewildering and arbitrary powers of the law. Mr Tulliver wants an education for his son so that Tom will be a 'match for the lawyers' and thereby immunised against the sense of class and educational victimhood that clearly bedevils Mr Tulliver himself.[40] At the same time, Mr Tulliver has a traditional puritan distrust of the intellect; he suspects that lawyers are creations of 'Old Harry', and understands education as primarily a ruse of power, if not a form of evil.[41] This is further complicated by the fact that Mr Tulliver believes in the innate superiority of his own 'brains', and, despite his manifest sexism, is gratified by what he takes to be his daughter's inherited mental gifts.[42] Indeed, while he thinks of Maggie's cleverness as a disturbing anomaly, a 'mistake of nature', it also flatters his belief that hereditary natural ability is ultimately more potent than any social hierarchy.[43] Through her subtle portrait of Mr Tulliver, Eliot clarifies the allure of an innatist conception of intelligence to the uneducated but 'proud' yeoman – and by implication, to the ambitious middle classes of her mid-Victorian present.[44] The concept of innateness allows intelligence to be experienced as the ultimate personal property – one that empowers its putative owner to transcend, at least in fantasy, hierarchies of education, class, and wealth. It is not incidental that Mr Tulliver's legal feud with Mr Wakem is also an effort to turn a fluid natural phenomenon into a productive, proprietary object: at stake are Mr Tulliver's rights as a mill owner to harness the power of the River Floss. Mr Tulliver's desire to quantify his children's mental capacities arises from the same anxious – and essentially economic – need to turn the river into a proprietary thing. However, in the case of rivers Mr Tulliver at least perceives the limits of his drive toward reification: 'water's a very particular thing; you can't pick it up with a pitchfork'.[45]

Throughout the 1850s and 1860s, Lewes often articulated his enthusiasm for Spencer's Lamarckian view of heredity.[46] In his 1856 essay, 'Hereditary Influence, Animal and Human', Lewes – sounding not entirely unlike Mr Tulliver – asserts: 'a whole dynasty of blockheads would never produce a man of genius by intermarriage with blockheads'.[47] As I have noted, Lewes eventually became more circumspect about the extent to which mental characteristics can be attributed to biological heredity, given that the evidence is obscured by environmental factors – the forces of social and cultural transmission.[48] This is a subject on which Eliot's thinking seems to have outrun Lewes's: his later suspicion of the scientific tendency to 'exaggerate the action of heredity' in constituting human intelligence is already manifest in Eliot's *Mill on the Floss*. Critics often take Mr Tulliver's verdicts about his children's aptitudes at face value, but as Michael Davis points out, Eliot's narrator never endorses Mr Tulliver's belief that Maggie has inherited his intelligence.[49] More than this, Maggie's 'quickness' is always treated as a matter of social reputation and self-image, and Eliot actually goes to great lengths to undercut Mr Tulliver's judgement that Maggie is Tom's intellectual superior in any bio-logically fixed, natural sense. To feminist readers, this is perhaps a disappointing, even perverse feature of the novel. A range of characters recognise Maggie as naturally gifted, even 'brilliant', and the Romantic-minded reader perhaps hopes that she will come to be feted as a genius in the pattern of the heroine of Madame de Staël's *Corinne* (1807) – a novel that Maggie herself reads, but finds dissatisfying.[50] On one level, Maggie's failure to live up to her early potential is an expression of the anti-heroic, deflationary impetus of Eliot's realism, which expresses itself partly as an effort to undercut Romantic models of genius and celebrity: the narra-tor specifies that Maggie will 'never be a Sappho or a Madame Roland or anything else the world takes wide note of'.[51] Equally obviously, this is an accurate reflection of the limited opportuni-ties available to women in provincial England in the 1820s and 1830s. Yet Eliot's commitment to realism does not fully account for how firmly the novel wrests our attention away from Maggie's supposed cleverness and on to Tom's supposed deficiencies. While Eliot certainly asks us to feel the tragedy of Maggie's 'unsatis-fied intelligence', much more narrative attention is lavished upon championing Tom's overlooked intellectual capacities.[52] The femi-nist narrative of Maggie's frustrated desire for an education is, at least superficially, marginalised by Tom's school narrative; and his experience of formal education is so humiliating as to make Maggie's yearning for his advantages seem ill founded. Yet if Eliot's focus on Tom's experience spoils any simple message about women's potential for genius or aptitude for education, it also enables Eliot to unfold an ambitious polemic about the cultural gendering of intelligence.

Stereotype threats and mistaken educations

In the first half of *The Mill on the Floss*, Eliot persistently asks the reader to reflect on how we judge the intelligence of others. She stages the question of intelligence as a question about attention and desire: what kind of objects does the person most often think about? Does the person tend to focus on abstract ideas and imaginary constructs, or on the details of the material world? This is the philosophical burden of the child Maggie's conversation with Luke, the head miller at her father's mill. Maggie, bored and treating the mill as her playground, tries to interest Luke in her books – one a tour guide of Europe, the other about exotic animals. Luke responds with what seems like standard peasant philistinism. He tells Maggie he is 'no reader' because:

'I'n got to keep count o' the corn; I can' do w' knowing so many things besides my work. That's what brings folks to the gallows, – knowin' everything but what they'n got to get their bread by. An' they're mostly lies, I think, what's printed i' the books.'[53]

Maggie raises a moral objection to Luke's attitude, asserting that he has an obligation to be interested in books because 'we ought to know about our fellow-creatures'.[54] Eliot's irony is trenchant here. Maggie's precocious cosmopolitanism prevents her from truly engaging with the fellow creature before her; she fails to notice the material conditions that force Luke to restrict his attention to corn-counting, while she is free to lounge in the mill and allow her imagination to roam. In case we have missed the point, the relative moral stakes of attending to abstractions versus attending to concrete particulars are reinforced when Luke points out that Tom's rabbits have died because Maggie has forgotten to feed them. Maggie's preoccupation with distant and exotic others blinds her to the claims of immediate and particular others – her brother and his rabbits, clearly, but also to Luke himself. Maggie's tendencies toward abstraction and bookishness – cited by her father as proof of her high intelligence[55] – Eliot here recasts as a form of morally culpable stupidity.

As Daston observes, the philosophical tradition has generally cast the difference between male and female minds in terms of a relative capacity for abstract reason. Since antiquity, the female intellect has been characterised as passive, emotional, and easily distracted by the details of the material world. Overwhelmed by the intensities of their own bodies and feelings, women are allegedly unable to grasp the general laws that govern political and intellectual life.[56] As Daston points out, these ancient clichés were granted fresh legitimacy in the nineteenth century as they were recast in the framework of evolutionary biology by Spencer, Darwin, Maudsley, Galton, and others.[57] In *The Mill on the Floss*, the traditional view of the limits of female intelligence is articulated by Mr Stelling, Tom's teacher: "'[Women] can pick up a little of everything, I dare say," said Mr. Stelling. "They've a great deal of superficial cleverness; but they couldn't go far into anything. They're quick and shallow."'[58] Tom and Maggie are obvious – and polemical – counter-examples to Mr Stelling's generalisation: Maggie demonstrates the allegedly masculine aptitude for abstract thought, while Tom shows a 'feminine' tendency to dwell on concrete particulars and on his own physical experience. Yet Eliot is not content merely to reverse gender stereotypes or to affirm the female capacity for reason. Instead, Eliot challenges the conventional identification of intelligence with abstract rationality and exposes the hidden psychological and social determinants of what manifests itself as intelligence. She does this not by glorifying Maggie's intellect but by asking us to adopt a more nuanced view of Tom's capacities than his parents or teacher do:

[Mr Stelling] very soon set down poor Tom as a thoroughly stupid lad [. . .] [Yet] Tom had never found any difficulty in discerning a pointer from a setter, when once he had been told the distinction, and his perceptive powers were not at all deficient. I fancy they were quite as strong as those of the Rev. Mr. Stelling; for Tom could predict with accuracy what number of horses were cantering behind him, he could throw a stone right into the centre of a given ripple, he could guess to a fraction how many lengths of his stick it would take to reach across the playground, and could draw almost perfect squares on his slate without any measurement. But Mr. Stelling took no note of these things; he only observed that Tom's faculties failed him before the abstractions hideously symbolized to him in the pages of the Eton Grammar [. . .].[59]

Eliot's defence of Tom's intellect is a covert defence of the 'feminine' intellect and its alleged bias toward the sensuous, the particular, and the emotionally charged. Eliot insistently reframes Mr

Tulliver's fixation on innate intelligence and prompts the reader to think in terms of the psychology of attention and motivation. The narrator observes: 'For getting a good flourishing growth of stupidity there is nothing like pouring on a mind a good amount of subjects in which it feels no interest.'[60] Tom is not 'slow' or 'dull' – he is merely focused on proving his masculinity in physical, often violent ways. Meanwhile Maggie shows the aptitude for geometry and Latin that Tom lacks, but Eliot similarly clarifies that this aptitude is also driven by her desire to learn. Latin and geometry fascinate Maggie because she identifies them as indirect routes to patriarchal power; they are boring to Tom because he has more immediate routes to that same power. Where many of the novel's characters treat intelligence as a fixed essence – Tom is 'slow', Maggie is 'quick' – Eliot's narrator is at pains to trace how their intellectual capacities are shaped by their feelings, especially their feelings about their gender and status. Indeed, when Tom feels humiliated by his own 'slowness' under Dr Stelling's tutelage, he experiences this as emasculation: 'Tom became more like a girl than he had ever been in his life before.'[61] In its emphasis upon the emotional dimensions of intellectual capacity, *The Mill on the Floss* anticipates the argument that Lewes would make in his *Problems of Life and Mind*: 'All cognition is primarily emotion. We only *see* what *interests* us. No phenomenon is interesting until it is illuminated by emotion, and we see, or foresee, its connection with our feelings.'[62]

Eliot's exploration of the psychological underpinnings of Tom's and Maggie's intellectual capacities also anticipates the work of modern psychologists on the impact of 'stereotype threats' on intellectual performance. A subfield of social psychology has dedicated itself to demonstrating that how we perform on intelligence tests is influenced by how we feel about our own intelligence; more precisely, it is influenced by how we feel about our social status. Feelings of inferiority, or simply the fear of being judged inferior by others, can substantially diminish performance, particularly in those who belong to groups subject to negative stereotyping about their intellectual ability. The psychologists Claude Steele and Joshua Aronson famously demonstrated that when African-American and white students with equivalent SAT scores were told they were taking a diagnostic intelligence test, the African-American students under-performed on the test relative to the white students; however, when the same test was presented as a simple problem-solving task, the performance gap between the groups disappeared.[63] The distorting effects of stereotype threats can work in the opposite direction, too: if test-takers are strategically primed to believe that they belong to an intellectually superior group, it can enhance performance. For instance, when female Asian-American students were prompted to reflect on their ethnicity prior to taking a maths test, it elevated their results relative to a control group – apparently because the students were bolstered by the positive stereotype of Asians possessing an innate talent for mathematics. However, when female Asian-American students were instead prompted to reflect upon their gender prior to taking the test, it depressed their results relative to the control group – apparently because they were demoralised by the stereotype of female inferiority at maths.[64]

Research into stereotype threats attempts to challenge the scientific neutrality of intelligence tests and lay bare the social and psychological contingencies of intellectual performance. In this, modern social psychologists are carrying on work that was first performed by novelists such as Eliot. The novel form was a unique space in which to explore the web of social and psychological factors generally occluded by both scientific and casual reifications of 'mental ability' as a fixed trait. Narrativising the process of intellectual formation and revealing the intricacy of its social embeddedness were also a means of countering the claims about women's mental inferiority issuing from the new evolutionary science. As Alaya has observed, Victorian scientific pronouncements about the deficiencies of the female intellect are generally audacious in their dogmatism: there is little, if any, effort to supply evidence or reasoning, so self-evident are the claims held to be.[65] In riposte, a novel such as *Mill on the Floss* offers not an equally bald counter-assertion but a 'thick description' of how intellectual potential is by turns nurtured and stultified by the pressure of gender norms. At the same time, Eliot emphasises that gender norms imprint on individuals in imperfect and often ironic ways: they can make Latin seem a seductive form of empowerment to a girl and an emasculating oppression to a boy.

Angelique Richardson has observed that fiction at a formal level 'tends to present a challenge to the idea of character as biologically produced and determined' insofar as it 'elaborately detail[s] the conditions necessary to existence'; this is especially true of the Victorian realist novel and its effort to document the interaction of individual and society, or organism and environment.[66] However, *The Mill on the Floss*'s focus on the social factors that shape the intellects of Tom and Maggie is much more than an unintended bias of its fictionality or its realism. Eliot's explicit project in the novel is to disillusion any reader – perhaps especially readers of Smiles's recently published *Self-Help* – who is 'strongly impressed with the power of the human mind to triumph over circumstances'.[67] Throughout the novel, Eliot's descriptive language strives to convey the social enmeshment of Tom's and Maggie's developing characters. As Michael Kearns has argued, this does not mean Eliot conceives of the mind as simply passive and impressible; rather, her favoured metaphor for the mind is that of 'a sentient web', and she generally employs descriptive language that emphasises 'texture and connectedness' when characterising the relationship between the individual and the environment.[68] In *The Mill on the Floss*, 'fibres' are Eliot's key trope for this. The trope appears eleven times in the novel and often with similar modifiers: 'tender', 'delicate', 'sensitive'. The 'fibres' of the novel's characters variously 'vibrate', 'thrill', answer to 'fondling', are 'touched' and 'stirred' by other characters. The word at once conveys Eliot's sense of the organic nature of the self and its susceptibility to social influence. This is not total susceptibility: Eliot sometimes uses 'fibre' too to suggest a resistant integrity in the self – an individuality that does not simply yield to external pressures. For example, 'Philip's letter had stirred all the fibres that bound [Maggie] to the calmer past': here, 'fibres' suggest both how Maggie is susceptible to Philip Wakem in the moment and how her emotional history provides an underlying resistance to that influence. In the case of this example, the self's capacity to resist external influence is not an innate disposition, but the complex sum of personal experience. Yet elsewhere the narrator does highlight that human beings are 'flesh and blood, with dispositions not entirely at the mercy of circumstances'.[69] In general, Eliot's fiction emphasises the plasticity of character: neither entirely fixed nor entirely malleable, character is formed through interaction between what Eliot thinks of as intrinsic 'organisation' – innate dispositions – and extrinsic influences, or social environment.[70] Yet Eliot's refusal of what we now think of as the nature/nurture dichotomy still admitted of corrective emphasis upon the determining force of 'nurture' on questions where she felt that 'nature' had been reified into an essentialist ideology. In *The Mill on the Floss*, Eliot's close tracing of the 'mistaken education[s]' of Maggie and Tom is an effort to show how the complexity of social circumstances confounds any effort to 'justly calkilate' the power of their innate intelligence.

Multiple intelligences

Eliot's defence of Tom's intellect is not only a camouflaged feminist argument, but an affirmation of the value of cognitive differences and of the diversity of human intelligence. Eliot suggests that Mr Stelling's conviction that there is one type of intelligence and that therefore 'one regimen' is suitable 'for all minds' is itself a form of stupidity, akin to a beaver obeying its instinct to build, regardless of circumstances.[71] Mr Stelling is one of the novel's satirical portraits of meritocratic aspiration. That Mr Stelling embodies the 'true British determination to push his way in the world' and 'rise by merit' within the ossified and supposedly unworldly structures of the Anglican Church is one of the novel's ironic comments on the incongruities produced by the collision of liberal individualism and traditional social structures.[72] It is also suggestive of the tendency of meritocratic aspiration to flourish in defiance of objective social realities (as discussed in the Introduction). The Victorian Anglican hierarchy was a chaotic patronage system primarily controlled by the aristocracy, not a profession 'open to talent'. In the 1850s, the Church was becoming notorious for its resistance to the new ideal of promotion by merit and its determination to 'reserve [. . .] large areas of its preferment to those with private connections', as Frances Knight writes.[73]

It is not accidental that Mr Stelling is both invested in the modern ideal of 'merit' and the proponent of an elitist and categorical conception of intelligence. He regards his own educational methods as an objective test of both intelligence and moral character, and so – contradictorily – believes that Tom's struggle to learn Latin proves his stupidity as well as his obduracy. Eliot at once satirises Mr Stelling's idea of himself as a 'first-rate man' and dwells on the unintended – or only half-intended – violence his teaching does to Tom, who experiences his lessons as 'bruises and crushings'.[74] Mr Stelling's error is less deliberate cruelty than a failure to recognise that Tom's intelligence is different in kind to his own. At the same time, that failure of recognition is obviously a form of class myopia: Mr Stelling is certain his teaching methods are the 'only right way' because he is raising Tom from his yeoman origins and furnishing him with the 'education of a gentleman'.[75] Mr Stelling is what Bourdieu calls a 'mystified mystifier': a pedagogue who unwittingly alchemises judgements about class and social status into judgements about intellectual capacity and thereby transmutes 'social truth into academic truth'.[76]

The notion of 'multiple intelligences' was popularised in the late twentieth century by the educationalist Howard Gardner, who was attempting to counter the hegemony of the IQ concept in American education. In 1983, he argued there were at least seven types of intelligence – not only the verbal and mathematical kinds assessed in IQ tests, but also 'bodily-kinaesthetic', 'interpersonal', 'intrapersonal', 'musical-rhythmic', and 'visual-spatial'.[77] Gardner's theory is often attacked for being unfalsifiable and therefore unscientific, but has enjoyed a popular currency, particularly among schoolteachers.[78] To an extent, Gardner himself acknowledges its non-scientific status, remarking that his model renders the evaluation of intelligence more a matter of 'artistic judgment than scientific assessment'.[79]

Gardner's concept of 'multiple intelligences' can be understood as a modern descendent of phrenology. As Stephen Jay Gould points out, phrenology, in contrast to the IQ concept, 'celebrated a theory of richly multiple and independent intelligences'.[80] And Eliot's pluralistic understanding of intelligence is perhaps in part a residue of her youthful interest in phrenology. In 1844 Eliot had travelled with her friend Charles Bray to have a cast of her head made and analysed by the phrenologist George Combe.[81] However, by the late 1850s Eliot shared Lewes's scepticism toward the science and confessed her 'intolerance' toward its often dogmatic partisans.[82] Eliot's representation of Maggie's and Tom's intellectual differences does not draw upon the language of phrenology, and the narrator does not suggest they arise from fixed biological differences. Instead, as we have seen, she steers us to attribute these differences primarily to social dynamics and psychological motives. At the same time, Eliot is always asking us to perceive the moral freight of converting the recognition of mental difference into judgements about intellectual superiority and inferiority, and this project extends far beyond her sympathetic portrayal of Tom's 'crushing' education.[83]

Mental superiority and struggles for recognition

The desire to be thought 'clever' is a keynote of Maggie's character as child: we learn that she 'only wanted people to think her a clever little girl', and that she was 'so proud to be called "quick" all her little life'.[84] This desire clearly springs from Maggie's belief that cleverness will exempt her from the usual oppressions of the female lot. Tom enlightens Maggie that a reputation for cleverness actually magnetises misogyny rather than immunising a woman against it:

> 'I think women are crosser than men', said Maggie. 'Aunt Glegg's a great deal crosser than uncle Glegg, and mother scolds me more than father does.'
> 'Well, *you'll* be a woman someday', said Tom, 'so *you* needn't talk.'
> 'But I shall be a *clever* woman', said Maggie, with a toss.
> 'Oh, I dare say, and a nasty conceited thing. Everybody'll hate you.'[85]

Maggie's childish desire to be found 'clever' is only one expression of what *The Mill on the Floss* diagnoses as a general human desire for 'mental superiority'. Throughout the novel, Eliot highlights how struggles to establish 'mental superiority' – a phrase that appears in the novel twice – carry the seeds of sadism, violence, and tyranny, even when they are apparently trivial or comic. Much of the novel's satire springs from narrator's relish in discerning dark political struggles in the play of children and in the minor domestic rivalries among and between the Tulliver and Dodson families. Eliot's narrator is always overtly partisan in these power struggles: her sympathies always lie with 'those less likely to be winners in the game of life', to quote from the novel itself, even as she emphasises the volatility of such struggles and the tendency of victims to become aggressors and vice versa.[86] Eliot's double perspective is especially apparent in the case of Tom. If Eliot is sympathetic to Tom's humiliation at the hands of Dr Stelling, she is biting in her critique of Tom's will to power, or, in Eliot's own language, his will to 'mastery'. Throughout the novel, Eliot attempts to expose Tom's will to mastery as not simply immoral but ridiculous and self-defeating:

> In very tender years, when [Tom] still wore a lace border under his outdoor cap, he was often observed peeping through the bars of a

gate and making minatory gestures with his small forefinger while he scolded the sheep with an inarticulate burr, intended to strike terror into their astonished minds: indicating thus early that desire for mastery over the inferior animals, wild and domestic, including cock-chafers, neighbours' dogs, and small sisters, which in all ages has been an attribute of so much promise for the fortunes of our race.[87]

The invocation of the 'fortunes of our race' places Tom's boyish aggression on a continuum with patriarchal and imperial forms of domination; sabre-rattling at animals and sisters is preparation for the adult business of subjugating wives, children, and other races. At the same time, Eliot casually diagnoses British imperial masculinity as being caught in a farcical master/slave dialectic: such masculinity can gain no more satisfying recognition from the women and other races it subjugates than an infant trying to impress sheep. Eliot evidently liked the image of Tom lording it over animals so much that she repeated it: Tom, in the midst of bullying Maggie, amuses himself by shooting peas at a 'superannuated bluebottle which was exposing its imbecility in the spring sunshine, clearly against the laws of Nature, who had provided Tom and the peas for the speedy destruction of this weak individual'.[88] Critics have rightly highlighted this passage as evidence of Eliot's critical awareness of an emergent Darwinian and Spencerian 'survival of the fittest' logic.[89] But the real satirical sting of the passage lies in the fact that Tom is projecting such a logic on to a creature which cannot possibly satisfy his need to be recognised as a superior being. Such intrinsically unequal and therefore doomed quests for recognition play out across the novel and suggest Eliot's absorption of G. W. F. Hegel's master/slave dialectic.

The master/slave dialectic – or more properly, 'lordship and bondage' – is part of Hegel's theory of self-consciousness.[90] Hegel claims that self-consciousness depends upon the recognition of another self-conscious being; it is only through such acknowledgement that a person gains affirmation of his or her reality and status. Full recognition depends upon reciprocity – each person must accord equal and independent existence to the other, and recognise that his or her own identity is in the power of the other. Hegel unfolds his argument as a parable about two abstract consciousnesses meeting in a state of nature. Initially, their confrontation escalates into a 'life-and-death struggle', where each consciousness tries to assert his independent, essential reality by annihilating the other.[91] But consciousness cannot gain assurance of its reality from an indifferent or dead object. The master/slave dialectic arises from the realisation that the recognition of a living other is necessary for a consciousness to prove its reality and worth to itself – just as Tom cannot gain recognition of his mental superiority from killing bluebottles but requires Maggie as an audience. In a master/slave conflict, a 'one-sided and unequal' form of recognition arises: one who surrenders out of desire to preserve his life and so becomes a slave, and a master who affirms his reality by treating the slave as a mere 'thing'.[92] But the master's triumph has destabilising irony at its core: his sense of his absolute power is dependent upon the recognition of his slave, and he regards the slave's recognition as worthless. In this way, the 'truth' of the master's consciousness is actually the despised consciousness of the slave.[93] And this same irony plays out in the slave's consciousness as well: the slave's mortal terror of his master and the labour he is forced to perform both grant him a certain independence and freedom of mind[94]

Isobel Armstrong has brilliantly demonstrated that Eliot's representation of power dynamics in domestic spaces and particularly within marriage in *Middlemarch* (1872) attests to her keen understanding of Hegel's master/slave dialectic. Eliot does not follow Hegel's parable of the master and the slave programmatically or with any precise fidelity to Hegel's metaphysics. Rather, she mobilises Hegel's 'structure of domination as a covert tracking device for bourgeois marriage meant that Eliot could stress the enormity and cruelty of its power relations', as Armstrong writes.[95] In *The Mill on the Floss*, the Hegelian structure of domination is a means of elucidating the moral stakes and the psychology of power underpinning modern ideas of merit and intelligence. Hegel's influence can be felt in the novel, first, in Eliot's emphasis upon the primacy of the desire for social recognition in human psychology, and second, in her efforts to demonstrate the intrinsic instability and hollowness of quests for 'mental superiority'.

One of the novel's moral fables about the desire for mental superiority centres on the minor character of Bob Jakin. At the start of the novel Bob is a child who, like young Jude Fawley in Hardy's *Jude the Obscure*, is employed by a local farmer to scare birds away from crops. Eliot ironises Maggie's childish conflation of Bob's mental capacities with his menial job: Maggie finds Bob alarming and thinks of bird-scaring not merely as his occupation but as his 'natural function'.[96] Maggie also extrapolates from Bob's ingenuity at hunting and trapping animals that he himself is bestial and 'wicked', even 'diabolical', though she does not 'distinctly know why'.[97] What is being ironised here is not merely the luridness of Maggie's childish imagination, but how perfectly a child will replicate adult social prejudices: if Maggie does not 'distinctly' know why she feels an aversion to Bob, the reader surely does. In any case, Eliot's narrator intervenes to spell out the point: '[Bob's] virtue, supposing it to exist, was undeniably "virtue in rags", which is notoriously likely to remain unrecognised (perhaps because it is seen so seldom).'[98] As this aside suggests, the purpose of this parable is not to celebrate the unrecognised virtues of the poor (though Bob does, in fact, turn out to be virtuous). Eliot is instead interested in exploring the human propensity to malign the intelligence of social inferiors, particularly when such inferiors demonstrate too much agency or make claims to equality. For it is not merely Bob's low social status that leads Maggie and later Tom to question his moral character, but the fact that he has 'more brains nor [he] know[s] what to do wi[th]' [sic]': he possesses an intelligence so lively and self-assured that it unsettles their understanding of the social hierarchy.[99] In other words, Bob is intelligence out of place in Rancière's sense: he spoils the supposed fit between minds and social positions, and this is the real reason Maggie and Tom both find him disconcerting.

Tom and Bob have a natural affinity because they share the same kind of practical intelligence: like Tom, Bob has 'a notion of things out o' door, a common sense'.[100] However, Tom can enjoy Bob's friendship and tolerate his 'superior knowingness' about the natural world only on the condition that Bob acknowledge his own status as an 'inferior'.[101] Bob has the audacity to imagine Tom as his equal, and this sparks a struggle for recognition. Their friendship ruptures when they quarrel over a coin-toss game and Tom demands that Bob recognise that Tom is his 'master', which Bob refuses to do. A physical fight ensues, and Eliot underscores that this is an existential struggle for Tom, who needs to wrest recognition not just of his physical strength but of his mental superiority from Bob: Tom does not merely want the coin, he wants Bob to 'give' it to him and thereby acknowledge his subservience. When Bob remains indomitable, Tom moralises his own desire for mastery and pronounces Bob a 'cheat', though the fact that they are arguing over a game of chance emphasises the morally

arbitrary nature of their struggle, which is at bottom over power
and class – as the symbol of the coin underscores.[102] Eliot's narrator comments that this episode illustrates Tom 'Rhadamanthine'
nature – his need to dominate and punish others under the guise
of justice – and it is clearly intended to foreshadow his later treatment of Maggie.[103] And as in the case of Maggie, Tom's need to
assert this mastery is self-defeating: he merely deprives himself of
the pleasures of a relationship between equals. 'An' I'n g'ien you
everything, an' showed you everything, an' niver wanted nothin'
from you,' Bob calls forlornly after Tom.[104] But, in fact, Bob did
want something from Tom: he wanted Tom to recognise him as
an equal.

In case we failed to notice the groundlessness of Maggie's and
Tom's childhood sense of superiority to Bob, Eliot transforms
Bob into their saviour when they are adults. Maggie and Tom
both come to feel ashamed of their childhood perceptions of him
when he offers them money in the wake of their father's bank-
ruptcy; Maggie proclaims that she now thinks him 'the kindest
person in the world!'[105] It is in fact Bob's 'triumphant knowingness' that delivers the Tulliver family from debt and enables Tom
to re-establish himself as a gentleman–businessman: it is Bob who
advises Tom to speculate in cargo.[106] Superficially, Bob here functions as a 'flat' helper or lackey archetype: his convenient mixture
of deference and shrewdness ensures that Tom recoups his gentlemanly identity – itself new and precarious – relatively quickly and
without too much exertion on his own behalf. However, Bob is
actually a disruptive figure in *The Mill on the Floss*; his speeches
– all in dialect – are too lengthy to function as merely comic or
picturesque interludes. And he does not shore up the naturalness
of Tom's status as a gentleman–businessman, but rather exposes
its hollowness.

Critics have observed that Eliot uses Tom's apprenticeship narrative to critique the Victorian ideal of the self-made businessman
and the Samuel Smilesian ethic of self-help, but Bob's centrality to
this critique has been generally overlooked.[107] Bob reappears in
the narrative just as Eliot seems to be constructing Tom's career
as an inspiring, Smilesean story about the rewards of pluck and
self-discipline. She undercuts this narrative abruptly and heavy-
handedly, instructing us not to confuse Tom with the archetype
of the 'industrious apprentice'.[108] The title of the chapter in which
Tom reveals that he has cleared his father's debts, 'The Hard-Won

'Triumph', can only be sardonic, since it is not Tom's virtuous labour that has enabled him to triumph, but Bob's canny investment scheme. In this way, Eliot clarifies that Maggie's and Tom's childhood impulse to stigmatise Bob's intelligence as animalistic or as a type of low cunning – they variously think of it as wickedness, cheating, sneaking, and theft[109] – is not only class prejudice but wilful self-ignorance, particularly in the case of Tom. Tom's successful speculation in cargo is another coin-toss game – one that Tom needs to moralise in order to maintain his own sense of own merit. Mr Tulliver more generously extends the meritocratic laurel to Bob himself when he learns of Bob's role in Tom's success:

> Bob's juvenile history, so far as it had come under Mr Tulliver's knowledge, was recalled with that sense of the astonishing promise it displayed, which is observable in all reminiscences of the childhood of great men.[110]

Eliot here mocks the meritocratic ideal as a just-so story designed to make success seem deserved, rational, and predictable. Bob's function in the narrative is to highlight just the opposite: he serves to expose the extent to which Tom's overweening superiority depends upon moral luck – and in particular, on the goodwill and intelligence of others.

Maggie's episode with the 'gypsies' is another parable about the instability of quests for mental superiority, and it also suggests Eliot's internalisation of Hegel's master/slave dialectic. *The Mill on the Floss* frequently highlights the tendency of the dominated to dominate others in their turn. This pattern repeats itself across the novel, where a character attempts to redress an experience of humiliation or powerlessness by lording it over a perceived inferior. For example, Tom avenges his intellectual humiliation at Dr Stelling's hands by humiliating Maggie and then Philip Wakem. Maggie's episode with the 'gypsies' is another of these compensatory quests for domination: Maggie tries to relieve her sense of 'blighting obloquy' within her family by becoming 'queen of the gypsies'.[111] Maggie's Romantic sense of identification with the Roma arises from her family's construction of her as an anomaly – too dark-complexioned, unruly, and clever to fit with their ideal of femininity. As is often noted, Maggie's otherness within her own family and the world of St Ogg's is ambiguously racialised: her mother complains that she looks like a 'mulatter'; she is said to be 'like a gypsy' and 'half wild'; she identifies with the 'dark woman' in stories and fairy tales; her 'brown skin' inspires her Uncle Pullet to identify her with Crazy Kate, the doomed heroine of a William Cowper poem.[112] Maggie's flight to the Roma camp initially appears like an attempt to embrace this racialised otherness: after vengefully smearing her blonde and favoured cousin Lucy with mud, Maggie feels a pariah within her family and so resolves to seek fellowship within a 'dark', stigmatised community. Yet as the title of the chapter indicates – 'Maggie tries to run away from her shadow' – her flight to the Roma is actually an effort to exorcise her sense of otherness, not to embrace it. And she flees to the Roma not in search of kinship but to enjoy a compensatory sense of 'supremacy'.[113] The comedy of the episode arises not merely from Maggie's naïveté or egotism, but from the partial sophistication of her colonial fantasy: she imagines that she will bring 'amusing and useful knowledge' to the Roma; that she will rule over them as a benevolent queen; that they will worship her cleverness.[114] She even attempts to instruct them in the history of colonialism, offering to inform them about Christopher Columbus.[115] When the Roma prove less receptive to her pedagogy than she hoped, her fantasy turns Gothic and she begins to fear that they are cannibals, perhaps even demonic.[116] Eliot here highlights the same psychological reflex that characterised Tom's and Maggie's relationship with Bob: when a presumed social inferior proves less than deferential, they are suspected of hyperbolic evil.

Throughout the chapter, Eliot highlights the extent to which Maggie's fantasy of colonial rule is the product of her avid reading and her investment in the idea of her exceptional intelligence. Books are what Maggie hopes to bring to the Roma; and it is recognition of her 'cleverness' that she most craves from them.[117] Although Eliot invites us to find Maggie's delusions of grandeur comic and charming, she also emphasises that they are not innocent: it is not just Maggie's precocious literariness but her 'excessive delight in [. . .] acknowledged supremacy' that leads her to imagine herself 'queen of the gypsies'.[118] However, the most telling detail of Maggie's fantasy is actually the anxiety that threatens it: she repeatedly worries that the Roma will think her an 'idiot'.[119] This refers back to Tom's mockery of Maggie after she cut her own hair: he says that she looks 'queer' and 'like the idiot we throw nutshells at at school'.[120] The fact that Tom invokes a specific person here makes clear that 'idiot' in this context is not merely colloquial; he means that Maggie is at risk of appearing intellectually disabled. This links to a wider familial discourse that casts Maggie as mentally deficient: her mother thinks she is 'half an idiot' and like a 'Bedlam creetur'; Tom constantly delights in telling her she is 'a stupid' or an 'idiot'; Uncle Pullet compares her to 'Crazy Kate'.[121] Maggie's anxiety that the Roma will 'set her down as an idiot' makes clear that this familial cruelty is not merely the perverse punishment meted out to a daughter considered unusually bright.[122] Mrs Tulliver actually elides Maggie's dark skin with her putative idiocy and madness; the possibilities that Maggie might be a 'mulatter' and 'half an idiot' are raised at the same time.[123] Similarly, it is Maggie's 'brown skin' that leads her Uncle Pullet to associate her with 'Crazy Kate'. That Maggie is pathologised for her unfeminine intelligence but also disparaged as mentally deficient captures the partial fluidity of the nineteenth-century hierarchy of mental capacity. Although white male rationality may be the stable apex of the hierarchy, the 'inferior' characteristics are somewhat fungible and may be conflated or played off against each other according to ideological convenience. Maggie's reputation for cleverness does not destabilise this hierarchy so much as demonstrate its tensile force: her unfeminine intellect means that she seems to conjure other abjected categories – blackness, madness, idiocy, savagery – in the minds of others, however casually or half-affectionately. And even as a child Maggie seems to intuit this. Her bid to become queen of the gypsies is a contradictory attempt both to assimilate the shame of her own outsider status within her family and to align herself imaginatively with patriarchal and colonial power. However, the fact that this effort is shadowed by the fear that the Roma will instead think her intellectually disabled suggests the precariousness of any such attempt to ascend the cultural hierarchy of minds, even in childish fantasy. Maggie's effort to elevate herself by casting the Roma as her inferior others instead confronts her with the dangers of being cast as an inferior other herself.

The superior power of misery

It is not, in fact, intellectual disability but physical disability that appears most prominently in *The Mill on the Floss*. Philip Wakem has curvature of the spine, a disability that endows him with a mixture of emotional sensitivity and self-consciousness that we are asked to recognise as the hallmarks of an artistic temperament. Like Maggie, Philip is defined by his 'cleverness', and there are many suggestions that he might grow up to be a talented artist, perhaps even a genius.[124] But as is the case with Maggie, this possibility is raised only to be undercut. Philip is the archetype of the wounded Romantic genius, but pointedly humbled by the laws of Eliot's realism. His deformity, his mercurial imagination, and his tendency to sarcasm and brooding vaguely recall Lord Byron, but he entirely lacks the glamour of the Romantic archetype he evokes. Philip's Romantic lineage is also evident insofar as he is the novel's most articulate advocate of *Bildung*: he urges Maggie to turn away from her quasi-Christian asceticism and pursue many-sided self-development, but it is clear that his ideals are as unattainable to him as they are to her.[125] Eliot is explicit that we are meant to understand Philip as a case study in the hard truth that 'ugly and deformed people' do not necessarily have compensatory talents or virtues.[126] Instead of being tormented by his genius in the pattern of a Romantic artist, Philip is tormented by his awareness of the 'mediocrity of [his] powers'.[127]

As Clare Walker-Gore points out, the intellectual and emotional affinities between Philip and Maggie prime the reader to expect a romantic relationship between them. However, it gradually becomes apparent that Philip's disability means that he primarily arouses 'pity' in Maggie; it requires the 'emphatically able-bodied masculinity' of Stephen Guest to awaken her sexuality.[128] Walker-Gore notes that while Maggie's erotic preference for Stephen over Philip is constructed as 'natural' in the novel, it is not by extension celebrated as moral; on the contrary, Eliot encourages us to feel moral discomfort at the way the 'law of sexual attraction' leads Maggie to 'select' the vacuous Stephen over the imaginative and intellectual Philip. Walker-Gore rightly perceives a prescient critique of eugenics in the novel, suggesting that Eliot foresaw how Darwin's theories would tempt people to confound the natural and the morally good, biological evolution and social progress.[129] As I have been arguing, Eliot's anti-eugenic thinking also extends into the realm of intellectual abilities, which Eliot suggests may be as morally arbitrary as physical ones – that is, if they are understood in reductively biological terms, as fixed and definite traits open to measurement and competitive ranking. It is Mr Stelling who articulates this logic most explicitly in the novel: 'A boy born with a deficient power of apprehending signs and abstractions must suffer the penalty of his congenital deficiency, just as if he had been born with one leg shorter than the other.'[130] Although this opinion is focalised through Mr Stelling and is clearly an object of irony, Eliot does, in fact, invite us to compare Tom's alleged 'slowness' to Philip's physical disability. In the schoolroom power struggles between them, Philip pits his 'cleverness' against Tom's physical prowess, and each boy succeeds in humiliating the other. While, superficially, Tom is the bully and Philip his pathetic victim, Philip has a psychological acuity that Tom lacks, and this makes the struggle between them more evenly matched than it appears at first sight. Despite the complexity of this dynamic, Eliot is also encouraging us to perceive the incommensurability of physical and mental qualities. The comedy and cruelty of their contest lies in the fact that they are effectively fighting on different fronts: Philip's 'cleverness' is a capacity different in kind to Tom's physical strength just as Tom's slowness at schoolwork is incomparable to Philip's physical disability, even if they are equally determined to weaponise their differences.[131] In case we miss this point, Eliot gives Tom a minor leg injury, which seems superficially to equalise the condition of the two boys. In fact, however, this crude and temporary physical equality only serves to underscore the profound and unpredictable mental differences between them: Tom's injury actually inspires Philip to feel more empathy with Tom rather than granting Tom any significant insight into Philip's experience of disability.[132]

The competition between Tom and Philip prompts us to perceive that conceptualising mental characteristics as if they were as empirically knowable as physical ones is a kind of category error. The narrator calls attention to the fact that such equivalencies between mental and physical characteristics are unstable metaphors, and ones that may lead us into absurdly literal thinking:

> Mr Stelling concluded that Tom's brain, being peculiarly impervious to etymology and demonstrations, was peculiarly in need of being ploughed and harrowed by these patent implements; it was his favourite metaphor, that the classics and geometry constituted that culture of the mind which prepared it for the reception of any subsequent crop [. . .] It turned out as uncomfortably for Tom Tulliver as if he had been plied with cheese in order to remedy a gastric weakness which prevented him from digesting it. It is astonishing what a different result one gets by changing the metaphor! Once call the brain an intellectual

stomach, and one's ingenious conception of the classics and geometry as ploughs and harrows seems to settle nothing. But then it is open to some one else to follow great authorities, and call the mind a sheet of white paper or a mirror, in which case one's knowledge of the digestive process becomes quite irrelevant. It was doubtless an ingenious idea to call the camel the ship of the desert, but it would hardly lead one far in training that useful beast. O Aristotle! if you had had the advantage of being 'the freshest modern' instead of the greatest ancient, would you not have mingled your praise of metaphorical speech, as a sign of high intelligence, with a lamentation that intelligence so rarely shows itself in speech without metaphor, – that we can so seldom declare what a thing is, except by saying it is something else?[133]

It is possible to perceive Eliot's sympathy with Lewes's dual-aspect monism here (which perhaps has its roots in their shared knowledge of Spinoza, whose *Ethics* (1677) she translated just before she commenced work on *The Mill on the Floss*). While Eliot emphasises the embodiment of the intellect, she also underscores that a fully materialist logic which treats the brain as the same kind of entity as the stomach is only one way of thinking about mental processes, and one that is just as unstable as other more hallowed and obviously poetic metaphors of mind. In this context, Eliot is also alerting us to how metaphors of mind can rigidify into educational dogma and invidious judgements about mental capacity. With a final flourish, Eliot's narrator points out that no lesser authority than Aristotle suggested that metaphorical speech is a sign of high intelligence; but given both the treacherousness of metaphors and their ubiquity in speech, how reliable can judgements about intelligence be?

Eliot repeatedly specifies that Philip's disability is not congenital but the result of an accident.[134] This reflects the novel's general emphasis upon the impact of contingency upon human character rather than upon essentialist forms of biological determinism. Such essentialism tends to be attributed to naïve or narrow-minded characters such as Mr Tulliver and Dr Stelling. In relation to Philip, such essentialist thinking is attributed to Tom, who is so impressed by Philip's drawing talent that he is prompted to wonder if Philip's 'crooked back might be the source of remarkable faculties'.[135] This speculation is akin to Tom's belief that Philip must be a 'rascal' because his father is Mr Tulliver's enemy; biological essentialism clearly justifies archaic forms of superstition and clannishness.[136]

And yet Eliot also suggests that there is, in fact, an indeterminist connection between Philip's disability and what Tom thinks of as his 'cleverness': Philip's acute self-consciousness about his disability has endowed him with both emotional intelligence and a precocious understanding of the tragic. In the novel's own language, Philip shares with Maggie 'the superior power of misery' or the 'gift of sorrow', and Eliot insists that it is this power that it is the real source of their intellectual superiority to Tom.[137] In this way, the novel covertly retains a Romantic faith in a link between suffering and genius even as it explicitly rejects the notion as sentimental wish-fulfilment.

The phrase the 'superior power of misery' appears when Eliot is musing over the difference between the child Maggie and a dog. Where Maggie feels shame and anger when Tom accuses her of being greedy with her jam-puffs, the dog Yap is loyal to Tom even when denied food. Eliot suggests that Maggie's misery is emblematic of the human capacity for inner conflict, a capacity which distinguishes human beings from animals and places them at 'a proud distance from the most melancholy chimpanzee'.[138] In the wake of Spencer's and Darwin's work, 'intelligence' could no longer be sanctified as the noble feature that distinguished humans from animals, and Eliot's remark suggests how a humanist ideal of tragic consciousness might be used as a secular means of preserving a sense of human exceptionalism. Yet in the rest of the novel, Eliot is not anxious to establish differences between human and animal intelligence; on the contrary, the novel is rich with metaphors and similes that analogise human social customs and animal behaviour.[139] Instead, Eliot is troubled by the reduction of intelligence to an amoral competitive trait. It is against this scientific and meritocratic conception of intelligence that Eliot leverages the idea of the tragic.

Critics have often read *The Mill on the Floss* through the prism of classical tragedy, and the novel certainly affirms what is often held to be the primary axiom of the genre: that great suffering ennobles the sufferer.[140] As the novel moves toward its conclusion and Maggie's conflict between her desires and her sense of duty intensifies, she is presented in increasingly exalted terms. In the latter half of the novel, Eliot emphasises Maggie's exceptional beauty and dignity with increasing insistence, and Maggie is granted a sombre rhetorical authority in a series of moral *agons* with Philip, Tom, and Stephen Guest. As critics often note, Maggie's dilemma

seems consciously constructed according to Hegel's definition of
tragedy as a conflict between equally legitimate but incompat-
ible ethical imperatives.[141] Eliot repeatedly suggests that Maggie's
condition of anguished ambivalence grants her not only tragic
insight, but a genuine intellectual superiority. In contrast, Tom's
moral absolutism is constructed as a reflection of his intellectual
limitations; when Maggie reproaches Tom that he does not 'have
a mind large enough to see that there is anything better than your
own [. . .] petty aims', she is only echoing the narrator's explicit
judgement.[142] That Maggie now possesses the gravity and pathos
of a tragic heroine is designed to give an unanswerable aesthetic
force to Eliot's remoralisation of the intellect: Maggie's tragic
intelligence towers over not just Tom's tyrannical moralism but
the preoccupation with innate cleverness, master/slave struggles
for 'mental superiority', and meritocratic ideals of success that
pervade the book.

In her deliberate conflation of intellectual superiority with tragic
insight, Eliot was self-consciously attempting to sustain what she
understood as an embattled Christian paradigm, albeit in secularised form. Eliot thought the Christian tradition was right to subor-
dinate the intellect to moral passions and virtues, and she wanted
to mount a secular defence of this position. She is explicit about
this project in *Middlemarch*:

> [. . .] though the opinion in the neighbourhood of Freshitt and Tipton
> had pronounced [Dorothea] clever, that epithet would not have
> described her to circles in whose more precise vocabulary cleverness
> implies mere aptitude for knowing and doing, apart from character.
> All her eagerness for acquirement lay within that full current of sym-
> pathetic motive in which her ideas and impulses were habitually swept
> along [. . .] If she had written a book she must have done it as Saint
> Theresa did, under the command of an authority that constrained her
> conscience.[143]

Eliot's desire at once to preserve and to secularise a Christian
perception of the intellect's necessary humility – its subservience
to faith and moral feeling – was already fully fledged in *Mill on the
Floss*. However, for Eliot this project entails not simply the idealisation of heroines whose intellectual aspirations are inseparable
from their 'sympathetic motives'; it entails an effort to vindicate
what was traditionally devalued as 'feminine' intelligence.

From emotional intelligence to moral genius

Daston notes that the Western philosophical tradition has allowed for the possibility that women have certain, if distinctly minor, intellectual virtues. Women are often credited with a natural aptitude for sociability or sympathy; if women's minds are irrational and childish, they might nonetheless be quick, lively, or intuitive.[144] In some contexts, such faint praise has granted scope for a more radical valorisation of women's intellects. For example, the historian Anthony La Vopa has shown that within the salon culture of the French Enlightenment, women's reputed social intelligence was often celebrated as equal or even superior to the scholastic rationality identified with men. In that context, 'feminine' intelligence, which was believed to manifest itself in an array of social talents – charm, tact, wit, sympathy, psychological insight – was, to a large extent, enshrined as an ideal for both men and women.[145] Eliot was fascinated by this tradition. In her 1854 essay 'Women in France: Madame de Sablé', she praises 'the women whose tact, wit, and personal radiance created the atmosphere of the salon, where literature, philosophy, and science, emancipated from the trammels of pedantry and technicality, entered on a brighter stage of existence'.[146] In that essay, Eliot takes the inferiority of the female intellect for granted and suggests it is grounded in physiology and evolution; indeed, she articulates the very perception of women's deficient capacity for abstract thought that she later critiques in *Mill on the Floss* ('phantasms of great ideas float through' women's minds, but women lack 'the spell that will arrest' such ideas and 'give them fixity').[147] However, as Barbara Pauk has argued, 'Women in France' paradoxically mobilises scientific sexism in order to mount a feminist argument.[148] Eliot suggests that the French salon culture demonstrates the special value of women's social intelligence and the desirability of women having equal access to education and intellectual debate:

> Let the whole field of reality be laid open to women as well as to man, and then that which is peculiar in her mental modification [. . .] will be found to be a necessary complement to the truth and beauty of life.[149]

As I have been arguing, Eliot's construction of Tom's and Maggie's mental capacities as children is clearly designed to challenge biological essentialism about sex and intelligence, particularly the traditional identification of masculinity with abstract reason and femininity with emotional particulars. Yet if Eliot moved away from the scientific sexism of 'Women in France', she retained a strong investment in rehabilitating the kinds of social and emotional intelligence traditionally identified with women.[150] Strikingly, Eliot's even-handedness in her depiction of Tom's and Maggie's forms of intelligence evaporates as the novel moves towards its conclusion. The question of the relative mental capacities of Maggie and Tom is eclipsed by the question of their relative kinds of moral intelligence, and on this ground, Eliot is willing to affirm Maggie's superiority. The narrator asserts that Tom's moral rectitude reflects the 'narrowness of [his] imagination and intellect', while encouraging the reader to perceive that Maggie's moral dilemmas emerge from her deep capacities for passion and empathy.[151] Eliot returns to the gendered dichotomy of abstract reason versus concrete, personal experience, but this is now framed as a matter not of different types of mental ability but of different moral philosophies. Tom and Maggie effectively switch positions and come to occupy their standard gendered roles: Tom exemplifies the masculine commitment to abstract principles, Maggie the feminine preoccupation with the personal, the emotional, the specific. Where Tom wields his own 'conscious rectitude of purpose' – his commitment to abstract ideas of sexual propriety and filial duty – against Maggie like 'a staff and a baton', Maggie is consumed by a 'passionate tumult' as Tom, Stephen, and Philip make conflicting appeals to her sympathies.[152] Yet we know from the first half of the novel that this apparently gendered moral conflict does not arise from any kind of natural difference in their intellects: as a child Tom has a 'tendency in his mind to details' and Maggie has a 'keen taste' for abstraction. (Eliot re-emphasises this point toward the end of the novel when Maggie resumes her studies in Latin and discovers she has an 'understanding quite equal to [. . .] peculiarly masculine studies'.[153]) And just as Eliot sought to reveal that the young Tom's preoccupation with empirical detail was an authentic form of intelligence, she now seeks to show that Maggie's emotionalism is an expression of her intellect. More, Eliot makes clear that Maggie's passionate feelings are not mere feelings at all; they involve her in taxing forms of self-analysis and moral deliberation. Maggie's *agons* with Tom illustrate not simply that her capacity for passion and sympathy exceeds his, but that her more supple and self-critical intellect gives her a greater insight into what Eliot calls 'that complex, fragmentary, doubt-provoking knowledge we call truth'.[154]

Maggie is the first in a triptych of Eliot heroines whose youthful intellectual promise is fulfilled not through any worldly achievement but by her incarnation of moral genius: her narrative clearly anticipates those of Dorothea Brooke in *Middlemarch* and the eponymous heroine of *Romola*. However, the fact that Eliot was not simply exalting an essentialist ideal of female altruism but positing emotional intelligence as an ideal for both men and women is clearest in the construction of the hero of her final novel, *Daniel Deronda*.

As with *The Mill on the Floss*, Eliot's valorisation of emotional intelligence in *Daniel Deronda* entails a critique of meritocratic conceptions of intellectual ability. Daniel Deronda is first established as an exemplary moral character through his principled rejection of the competitive examination system at the University of Cambridge. Daniel is repelled by the competitive exam system for the same reason he is repelled by gambling in the opening scenes of the novel: it is a zero-sum game, where 'our gain is another's loss'.[155] At this stage of the novel, Daniel, unaware of his Jewish ancestry, is anxious about the possibility he is illegitimate and eager to establish that he is an English gentleman 'to the backbone'.[156] Significantly, however, Eliot suggests that Daniel's preference for self-sacrifice over competition – he would rather 'be the calf than the butcher' – is the first sign that he is, in fact, better than the upper-class Englishness to which he aspires: Eliot pointedly contrasts him to Robert Clive, one of the notoriously brutal architects of the British empire in India. Eliot here clearly links the competitive culture of cram at Cambridge to the ruthlessness of British imperial masculinity, and constructs Daniel's unfitness for both as proof of his moral and intellectual depth. In the end, Daniel fails to win a mathematics fellowship because he neglects his studies in favour of helping his hapless friend, Hans Meyrick, to succeed. Daniel's noble failure serves to highlight the moral claims and contingencies – in this case, the claims of friendship and Meyrick's misfortunes – that are excluded from meritocratic justice.

Daniel's disenchantment with Cambridge is clearly designed to allow Eliot to critique the narrowness of the curriculum at the ancient English universities and the tendency of examination culture to encourage rote learning at the expense of 'the principles which form the vital connections of knowledge'.[157] Eliot is also highlighting that the ancient English universities do not foster *Bildung* in the holistic, 'many-sided' sense that Daniel craves and that Eliot identifies with European education.[158] Castle suggests that Victorian novelists generally narrowed and institutionalised the Romantic ideal of *Bildung* by identifying it with Oxford and Cambridge, but in the case of *Deronda Deronda* we find just the opposite: Eliot uses the ideal of *Bildung* order to expose the sterility of English university culture, and in particular the upper-class English notion of the 'first-class' or 'first-rate' mind.[159] Eliot encourages us to perceive the link between the idle taste for gambling, archery, and blood sports within the novel's English aristocratic milieux and the competitive exam culture Daniel encounters at Cambridge. We are invited to appreciate that Daniel's 'second-rateness' in terms of the Cambridge examination culture actually attests to the immeasurable nature of his moral and intellectual qualities.[160] Although Eliot repeatedly hints that Daniel did, in fact, have the ability to triumph at Cambridge – everyone agrees that 'he might have taken a high place if his motives had been of a more pushing sort' – he must renounce all such ambition for 'personal priz[es]': he will be a hero not of merit but of moral genius.[161] Like other Eliot heroines before him, Daniel's genuine 'rarity' lies in his 'fervour of sympathy, an activity of imagination on behalf of others'.[162]

As many critics have observed, Daniel Deronda is clearly constructed as a feminine or 'womanly' hero.[163] His 'plenteous, flexible sympathy', his impulse toward self-sacrifice, and his sense of identification with the marginalised and oppressed all recall Eliot's other heroines of moral imagination: Maggie, Romola, and Dorothea.[164] Also like Eliot's prior heroines, Daniel has a high intelligence and a creative or 'poetic' temperament that does not result in any works of art or scholarship, but in a nebulous desire 'to make a little difference for the better' (though, of course, in his case this desire assumes the more definite shape of Zionism by the novel's end).[165] Yet *Daniel Deronda* is perhaps Eliot's most radical argument on behalf of emotional intelligence insofar as the novel is her fullest effort to demonstrate that it is not simply a feminine capacity or vocation but the disavowed core of what is conventionally esteemed as masculine reason.

Eliot discusses emotional intelligence – what she calls 'the emotional intellect' – explicitly in *Daniel Deronda*.[166] The phrase

appears at the pivotal moment when Daniel is attempting to rationalise his own receptivity to the oracular Zionism of Ezra Mordecai
Cohen. Eliot devotes an entire chapter to Daniel's inward debate
on this subject. Eliot is simultaneously attempting to justify the
novel's swerve away from realism and the decadent mores of the
English aristocracy and into a realm of romance that can accom-
modate the religious idealism of the novel's Jewish plot. On the
face of it, Daniel's willingness to become Mordecai's disciple is
unaccountable because Daniel does not yet know about his Jewish
ancestry and has so far been presented as a cautious, basically
secular character. Eliot invokes the 'emotional intellect' in order
to defend Daniel's reverence for Mordecai:

> Suppose [Mordecai] had introduced himself as one of the strictest rea-
> soners: do they form a body of men hitherto free from false conclusions
> and illusory speculations? The driest argument has its hallucinations,
> too hastily concluding that its net will now at last be large enough to
> hold the universe. Men may dream in demonstrations, and cut out an
> illusory world in the shape of axioms, definitions, and propositions,
> with a final exclusion of fact signed Q.E.D. No formulas for think-
> ing will save us mortals from mistake in our imperfect apprehension
> of matter to be thought about. And since the unemotional intellect
> may carry us far into a mathematical dreamland where nothing is but
> what is not, perhaps an emotional intellect may have absorbed into
> its passionate vision of possibilities some truth of what will be – the
> more comprehensive massive life feeding theory with new material, as
> the sensibility of the artist seizes combinations which science explains
> and justifies. At any rate, presumptions to the contrary are not to
> be trusted. We must be patient with the inevitable makeshift of our
> human thinking [. . .].[167]

Eliot here suggests that the ideal of a pure, mathematical rationality is chimerical and itself a form of irrationality. By contrast,
the 'emotional intellect' is able to approach the 'truth' because
it has no such illusions about its own purity: it acknowledges
the imperfection of reason. This argument is not simply asserted
by the narrator but dramatised throughout the chapter as Eliot
strives to show that Daniel's 'perceptive sympathetic emotiveness'
demands complex ratiocination and calls upon all the resources of
his education and wide reading. Like Maggie's tragic conflict in
The Mill on the Floss, Daniel's crisis in Chapter 41 is presented by

Eliot as a philosophical drama: the complexity of Daniel's feelings leads him into a rigorous interrogation of his own values and his understanding of history, politics, and religion. This is not just a matter of Eliot revealing that Daniel's intellect is influenced by his emotions, but of revealing that Daniel's 'emotions are themselves suffused with intelligence and discernment', to borrow a phrase from Nussbaum.[168]

Sally Shuttleworth observes that Eliot often calls upon Victorian psychology to justify her moral positions.[169] Eliot's construction of the 'emotional intellect' in her novels tends to blur the distinction between fact and value: she presents the inseparability of the intellect and the emotions as a fact about the human mind, but also consecrates the 'emotional intellect' as a moral ideal and as the special gift of heroes and heroines such as Maggie, Daniel, and Dorothea. This sleight of hand is discernible in the passage quoted above. The emotional nature of Daniel's intellect is presented as a reflection of the 'inevitably makeshift' nature of all human thought, but also as a privileged insight which confirms that Daniel possesses 'the sensibility of an artist'. In this way, Eliot clearly retains an investment in the figure of the Romantic genius, even if her heroes and heroines must forfeit any dreams of 'personal pre-eminence' for the sake of moral and collective goods.[170] It is clearly important to Eliot that the reader knows or at least suspects that Daniel, Dorothea, and Maggie are exceptionally clever before we are asked to appreciate that their real genius is moral, not intellectual.

Gillian Beer has observed that the narrator of *Middlemarch* is alien to the town of Middlemarch: 'the disparities between topic and writing are striking. The town of Middlemarch is provincial: the writing of *Middlemarch* is urban, cosmopolitan even. The concerns of the people are local; the writing, polymathic.'[171] In a similar vein, David Kurnick has remarked that *Middlemarch* is a book that refuses to extend its own 'intellectual riches' to any of its characters; the narrator effectively monopolises intellectual sophistication.[172] There is a similar tension between the famously scholarly and cerebral omniscience of Eliot's narrators and Eliot's commitment to elevating moral and emotional intelligence over any form of intellectual superiority or distinction. The tension is also perceptible in some of Eliot's most famous statements about egotism, sympathy, and ethics: 'We are all of us born in moral stupidity, taking the world as an udder to feed our supreme selves'; 'the quickest of us walk about well wadded with stupidity'; 'hatred of innocent human obstacles was a form of moral stupidity not in Daniel's grain'.[173] These statements – the first two from *Middlemarch*, the third from *Daniel Deronda* – aim to awaken the reader to the moral claims of others, but it is significant that they do so by arousing the reader's presumed intellectual vanity. Eliot is partly using 'stupidity' in the etymological sense of a stupor or a form of insensibility, but it still carries the more colloquial force of insult. In effect, Eliot's formidably intellectual narrators try to shame us out of egotism by suggesting that it is an embarrassing form of mental inferiority. It is open to question whether this strategy does not simply reinforce the preoccupation with mental superiority that is one of the prime objects of Eliot's moral critique.

If Eliot does not fully share her magisterial intellect with any of her characters, she is nevertheless generally committed to endowing secondary and minor characters with lively and unexpected forms of intelligence. Her effort to vindicate the overlooked intelligence of Tom Tulliver and Bob Jakin in *Mill on the Floss* is actually a ubiquitous moral imperative in her novels. Eliot's famous critiques of human egotism are frequently not injunctions to sympathy but injunctions to respect the intelligence of another. Here is a representative example from *Daniel Deronda*:

> [. . .] self-confidence is apt to address itself to an imaginary dullness in others; as people who are well off speak in a cajoling tone to the poor, and those who are in the prime of life raise their voice and talk artificially to seniors, hastily conceiving them to be deaf and rather imbecile. Gwendolen, with all her cleverness and purpose to be agreeable, could not escape from that form of stupidity; it followed in her mind, unreflectingly, that because Mrs. Arrowpoint was ridiculous she was also likely to be wanting in penetration.[174]

As this passage suggests, Eliot's narrators often highlight the fact that it is not merely egotism but social conventions – here, condescension toward the poor, the elderly, and 'ridiculous' lady novelists such as Mrs Arrowpoint – that make the intelligence of others seem negligible. In the next chapter, I explore how Hardy – himself a close reader of Eliot's novels – also attempts to vindicate overlooked forms of intelligence. However, in his novels we find a more overtly political effort to critique the tendency of the powerful to address themselves to an 'imaginary dullness in others'.

Notes

1 George Eliot, *Impressions of Theophrastus Such* (New York: A. L. Burt, 1900), pp. 70–1.

2 For example, Such's speculations in 'Shadows of a Coming Race' anticipate contemporary anxieties about artificial intelligence and its implications for humanity. See *Theophrastus Such*, pp. 139–44, and Helen Small, 'Artificial Intelligence: George Eliot, Ernst Kapp, and the Projections of Character', 19 *Interdisciplinary Studies in the Long Nineteenth Century* 29 (2020). Available at: <https://19 .bbk.ac.uk/article/id/1993/> (last accessed 24 November 2021).

3 Theophrastus Such/Eliot is alluding to Samuel Johnson's claim that Newton would have written a great epic poem if he had devoted himself to poetry rather than mathematics. In response to an interlocutor who asserts that men have different kinds of intellectual aptitude, Johnson replies, 'No, sir. It is only that one man has *more mind* than another. He may direct it differently; he may by accident desire to excel in this study or in that. Sir, the man who has vigour may walk to the east, just as well to the west.' As Cyril Burt observed, Johnson was here articulating the same belief in general intelligence that Galton and later intelligence testers were attempting to substantiate. See James Boswell, *Life of Johnson* [1791], ed. George Birkbeck Hill (New York: Harper & Bros, 1891), p. 38. Also see Burt, 'Historical Sketch of the Development of Psychological Tests', pp. 14–15.

4 It is clear from Eliot's notebooks that she was familiar with Galton's work at least via her reading of Darwin; in 1872, she records her interest in Galton's claim that three generations of a particular family shared the same tic while sleeping. See Jane Irwin, *George Eliot's Daniel Deronda Notebooks* (Cambridge: Cambridge University Press, 1996), p. 242. Her letters reveal that she met Galton casually at least once: Galton, Darwin, and Eliot all walked out of a séance together in contempt. See K. M. Newton, *George Eliot for the Twenty-First Century: Literature, Philosophy, Politics* (Basingstoke: Palgrave Macmillan, 2018), p. 55. More significantly, Eliot was aware that Galton took a scientific interest in her mental abilities. As noted in the Introduction, Sully questioned Eliot about her 'visualising power' on Galton's behalf at

some point in the 1870s. See Collins, *George Eliot: Interviews and Recollections*, p. 197.

5 See Nancy Paxton, *George Eliot and Herbert Spencer: Feminism, Evolutionism, and the Reconstruction of Gender* (Princeton, NJ: Princeton University Press, 1991).

6 See, for example, K. K. Collins, 'G. H. Lewes Revised: George Eliot and the Moral Sense', *Victorian Studies* 21.4 (1978), pp. 463–92; Michael Davis, *George Eliot and Nineteenth-century Psychology: Exploring the Unmapped Country* (London: Routledge, 2016); Rylance, *Victorian Psychology*; Angelique Richardson, 'George Eliot, G. H. Lewes, and Darwin: Animals, Emotions, and Morals', in *After Darwin: Animals, Emotions and the Mind*, ed. Richardson (Amsterdam: Rodopi, 2013), 136–71; and Sally Shuttleworth, *George Eliot and Nineteenth-century Science: The Make-Believe of a Beginning* (Cambridge: Cambridge University Press, 1984).

7 Paxton, p. 4.

8 Rylance, p. 280.

9 On the Spinozan origins of Lewes's dual-aspect monism, see Davis, pp. 13–19, and Reed, *From Soul to Mind*, pp. 146–51. On Lewes's dual-aspect monism more broadly and its conciliatory politics, see Rylance, pp. 280–4.

10 George Henry Lewes, *Problems of Life and Mind, Third Series, Part 2* (Boston: Houghton, Osgood & Co., 1880), p. 391.

11 George Henry Lewes, *Physiology of Common Life* (Edinburgh: William Blackwood & Sons, 1859), pp. 375–411.

12 Rylance, p. 272.

13 Lewes, *Physiology of Common Life*, p. 5.

14 Lewes calls craniometry 'one of the most [. . .] misleading applications of arithmetic to life'. See *Physiology of Common Life*, pp. 181–2. On Lewes's hostility to Ferrier's work and suspicion of brain-localisation theories, see M. A. B. Brazier, 'Historical Introduction: The Discoverers of the Steady Potentials of the Brain', in *Brain Function*, ed. Brazier (Berkeley: University of California Press, 1963), pp. 2–3.

15 George Henry Lewes, *Problems of Life and Mind. First Series: The Foundations of a Creed*, vol. 1, 3rd edition (London: Trübner & Co., 1874), pp. 173–5.

16 Ibid., p. 124.

17 Reed, p. 153.

18 George Henry Lewes, *Problems of Life and Mind. Third Series. The Study of Psychology* (London: Trübner & Co. 1879), p. 152.

19 On this point, see Collins, 'Lewes Revised', p. 469.

20 Spencer, *Principles of Psychology*, p. 586.

21 George Henry Lewes, *Problems of Life and Mind. Third Series. Mind as a Function of the Organism* (Boston: Houghton, Osgood & Co., 1880), p. 441.

22 Ibid., p. 407.

23 On the influence of both Darwin and Spencer on Lewes, see Rylance, pp. 252–329.

24 Ibid., p. 442.

25 George Henry Lewes, 'The Lady Novelists', *Westminster Review* 58 (1852), pp. 129–41, pp. 131–2.

26 Kyriaki Hadjiafxendi, 'Gender and the Woman Question', in *George Eliot in Context*, ed. Margaret Harris (Cambridge: Cambridge University Press, 2013), 137–44, p. 143.

27 Jill Matus, *Shock, Memory, and the Unconscious in Victorian Fiction* (Cambridge: Cambridge University Press, 2009), pp. 129–31.

28 Martha Nussbaum, *Upheavals of Thought: The Intelligence of the Emotions* (Cambridge: Cambridge University Press, 2001), p. 3.

29 See Merve Imre, 'The Politics of Feeling', *New Yorker* (19 April 2021), pp. 64–8; and Daniel Goleman, *Emotional Intelligence: Why It Can Matter More Than IQ* (London: Bloomsbury, 1996).

30 On the centrality of ideas about emotional control to Victorian psychology and self-help culture, see Athena Vrettos, 'Victorian Psychology', in *A Companion to the Victorian Novel*, ed. Patrick Brantlinger and William B. Thesing (Oxford: Blackwell, 2005), pp. 68–74.

31 See Thomas Vargish, *The Providential Aesthetic in Victorian Fiction* (Charlottesville: University Press of Virginia, 1985).

32 As K. M. Newton remarks, Eliot's novels articulate a consistent hostility to laissez-faire capitalism, even if she 'cannot commit fully to any alternative'. See Newton, *George Eliot for the Twenty-First Century*, pp. 36–7 and p. 30. See also Dermot Coleman, *George Eliot and Money: Economics, Ethics, and Literature* (Cambridge: Cambridge University Press, 2014), pp. 139–57.

33 Mary Jean Corbett, *Family Likeness: Sex, Marriage, and Incest from Jane Austen to Virginia Woolf* (New Haven, CT: Cornell University Press, 2008), p. 119.

34 Eliot, *The Mill on the Floss*, ed. A. S. Byatt (London: Penguin, 1979), pp. 59–60.

35 Ibid., p. 68.

36 Ibid., pp. 68–9.
37 Flavia Alaya, 'Victorian Science and the "Genius" of Woman', *Journal of the History of Ideas* 38.2 (1977), 261–80, p. 265.
38 Eliot, *Mill*, p. 385.
39 Suzanne Graver, *Eliot and Community: A Study in Social Theory and Fictional Form* (Berkeley: University of California Press, 1984), pp. 14–27.
40 Eliot, *Mill*, p. 68.
41 Ibid., p. 63.
42 Ibid., p. 68.
43 Ibid., p. 71.
44 Ibid., p. 275.
45 Ibid., p. 226.
46 See Rylance, p. 300.
47 Lewes, 'Hereditary Influence, Animal and Human', *Westminster Review* 66 (1856), 135–62, p. 156.
48 Lewes, *Problems, Study of Psychology*, pp. 151–2.
49 Davis, p. 61. For a critic who extrapolates Eliot's own views on heredity from Mr Tulliver's, see, for example, Felicia Bonaparte, *Will and Destiny: Morality and Tragedy in George Eliot's Novels* (New York: New York University Press, 1975), pp. 62–5.
50 Eliot, *Mill*, p. 432.
51 Ibid., p. 320.
52 Ibid., p. 253.
53 Ibid., p. 81.
54 Ibid., p. 81.
55 Ibid., p. 66.
56 Daston, pp. 209–35.
57 Ibid., p. 225. On this topic, see also Russett, pp. 49–103.
58 Eliot, *Mill*, pp. 220–1.
59 Ibid., pp. 207–8.
60 Ibid., p. 405.
61 Ibid., p. 310.
62 Lewes, *Problems, Study of Psychology*, p. 42.
63 C. M. Steele and J. Aronson, 'Stereotype Threat and the Intellectual Test Performance of African Americans', *Journal of Personality and Social Psychology* 69 (1995), pp. 797–811.
64 Margaret Shih, Todd L. Pittinsky, and Nalini Ambady, 'Stereotype Susceptibility: Identity Salience and Shifts in Quantitative Performance', *Psychological Science* 10.1 (1999), pp. 80–3.
65 Alaya, p. 265.

66 Richardson, 'Darwin and Reductionisms: Victorian, Neo-Darwinian and Postgenomic Biologies', *19: Interdisciplinary Studies in the Long Nineteenth Century* 11 (2010). Available at: <https://doi.org/10.16995/ntn.583> (last accessed 24 November 2021).

67 Eliot, *Mill*, p. 138.

68 Michael S. Kearns, *Metaphors of Mind in Fiction and Psychology* (Lexington: University of Kentucky Press, 1987), p. 218.

69 Eliot, *Mill*, p. 244.

70 For an excellent article on Eliot's emphasis on the plasticity of both matter and character, see Pearl S. Brilmeyer, 'Plasticity, Form and the Matter of Character in *Middlemarch*', *Representations* 130.1 (2015), pp. 60–83.

71 Eliot, *Mill*, pp. 206 and 208.

72 Ibid., p. 203.

73 Frances Knight, *The Nineteenth-Century Church and English Society* (Cambridge: Cambridge University Press, 1995), p. 161.

74 Eliot, *Mill*, pp. 205 and 210.

75 Ibid., p. 208.

76 Pierre Bourdieu, *Homo Academicus* (Stanford, CA: Stanford University Press, 1988), p. 207.

77 Howard Gardner, *Frames of Mind: The Theory of Multiple Intelligences, Twentieth-Anniversary Edition* (New York: Basic Books, 2004), pp. 73–237.

78 See John White, *The Child's Mind* (Abingdon: Taylor & Francis, 2002), pp. 92–7.

79 Gardner, p. 63.

80 Gould, p. 22.

81 Davis, p. 12.

82 Eliot in letter to Sarah Hennell in 1857. Qtd in Bernard Semmel, *George Eliot and the Politics of National Inheritance* (Oxford: Oxford University Press, 1994), p. 34.

83 Eliot, *Mill*, p. 210.

84 Ibid., p. 121 and p. 221.

85 Ibid., p. 216.

86 Ibid., p. 431.

87 Ibid., p. 153.

88 Ibid., p. 147.

89 Richardson, 'Eliot, Lewes, and Darwin', p. 146; and Shuttleworth, *George Eliot*, pp. 60–1.

90 G. W. F. Hegel, *Phenomenology of Spirit*, trans. A. V. Miller (Oxford: Oxford University Press, 1977), pp. 111–19.

91 Ibid., p. 114.

92 Ibid., p. 116.

93 Ibid., p. 117.

94 Ibid., pp. 118–19.

95 Armstrong, 'Eliot, Hegel, and *Middlemarch*', 19: *Interdisciplinary Studies in the Long Nineteenth Century* 29 (2020). Available at: <https://doi.org/10.16995/ntn.1992> (last accessed 24 November 2021).

96 Eliot, *Mill*, p. 101.

97 Ibid.

98 Ibid., p. 102.

99 Ibid., p. 501.

100 Ibid., p. 69.

101 Ibid., p. 101.

102 Ibid., pp. 104–6.

103 Ibid., p. 107.

104 Ibid., p. 106.

105 Ibid., p. 327.

106 Ibid., p. 456.

107 Karen Bourrier, *Measure of Manliness*: *Disability and Masculinity in the Mid-Victorian Novel* (Ann Arbor: University of Michigan Press, 2015), pp. 76–102; and Tamara Ketabgian, *Lives of Machines: The Industrial Imaginary in Victorian Literature and Culture* (Ann Arbor: University of Michigan Press, 2011), pp. 134–9.

108 Eliot, *Mill*, p. 406.

109 Ibid., p. 101, p. 104, and p. 107.

110 Ibid., p. 456.

111 Ibid., p. 171.

112 As Alicia Mireles Christoff notes, the darkness of Maggie's skin is highlighted at least seventeen times in the novel. See Christoff, *Novel Relations: Victorian Fiction and British Psychoanalysis* (Princeton, NJ: Princeton University Press, 2019), p. 102; and Eliot, *Mill*, p. 60, p. 168, p. 432, and p. 493.

113 Eliot, *Mill*, pp. 554–5.

114 Ibid., pp. 173–6.

115 Ibid., pp. 173–5.

116 Ibid., p. 177.

117 Ibid., pp. 172–3.

118 Ibid., pp. 554–5.

119 Ibid., p. 169 and p. 171.

120 Ibid., p. 120.

121 Ibid., p. 146, p. 60, and p. 493.

122 Ibid., p. 171.

123 Ibid., p. 60.

124 Ibid., pp. 260–1.

125 Ibid., p. 402.

126 Ibid., p. 403.

127 Ibid., p. 633.

128 Clare Walker-Gore, *Plotting Disability in the Nineteenth-Century Novel* (Edinburgh: Edinburgh University Press 2019), p. 183.

129 Ibid., pp. 184–6.

130 Eliot, *Mill*, p. 243.

131 Ibid., pp. 234–50.

132 Ibid., pp. 257–8.

133 Ibid., pp. 208–9.

134 Ibid., p. 233 and p. 543.

135 Ibid., p. 235.

136 Ibid., p. 233.

137 Ibid., p. 269.

138 Ibid., p.100.

139 For an analysis of the animal metaphors and imagery in *Mill on the Floss*, see Corbett, *Family Likeness*, pp. 115–43, and Richardson, 'Eliot, Lewes, and Darwin'.

140 See Terry Eagleton, *Sweet Violence: The Idea of the Tragic* (Oxford: Wiley, 2003), pp. 23–40.

141 See K. M. Newton, *Modern Literature and the Tragic* (Edinburgh: Edinburgh University Press, 2008), p. 71.

142 Eliot, *Mill*, p. 449.

143 Eliot, *Middlemarch*, ed. Rosemary Ashton (Penguin: London, 2003), p. 86.

144 Daston, pp. 215–21.

145 Anthony La Vopa, *The Labour of the Mind: Intellect and Gender in Enlightenment Cultures* (Philadelphia: University of Pennsylvania Press, 2017), pp. 1–19.

146 Eliot, 'Women in France', in *Selected Critical Writings*, ed. Rosemary Ashton (Oxford: Oxford University Press, 1992), p. 39.

147 Ibid., p. 40.

148 Barbara Pauk, 'Evolution of Woman: George Eliot's Woman in France: Madame de Sablé', *Cahiers Victoriens & Edouardiens* 73 (2011), pp. 37–50.

149 Eliot, 'Women in France', p. 68.

150 As Paxton suggests, 'Women in France' reflects Eliot's struggle to

reconcile her own feminist beliefs with anti-feminist evolutionary arguments made by Spencer in particular. See Paxton, p. 39.

151 Eliot, *Mill*, p. 579.

152 Ibid., p. 579.

153 Ibid., p. 240 and p. 380.

154 Ibid., p. 579.

155 Eliot, *Daniel Deronda*, ed. Terence Holt (London: Penguin, 1995), p. 337.

156 Ibid., p. 183.

157 Ibid., p. 180.

158 Ibid., p. 364.

159 Ibid., p. 178. See Castle, pp. 47–62.

160 Eliot, *Daniel Deronda*, p. 178 and p. 364.

161 Ibid., p. 179.

162 Ibid., p. 751 and p. 179.

163 See, for example, Elizabeth Sabiston, *Private Sphere to World Stage from Austen to Eliot* (London: Routledge, 2008), pp. 153–5.

164 Eliot, *Daniel Deronda,* p. 364.

165 Ibid.

166 Ibid., p. 514.

167 Ibid., p. 514.

168 Nussbaum, p. 1.

169 Shuttleworth, *George Eliot*, p. 189.

170 Eliot, *Daniel Deronda*, p. 273.

171 Gillian Beer, 'What's Not in Middlemarch?', in *Middlemarch in the Twenty First Century*, ed. Karen Chase (Oxford: Oxford University Press, 2006), 15–35, p. 17.

172 David Kurnick, 'Erotics of Detachment: "Middlemarch" and Novel-reading as Critical Practice', *ELH* 74.3 (2007), 583–608, p. 583.

173 Eliot, *Middlemarch*, p. 211 and p. 194; and Eliot, *Daniel Deronda*, p. 175.

174 Eliot, *Daniel Deronda*, p. 45.

2

Thomas Hardy and the Value of Brains

In one of the most celebrated passages in Thomas Hardy's *œuvre*, Henry Knight, the rationalist hero of *A Pair of Blue Eyes* (1873), has a dramatic reckoning with the implications of Darwinian science and deep geological time. Dangling off the face of a cliff, he realises he is eye to eye with a trilobite fossil, and this prompts him to contemplate his own mortality and the fragility of civilisation as if they were equivalent. Knight readily perceives himself as an incarnation of humanist ideals, and so understands the 'dignity of man' to be at stake in his predicament – a presumption that Hardy ironises but also encourages us to take seriously, at least insofar as we are asked to read the situation as an allegory of humanism in crisis.[1] Throughout the scene, Hardy emphasises that the evolutionary perspective on humanity is humiliating for a man like Knight: he is distressed not simply by an atheistic sense of death's finality, but by the idea that he will be 'with the small *in* his death' (my emphasis).[2] This formulation is odd but revealing.

Knight experiences his animal status as a catastrophic form of downward mobility – the trilobite is like an 'underling' who has the temerity to address him on terms of equality, and he imagines he will somehow continue to feel degraded by their intimacy even when he too is a fossil.[3] In this state of extreme physical vulnerability, we might expect Knight to invest little value in his mental capacities. In fact, his abjection makes his sense of intellectual superiority all the more potent:

> Most men who have brains know it, and few are so foolish as to disguise this fact from themselves or others, even though an ostentatious display may be called self-conceit. Knight, without showing it much,

knew that his intellect was above the average. And he thought – he could not help thinking – that his death would be a deliberate loss to earth of good material; that such an experiment in killing might have been practised upon some less developed life.[4]

Knight's sense of having been reduced to the same level as a trilobite, a form of 'intelligence [un]worthy of the name', paradoxically intensifies his sense of his high place within an exclusively human hierarchy of 'brains'.[5] Yet this hierarchy is not really an alternative system of value. Knight appraises his own intelligence in evolutionary and thoroughly materialist terms: it is precious not because it constitutes a moral or spiritual dimension to his nature, nor even because it will deliver concrete benefits to humanity (Knight is a critic and something of a dilettante) but because it is 'good material', more worth preserving than other 'less developed' forms of life. Hardy here allegorises not only the high Victorian struggle to 'find a scale for the human' in the vastness of Darwinian evolution, but also anticipates how that struggle would generate eugenicist modes of logic in the final decades of the century.[6]

Strikingly, Knight finds the eugenicist perspective on his death consoling: it compensates him for at least some of the pride that evolutionary thinking has cost him. Likewise, he appears to find it gratifying to conceptualise himself in statistical terms: his death will be especially regrettable because his brains are 'above average'. Although Hardy encourages us to pardon Knight for being conscious of his mental gifts, he suggests there is something transgressive in Knight's train of thought when he writes that Knight 'could not help thinking' of his death as an exceptional tragedy. There is a troubling vagueness to the phrase 'some less developed life': does Knight simply think it would be better if a 'zoophyte', 'mollusc' or 'shell-fish' died in his place, or also that it would be better if a human being of lesser intelligence did?[7] And better according to what calculus? Although I have described Knight's logic as 'eugenicist', its ultimate rationale is obscure: the 'earth' itself seems to be the only potential loser or beneficiary in relation to his survival. 'Earth' arguably suggests 'humanity' in this context, but Hardy's choice of this word is surely deliberate, since it conveys materiality and abstraction at once: it implies that Knight, having come to understand his own intelligence in scientific terms, cannot see what meaning it might have except as organic matter, or in relation to planetary processes.

Knight's evaluation of his own brains on the cliff face in *A Pair of Blue Eyes* reflects Hardy's sensitivity to the implications of the biologisation of human intelligence, especially its reconceptualisation as an unequally distributed evolutionary attribute that can be imagined in statistical terms and used to create hierarchical scales of human worth. Hardy has often been understood as a melancholy student of late Victorian biological determinism, his magpie reading of contemporary science and psychology feeding his sense of the supremacy of the tragic in both art and life.[8] Yet critical discussions of the significance of evolutionary and hereditarian thought in Hardy's work have not closely scrutinised how these shaped his understanding of intelligence, and for this reason, have often under-estimated how strenuously he sought to think equality after Darwin. Hardy's final three novels are pervaded by, and — in the cases of *Tess* and *Jude* – often complicit in, the late Victorian biopolitics of intelligence. Yet they are also concerned to reveal how the intelligence of both major and minor characters exceeds their social positions and eludes modern efforts to measure and rationalise intellectual capacities. These novels counter the scientific reification of intellectual inequality in various ways: by making an egalitarian poetry out of the interrelations between and amongst human beings and non-human nature, a strategy prominent in *The Woodlanders*; by insisting upon the fundamentally political and contestable nature of judgements about mental worth, a strategy apparent in all three novels; and by positing extreme suffering as the authentic ground of intellectual value, a strategy favoured in both *Tess* and *Jude*.

Measuring minds in *The Woodlanders*

In *The Woodlanders*, Hardy's interest in mental measurement is encapsulated in the subplot involving a minor rustic character, the servant woman Grammer Oliver. The gentleman scientist Edred Fitzpiers contracts to procure Grammer Oliver's brain upon her death, so that he may dissect it and probe the mystery of its freakish, masculine size. Grammer Oliver's peasant materialism initially appears compatible with Fitzpiers's interest in craniometry, but her bargain soon comes to feel Faustian to her: she worries that the brain she was happy to treat as a commodity and scientific specimen may, in fact, be the locus of her soul.[9] In context, the Grammer Oliver episode resonates as a comic allegory of the novel's wider concern with how the forces of modernity collide with folk traditions in rural England. Yet Grammer Oliver's belated qualms about her soul do not merely attest to the tenacity of supernatural belief among the peasantry. The fact that Grammer Oliver sells her brain ostensibly to science but more truly to gratify the whim of a bored aristocrat makes the transaction appear akin to prostitution, or a peculiarly macabre *droit de seigneur*. Fitzpiers's attempt to acquire Grammer's brain is clearly intended to parallel his seduction and marriage of the novel's heroine, Grace Melbury; in both cases, a lower-class woman piques the interest of an aristocratic man of science on account of the exceptional nature of her mind. Fitzpiers treats both women as objects of scientific curiosity and collection, and this establishes an imaginative link between the mental refinements Grace has attained through education and Grammer's 'fine brain'.[10] The parallel in turn sets up the question of whether intelligence is primarily inborn or acquired, even as it foregrounds the distorting effects of Fitzpiers's power relationships with both women upon his capacity to arbitrate what Galton had recently christened the 'nature/nurture' distinction.[11]

As I outlined in the Introduction, the late nineteenth-century enthusiasm for craniometry was entangled with the larger scientific quest to devise an objective test of intelligence. Interest in measuring skulls was driven by the misconception that skull and brain size are reliable indices of intelligence, and the practice was central to the efforts of nineteenth-century anthropologists to establish the intellectual inferiority of non-European peoples.[12] It motivated the accumulation of vast private and public collections of human skulls, since large numbers of measurements were needed to place the study of racialised mental difference on an 'objective' footing and render it amenable to statistical analysis. One of the most prominent exponents of the technique, the French anatomist Paul Broca, also believed that it could prove the intellectual inferiority of women and the lower classes – an assumption implicit in Fitzpiers's curiosity about the size of Grammer Oliver's brain.[13] As also noted in the Introduction, craniometry was among the methods Galton used to measure intelligence in the anthropometric laboratory he set up in London in 1884, and it was part of his research at the University of Cambridge in 1885, where he sought to correlate the exam results of students with their skull measurements.

Fitzpiers's interest in craniometry marks him out as a kind of anthropologist in Little Hintock; he studies the 'natives' and attempts to collect skulls and brain specimens with a presumption of intellectual detachment, though Hardy makes clear that he is, in fact, driven by his narcissism and libido. Jane Bownas aptly identifies Fitzpiers's assumptions as an illustration of the logic of 'internal colonialism': as Foucault observed, the techniques of domination that European powers deployed against colonial populations often resurfaced as means of controlling domestic populations.[14] Indeed, Fitzpiers appears to conceive of himself as a kind of colonial administrator: he arrives determined to 'inaugurate a new era' of 'advanced ideas and practices' and shows a lofty disdain for established beliefs, while treating the local women as his sexual chattel.[15] The villagers regard Fitzpiers as a kind of necromancer, and Hardy asks us to see that are some grains of truth in this perception, at least insofar as his scientific research has a pronounced mystical bent. More precisely, Fitzpiers's science is informed by his idealist metaphysics, and such metaphysics are in his case a monstrous form of magical thinking, a refusal to believe in the existence of a world beyond his own desires.[16] Hardy discredits Fitzpiers's investment in measuring minds both morally and epistemologically: it represents not an authentic curiosity about the nature of other minds, but a wish at once to possess and to negate the reality of others. Significantly, Hardy grants Grammar Oliver herself the prerogative of critiquing the theory of intelligence implicit in Fitzpiers's interest in craniometry. Grace enquires: 'Was [Fitzpiers] really made for higher things? Is he clever?'[17] Grammar Oliver replies, 'Well no. How can he be clever? [. . .] These young men – they should live to my time of life, and then they'd see how clever they were at five and twenty!'[18] There is a neatly ironic chiasmus here. For Grammar Oliver, apparently the superstitious rustic, intelligence is not a metaphysical given but thoroughly secular and empirical: it is acquired over time, through worldly experience. Meanwhile, Fitzpiers, apparently the detached scientist, is possessed by the desire to fathom metaphysical essences, and 'scarcely able to distinguish between reality from fancy'.[19] Fitzpiers's dual identity as aristocrat and scientist underscores the power of the modern sciences of mental measurement to legitimise ancient class distinctions. Likewise, Fitzpiers's self-serving amalgam of idealism and materialism calls attention to the capacity of science to be pressed into the service of ideology.

Rancière suggests that the insidious power of the idea of intellectual inequality lies partly in the fact that its exponents justify it on spiritual or material grounds according to convenience:

> The superior minds want neither a superiority that would be only material nor a spirituality that would make them the equals of their inferiors. They lay claim to the differences of materialists in the midst of the elevation that belongs to immateriality. They paint the cranioscopist's skulls with the innate gifts of intelligence.[20]

This is true of Fitzpiers, whose sense of superiority is so absolute that it leads him to suggest to Grace that he belongs to a different 'tribe' or 'species' to the labouring classes but who is nonetheless uncertain about whether that superiority is a gift of birth or education[21]:

> '[. . .] I dare say I am inhuman, and supercilious, and contemptibly proud of my poor old ramshackle family; but I do honestly confess to you that I feel as if I belonged to a different species from the people who are working in that yard'.
> 'And from me too, then. For my blood is no better than theirs'.
> [. . .] It was, indeed, a startling anomaly that this woman of the tribe without should be standing there beside him as his wife [. . .]
> 'Ah YOU – you are refined and educated into something quite different', he said, self-assuringly.[22]>

Fitzpiers is primarily eager to establish that there are, in Rancière's terms, 'two humanities', one in possession of an 'active intellectual faculty' and capable of refined thoughts and grand actions, the other consigned to the realm of 'passive materiality'.[23] When Grace protests that she falls on the wrong side of the 'species' division Fitzpiers imagines, it is easy enough for him to reconfigure its terms, since whether the ground of the division is biology or education matters less than the maintenance of the division itself.

Hardy makes clear that Fitzpiers's craniometry is less a science than a form of occultism that invests unequal social relations with mystical authority. This perception is reinforced by the parallel Hardy establishes between craniometry and phrenology. Grace's father is confident that she constitutes worthwhile 'material' for an education because he has consulted phrenologists on the matter:

'Her fortune has been told by men of science – what do you call 'em — phrenologists.'[24] As Hardy's characterisation of it as a form of fortune-telling suggests, phrenology had lost much of its scientific credibility by the second half of the nineteenth century, but it led a busy afterlife as a form of popular entertainment and folklore. In identifying phrenology with Mr Melbury, the ambitious provincial merchant, and craniometry with Fitzpiers, the mystical amateur scientist, Hardy charts quite precisely the development of the science of mental measurement in the nineteenth century. Craniometry was sometimes called the 'new phrenology' because it promised to succeed where phrenology had failed and to decipher the secret correspondence between mental and physical characteristics.[25] In *The Woodlanders*, the dubiousness of both methods of ascertaining mental worth is underscored by the acquisitive motives of the men who subscribe to them. Mr Melbury's naïve faith that phrenology has proven his daughter's natural aptitude for education is matched by his naïve and mercenary conception of education itself: 'You can't teach her anything new. She's been too far among the wise ones to be astonished at anything she can hear among us folk in Hintock.'[26] Mr Melbury fetishises education because he imagines that it confers a static, incontrovertible form of social power. In his fantasy, education is not a process but a property with a fixed value. This logic obviously turns education into a sterile, self-negating enterprise, the opposite of the humanist ideal of *Bildung*: one gains an education so that one never has to learn anything new, nor ever be surprised.

In a quieter way, *The Woodlanders* articulates a disenchantment with formal education as complete as we find in *Jude*. And like that novel, *The Woodlanders* is a kind of nihilistic *Bildungsroman*: Grace gains an education only to realise there was nothing worth learning; the truly valuable knowledge is the rustic wisdom she grew up among in Little Hintock, and the effort to extend beyond it brings only self-estrangement and destruction. Hardy's pessimism about education and social mobility in his last novels can seem perverse given that opportunities for both were expanding toward the end of the century. Nevertheless, Hardy's insistence upon the class-bound nature of the education system accurately reflects the elusiveness of such opportunities as well as the broadly elitist effects of meritocratic reform, which overwhelmingly favoured upper- and middle-class men (see the introduction, pp. 17–30). Beyond this, Hardy's jaundiced view of education needs to be understood in the context of the rise of scientific discourses of innate intelligence, which, taken to their extreme conclusion, could make education seem a superficial, largely diagnostic process, capable of measuring and classifying but not of substantially improving a person's intellectual capacities It is this essentialist and deterministic understanding of intelligence that partly accounts for the stagnant nature of Grace's *Bildung* plot – that is, the failure of her education to produce any significant moral or intellectual development – as well as the motif of blighted growth that runs throughout the novel. For as the rest of the novel makes clear, the allegory of class and gender domination encoded in Fitzpiers' purchase of Grammer Oliver's brain applies equally to Grace: her brain, no less than Grammer Oliver's, is subject to the logic of reification, both in the sense that it is a commodity to be bought and sold by men, and in the sense that her intelligence is conceptualised by men as essentially fixed natural endowment, only somewhat 'refined' or 'finished' by education.[27]

Although Mr Melbury boasts of his Grace's natural fitness for education, it is important that the novel never straightforwardly vindicates his paternal pride, and indeed does much to suggest that it is misplaced. The fact that Grace's supposed mental superiority is primarily registered in the class-conscious, reifying discourses of her father and Fitzpiers casts doubt on its reality; for much of the novel, it seems to signify nothing more than 'a veneer of artificiality'.[28] When Grace is disillusioned by Fitzpiers, she becomes an avid reader, and this turn toward books seems to mark the beginning of a morally serious form of self-cultivation, in contrast to the spurious kind she acquired at school.[29] Yet Grace remains a curiously flat, superficial character; Hardy never endows her with the kind of vibrant inner life we would expect of a *Bildung* progatonist (nor, indeed, of a Hardy heroine: Hardy himself apparently struggled to invest her with imaginative energy, considering her 'too commonplace and straitlaced' to be capable of real passion or worthy of a 'fine tragic ending').[30] At the novel's end, Hardy reduces Grace's interiority to a homily: she comes to learn 'how little accomplishments and culture weigh beside sterling personal character'.[31] Hardy even limits the extent to which Grace is permitted to gain tragic depth in the aftermath of her moral awakening, since it leads only to further compromise: after Giles Winterborne has sacrificed his life for her, she reconciles herself to a debased marriage with Fitzpiers, and the grandeur and pathos of the novel's tragic conclusion is instead conferred upon the peasant girl who loved Giles unrequitedly, Marty South.

On the most obvious level, this aggrandisement of the novel's rustic characters at the expense of their educated counterparts reaffirms old moralistic understandings of the intellect. As Daston notes, the Victorian psychologists and scientists never fully succeeded in detaching the category of 'intelligence' from its freight of moral and religious meanings.[32] Such meanings are woven into the romance fabric of *The Woodlanders*: Fitzpiers's sophistication marks him out as a devil or Faust archetype, while Giles's simplicity reflects his status as a Green Man/Christ figure; Grace's education is the cause of her fall into class consciousness and treachery to Giles, whereas Marty, the peasant girl, is defined by her sublime fidelity to him. Yet the novel's engagement with the new scientific conception of intelligence goes beyond simple moral rejection. It is, in fact, Hardy's endorsement of the biological model of intelligence that underpins both the novel's egalitarian politics and its moral vision.

Throughout *The Woodlanders*, Hardy contests the idea that social class is a simple emanation of mental worth. As I outlined in the Introduction, this ancient prejudice had gained fresh prestige from Galton's eugenics as well as from Spencer's Social Darwinism, both of which suggested that social hierarchies reflect underlying biological differences, and that social position is a relatively transparent signifier of intelligence. *The Woodlanders* contests this assumption at the basic level of plot: the narrative springs from George and Grace Melbury's failure to distinguish between social position and inner qualities. Crucially, this is not simply a failure to hold Giles's moral goodness at its proper value; it is a failure to recognise the profundity of his intelligence. Where Hardy ironises the highly abstract and mystical nature of Fitzpiers's intellectual pursuits, he emphasises the embodied intelligence entailed by Giles's agricultural work. Fitzpiers's intellectuality is a form of solipsism that renders him not just morally callous, but stupid about basic empirical realities – a fact symbolised by the episode where he mounts the wrong horse, drifts asleep while riding, falls on his head, and then drunkenly reveals his sexual infidelities to Grace's father. Fitzpiers's desire to abstract himself from the natural world through 'transcendental philosophy'[33] renders him much more vulnerable to bodily, instinctual impulses than Giles, whose acceptance of his interconnection with nature enables him to transcend such impulses – a paradox captured at the novel's close when he dies exposed to the elements rather than give way to sexual temptation with Grace. In this way, the novel schematically inverts the values conventionally ascribed to physical and mental labour, and lower- and upper-class men: where Giles exemplifies introspection and 'scrupulous delicacy', Fitzpiers is prey to his grossest instincts and appetites.[34]

Hardy's emphasis upon the 'intelligen[ce]' manifested in Giles's 'intercourse with nature' extends to Marty too.[35] It is in relation to her that the novel makes its most explicit statement about the arbitrariness of social class:

> As with so many right hands born to manual labour, there was nothing in its fundamental shape to bear out the physiological conventionalism that gradations of birth show themselves primarily in the form of this member. Nothing but a cast of the die of Destiny had decided that the girl should handle the tool; and the fingers which clasped the heavy ash haft might have skilfully guided the pencil or swept the string, had they only been set to do it in good time.[36]

The purpose of this passage is to establish Marty's natural equality with Grace, not to lament that Marty has been denied opportunities for more refined occupations: as the rest of the novel makes clear, education and social mobility are, at best, mixed blessings. Grace's failure to appreciate Giles's love until too late is duplicated in Giles's failure to hold Marty's love at its proper value, and the pathos of this latter tragedy is amplified by the fact that it is repeated at the level of the novel's distribution of narrative attention. Hardy persistently encourages us to regret that Grace, rather than Marty, is the novel's heroine, or at least to recognise that Marty has equal claim to the role. The wistful passage quoted above serves to underscore that Grace's status as heroine is as arbitrary as her acquisition of education and social mobility; she does not possess any particular mental qualities that elevate her above Marty. The fact that the novel's conclusion focuses on the tragedy of Marty's unrequited love and she utters the novel's final words further underscores her status not only as Giles's might-have-been wife but as the novel's might-have-been heroine.

The confidence with which Hardy undermines distinctions between mental and physical labour, intellect and instinct in *The Woodlanders* is surely due in part to his reading of Darwin and

Spencer. In *The Principles of Psychology*, Spencer argued that 'the commonly assumed *hiatus* between Reason and Instinct has no existence [. . .] The growth of intelligence is throughout determined by the repetition of experience.'[37] Darwin famously contends that much of what appears merely instinctual in animals can, in fact, be considered a form of reason, and that human reason must be understood as an adaptive development from such rudimentary acts.[38] However, where in Darwin and Spencer this perception of the organic, adaptive nature of intelligence sharpens the significance of the relative degrees of it possessed by individuals and groups, Hardy uses it in *The Woodlanders* to challenge the legitimacy of conventional social judgements about mental capacities.[39] In particular, the novel refutes what Rancière calls the 'opposition between the golden race and the iron race, any hierarchy – even an inverted one – between men devoted to manual work and men destined to the exercise of thought'.[40] Ventriloquising Jacotot, Rancière emphasises that intellectual emancipation consists not in 'opposing manual knowledge, the knowledge of the people, the intelligence of the tool to the science of schools or the rhetoric of the elite', but in recognising that there

> are not two levels of intelligence, that any human work of art is the practice of the same intellectual potential. In all cases, it is a question of observing, comparing, and combining, of making and noticing how one has done it [. . .] The fabrication of clouds is a human work of art that demands as much – neither more nor less – labour and intellectual attention as the fabrication of shoes or locks.[41]

Hardy's loving attention to the particulars of Marty's manual labour leads us to feel that her work cannot be understood as a mere waste of her mental capacities, harsh and socially degrading though it may be. Describing her making spars for thatching, Hardy highlights that her labour is mental as well as physical, demanding not just 'dexterous' hands but 'critical' attention.[42] Similarly, Hardy emphasises that Giles's and Marty's knowledge of the woodlands constitutes a sophisticated form of expertise. Where the novel deflates Fitzpiers's pretensions to esoteric knowledge, it suggests that Giles and Marty have authentically deep insight into the nature of things – a kind of literacy in the language of the woods. This is not because the novel romanticises instinctual, embodied wisdom at the expense of scientific knowledge; rather, it aims to break down such distinctions. Marty's and Giles's understanding of the woods is so profound that it appears instinctual and even magical to Grace, but it is, in fact, the product of patiently accumulated observation and experiment – a means of knowing that proceeds by the same principles as Fitzpiers's study of brain tissue:

> The casual glimpses which the ordinary population bestowed upon that wondrous world of sap and leaves called the Hintock woods had been with these two, Giles and Marty, a clear gaze. They had been possessed of its finer mysteries as of commonplace knowledge; had been able to read its hieroglyphs as ordinary writing; to them the sights and sounds [. . .] which had to Grace a touch of the uncanny, and even the supernatural, were simple occurrences whose origin, continuance, and laws they foreknew [. . .] together they had, with the run of the years, mentally collected those remoter signs and symbols, which seen in few, were of runic obscurity, but all together made an alphabet.[43]

The ecological vision articulated in passages such as this also offers a critique of the the late Victorian preoccupation with classifying and quantifying mental differences. As John Heaney argues, *The Woodlanders* marks a shift in Hardy's attitude toward Darwinian evolution.[44] Key passages in Hardy's earlier novels, the cliff scene in *A Pair of Blue Eyes* perhaps most famous among them, depict evolutionary monism as a devastating blow to human dignity and happiness. However, in *The Woodlanders*, the collapse of the distinction between humanity and nature, while still clearly tragic, no longer resonates as a mere degradation or loss of meaning; instead, the novel finds nobility and enchantment in the thoroughly organic nature of the human. Most strikingly, the novel's characters are persistently likened to trees, and this analogy enables Hardy to cast the human desire for flourishing in lushly poetic terms, as a beautiful urge toward growth. William Cohen captures this aptly when he notes that the novel's characters are frequently imagined as 'rooted, budding, leafy and abloom'.[45] This is not to suggest that the Hardy retreats to a pre-Darwinian pastoralism; he is careful to emphasise that trees, no less than animals and humans, are engaged in a struggle for existence pervaded by conflict and waste.[46] Nonetheless, Hardy's insistence upon the 'arboreality' of the human, to borrow Cohen's phrase, enables him to conduct an immanent critique of the hierarchical conception of human intelligence which emerged from Victorian psychology and evolutionary theory.[47] In *The Woodlanders*, the perception that human intelligence is a wholly natural phenomenon, subject to the same processes of adaptation as animal and plant life, does not serve to validate human forms of competition and hierarchy as it does in the writings of Spencer and Galton; rather, it serves to make human differences, particularly those entrenched by class, appear negligible, a narcissism of small differences. If human intelligence is produced by same adaptive processes as the growth of trees, what do mental variations between humans really signify? Fitzpiers's conviction that he belongs to a different 'species' to the labouring classes is rendered absurd by the novel's ecological vision, which dwarfs human categories and distinctions.

The felicity of Hardy's analogies between humans and trees in *The Woodlanders* often hinges upon the idea of silviculture, and thereby highlights not only the naturalistic status of human beings but human agency in interaction with non-human nature. Crucially, the metaphor of silviculture underscores that humans have the power to tend or damage one another's natural development. Giles's empathic intelligence is symbolised by his 'marvellous power of making trees grow',[48] while Fitzpiers's arrogance is evident in his destruction of the elm that John South fancies is linked to his mortality. Likewise, we are invited to perceive the connection between Mr Melbury's reification of his daughter's intelligence as a commodity on the marriage market and his business as a timber merchant. Fred Reid suggests that such silviculture metaphors derive from Hardy's reading of the 'Individualism' chapter of Mill's *On Liberty* (1859), in which Mill writes that human nature is 'not a machine to be built after a model, and set to do exactly the work prescribed for it, but a tree, which requires to grow and develop itself on all sides, according to the tendency of the inward forces which make it a living thing'.[49] Mill is here drawing upon Wilhelm von Humboldt's organicist concept of *Bildung*, and making a larger argument for an education system that would nurture individualism rather than conformity. Grace's experience of formal education has stifled any such holistic or personal mode of self-development: 'Cultivation had so far advanced in the soil of Miss Melbury's mind as to lead her to talk of anything save of that she knew well, and had the greatest interest in developing: herself.'[50] Yet a Romantic ideal of *Bildung* persists at the level of the novel's arboreal imagery and metaphors, suggesting that a richer and more enlightened conception of human flour-ishing is imaginable, even if the potentialities of Grace, Marty, and Giles have been tragically undercut. In its vision of human nature as a dynamic living thing, treelike in both its capacity for growth and its susceptibility to damage, *The Woodlanders* attempts to counter the reification of intelligence as a fixed, measurable entity. The novel is thus not a simple Romantic lament that 'Nature has lost its soul to modern science,' as Mary Jacobus has it.[51] It is pre-cisely in and through Hardy's acceptance of a biological and evo-lutionary understanding of intelligence that he is able to preserve a Romantic sense of the immeasurability of minds.

Tragedy's mental harvest in *Tess of the d'Urbervilles*

Where the ideological uses of the concept of innate intelligence are often under critique in *The Woodlanders*, the rhetoric of innateness is frequently used to assert the intellectual worth of the heroine of *Tess of the d'Urbervilles*: the narrator continually insists that Tess Durbeyfield is 'clever', and has 'naturally quick-ness', a 'rar[e] intelligence', or a 'naturally bright intelligence'.[52] This forms part of a larger discourse, often articulated by Tess's lover, Angel Clare, but certainly amplified by the narrator, which frames Tess as a pagan child of Nature, an instinctive sensualist and critic of 'social law'.[53] At times, this discourse shades into the deterministic logic of literary naturalism. Hardy wrote *Tess* in the wake of reading August Weismann's *Essays upon Heredity* (1889) and in a climate in which hard hereditarian discourses were gaining cultural ground.[54] Hardy certainly hints that Tess may carry a hereditary moral defect.[55] Yet as William Greenslade has shown, these suggestions of degeneration are strategically ambigu-ous: at least part of their purpose was to mitigate Tess's responsi-bility for her fate and thereby allow Hardy to handle the subject of an 'impure' woman with greater artistic impunity.[56] Although the question of the heritability of intelligence loomed large in scientific debate and there was an intense fascination with both the figure of the 'degenerate' genius and the emerging scientific category of 'feeble-mindedness' at the fin de siècle, Tess's 'bright intelli-gence' is never linked to her heredity or to notions of degeneracy.[57] Her intelligence is nonetheless constructed in markedly biological terms, and it is this which partly accounts for the novel's tendency to divide feminist readers.

As Dale Kramer observes, Hardy oscillates between constructing Tess as exceptional and suggesting she is an average or 'standard' woman.[58] This is true also of his representation of her intelligence. To an extent, Hardy constructs Tess as a meritocratic heroine, a 'naturally' clever young woman who would have risen above her humble origins if misfortune had not intervened. Tess is haunted by a sense of unrealised intellectual potential: she points out that her teachers said she had 'great aptness' and she would have become a teacher herself if circumstances had not forced her to leave school early.[59] The concept of latent 'ability' is always necessarily spectral insofar as it has a tautological relationship with whatever success or accomplishment it purports to predict. As Rancière observes, attributions of superior 'ability' or 'intelligence' often illustrate the *virtus dormitiva* fallacy: the terms are used to explain a successful performance they can only redescribe. Rancière articulates the logic thus: '"This man does better than the other because he is smarter." This means precisely: he does better because he does better.'[60] Ruth suggests that such tautological logic is what made the exam appear a form of 'social magic' in mid-Victorian culture: it could 'bypass the actual work necessary to earn identity' and 'disclose history in advance of itself'.[61] Hardy is sensitive to the fact that this meritocratic temporality produces a special kind of disappointment, perhaps especially when it meshes with an education system that aims at identifying 'promising' poor students, either to recruit them as 'pupil-teachers' or to select them as scholarship candidates.[62] This is the disappointed class that Tess counts herself among: those whose apparent promise when young did not come to any clear fruition and which therefore sustains a paradoxical life as a future gift forever located in the past and an innate possession of which she has been somehow dispossessed.

By the fin de siècle, the concept of general ability was increasingly inflected by the logics of eugenics and Social Darwinism, so that society and everyday life could be imagined as an arena in which innate biological worth was under competitive examination. Read through the prism of this meritocratic, biologised model of intelligence, Tess's tragedy is that she is an innately superior individual who would, in a rationally organised society, assume a high place in the social hierarchy, but instead finds her 'rare' intelligence 'wasted' for 'want of chances'.[63] As I have suggested, Tess appears to think of herself in this way to some degree. The narrator also sometimes seems to appraise her in Social Darwinist terms, as an especially fit competitor in the struggle of life. For example, the narrator remarks that Tess under-estimates her employability because she is not aware of the 'rarity' of her level of 'intelligence, energy, health [. . .] in any sphere'.[64] Although Hardy never makes the connection explicitly, Tess's 'natural' intelligence is also open to being interpreted as a sign of her aristocratic lineage, and thus to being understood in the class-laden terms of late Victorian eugenic discourses.[65] Yet Hardy's narrator explicitly refutes the idea that class bears any relationship to intellectual capacity, specifying that both stupidity and genius can be found among the peasantry.[66] Moreover, the meritocratic and Social Darwinist interpretations of Tess run against the grain of the novel's larger tragic vision and emphasis upon the value of altruism, or what Tess describes as 'loving-kindness'.[67] The difference between *Tess* and meritocratic–individualist Victorian *Bildungsromane* such as *Jane Eyre* or *David Copperfield* can be discerned in Tess's anguished sense of injustice that she, rather than the other lovesick girls at Talbothay's dairy, is sexually selected by Angel.[68] Although she knows herself to be 'cleverer, more beautiful' than them, she nonetheless feels compunction for the unchosen girls, and Hardy too encourages us to enter vividly into their suffering.[69] Hardy indicates that Tess's compassion is partly born of a misplaced sense of sexual guilt, but it is also clearly traceable to the fact that she too was overlooked by Angel in an earlier moment of sexual choosing, the dance on the green.[70] Where *Jane Eyre* and *David Copperfield* seek to vindicate the exceptional worth of a protagonist who has been unjustly overlooked by society, Hardy lingers upon the extent to which recognition of his heroine's merits means suffering for the unchosen and thereby makes the reader's recognition of Tess's 'natural' superiority morally fraught.

Tess's gender also complicates the significance of Hardy's emphasis on her exceptional intelligence. Although women's educational and professional opportunities improved significantly in the second half of the nineteenth century, the new scientific discourses on intelligence tended to cast women as essentially inferior, often aligning their mental capacities with those of children and 'primitive' peoples.[71] Rachel Ann Malane has argued that Hardy essentialises and denigrates Tess's intelligence in exactly these terms.[72] She notes that Hardy emphasises the physiology of Tess's mental life and claims that he is attempting to convey the volatility and irrationality of the female brain, citing this sentence as part of her evidence: '[Tess] was such a sheaf of susceptibilities that her pulse was accelerated [. . .] her blood driven to her finger-ends, and the cool arms flushed hot.'[73] Yet Hardy regarded all of human life as a 'physiological fact'[74] and his constructions of both male and female characters across his novels are attempts to represent what Suzanne Keen calls his 'embodied, affective theory of mind'.[75] While the narrator of *Tess* certainly dwells on Tess's beauty and subjective physical experience with a troubling erotic intensity, this does not by itself entail biological essentialism about the nature or quality of her mind.[76] Hardy is plainly less interested in Angel's physical being than in Tess's, but he emphasises the physiology of Angel's mental life too. For example, after learning of Tess's relationship with Alec, Angel becomes 'eaten out with thinking, withered by thinking; scourged out of all his former pulsating, flexuous domesticity'.[77]

As discussed in the Introduction, the late Victorian biologisation of the mind led to the hypothesis that intelligence was correlated with, or even a form of, sensory acuity, and the early intelligence tests by Galton and his American disciple, McKeen Cattell, were efforts to measure physical abilities, response times, and sensory discrimination.[78] This meant that in the 1890s, the assumptions of the mental testing movement dovetailed with the discourses of aestheticism and decadence, which also identified acute sensory receptivity with genius. Throughout *Tess*, Hardy encourages us to recognise that Tess's physical and emotional 'susceptibilities' constitute a profound form of intelligence. This discourse can, at times, seem to represent Tess's mind in standard sexist terms, as passive and derivative rather than active and original. For example, Hardy suggests that part of Tess's intelligence consists of an aptitude for imitation, which enables her to assimilate Angel's educated discourse easily.[79] In this, Hardy is probably echoing Darwin, who claimed that the female intellect was characterised by imitativeness and 'rapid perception' – qualities which reflected its general inferiority and kinship with the mentalities of 'lower races' and a 'past and lower state civilisation'.[80] Yet this emphasis upon Tess's 'quickness' also serves to establish how she and Angel are able to transcend the divides of class and education in order to speak on terms of equality.[81] Moreover, Hardy's focus upon the receptivity of Tess's mind resonates with the discourses of fin de siècle aestheticism and decadence, which blurred gendered distinctions between active and passive forms of intelligence and celebrated 'receptivity' as the precondition of a 'quickened, multiplied consciousness', in Walter Pater's famous phrase.[82] When Hardy describes Tess as 'impressionable', it may sound as if he is constructing her as girlishly naïve or pliable.[83] However, in context, it is clear that he is drawing upon the logic of aestheticism to account for how a peasant woman might experience the world more intensely than her social superiors: 'The impressionable peasant leads a larger, fuller, more dramatic life than the pachydermatous king.'[84] The metaphor of skin here is not merely proverbial: it captures how Hardy conceptualises Tess's intelligence as at once biological and aesthetic. It is linked to, or perhaps even based upon, an exquisite bodily sensitivity; and it means Tess is a kind of natural aesthete, experiencing life as it were a play. If, at times, Hardy uses this kind of aestheticised materialism to underscore Tess's exceptional qualities and frame her as a kind of natural aristocrat, at other times the same discourse has an egalitarian force. In one of his moments of moral clarity, Angel thinks:

> Tess was no insignificant creature to toy with and dismiss; but a woman living her precious life – a life which, to herself who endured or enjoyed it, possessed as great a dimension to the life of the mightiest to himself. Upon her sensations the whole world depended to Tess.[85]

The emphasis remains upon Tess's sensuousness and susceptibility to intense aesthetic experience, but here this does not make her special but representative; she might be anyone at all. As Rancière would suggest, the novel's egalitarianism consists in this affirmation of Tess's capacity 'to experience any emotion or passion whatsoever' and its effort to blur the distinction between refined aesthetic consciousness and ordinary bodily sensations, the perceptions of an aristocrat and those of a peasant.[86]

Like *The Woodlanders*, *Tess* mounts an ethical and egalitarian attack on mind–body dualism, though in *Tess* this is also clearly an indictment of Christian sexual morality, and this has complex consequences for Hardy's construction of Tess's intelligence. Where, in *The Woodlanders*, Hardy's celebration of Giles's embodied intelligence carefully excluded his sexuality, Tess's 'bright intelligence' clearly includes hers. This is partly because we come to appreciate Tess's intelligence through the prism of Angel's infatuation with her, though Hardy also underscores the limitations of Angel's perspective. Angel, impressed by Tess's capacity for a kind of nihilistic eloquence, marvels that a 'milkmaid' should experience what he understands as an epochal sense of existential dread – 'the ache of modernism' – and muses that the vanguard of intellectual thought only crystallises 'sensations' which have been 'vaguely grasped' by ordinary people for centuries.[87] Angel is being ironised at this moment insofar as the reader knows that Tess's pessimism flows from concrete experiences – poverty, rape, social ostracism, the death of her child – rather than being hazy intimations of the zeitgeist. But this irony reinforces rather than undercuts Angel's egalitarian point that ideas exalted into 'ology' and 'ism' have their origins in ordinary 'sensations'.[88] Moreover, the narrator echoes the claim and radicalises it: 'Tess's passing corporeal blight had been her mental harvest.'[89] The use of the phrase 'passing' here suggests that 'corporeal blight' refers to Tess's experiences of rape, pregnancy, and childbirth. When empiricist philosophers such as Bain or Mill argued that all ideas are traceable to sensations, such stigmatised female bodily experiences were, of course, not the examples they were eager to provide to illustrate their arguments – indeed, they were precisely the kind of gross materialities that needed to be repressed if their philosophy was to be considered respectable – but Hardy's comment spells out how such 'sensations' are necessarily entailed by their and Angel's logic.[90] Even if 'corporeal blight' is a somewhat vague formulation, the reader knows enough of Tess's story to infer that the taboo dimensions of her bodily experience are being invoked.[91] What is radical here is that Hardy specifies that such experiences are a 'mental' harvest. They do not amount merely to the 'dumb' suffering Angel associates with the 'unrecorded rank and file of the English nation', from which Angel wrongly presumes that Tess descends and about which he cannot summon any curiosity.[92] Nor has such suffering simply endowed Tess with emotional depth. Hardy's specification of 'mental' harvest is crucial: Tess's harrowing experience of sex and maternity has made her, in Hardy's terms, an authentic intellectual, which is to say, an unflinching pessimist; and Angel, fancying himself her tutor, is really her apprentice in 'the hobble of being alive', in Tess's own phrase.[93] There is a queasy undertow to this logic insofar as it seems to invite the reader to understand Tess's experience of rape in somewhat positive terms, as an emancipation of her intellect and expansion of her personality. In the same vein, the narrator asserts that a more enlightened society would recognise that Tess's relationship with Alec has been a 'liberal education' which had changed her from a 'simple girl' to a 'complex woman'.[94] Even so, Hardy's emphasis on the intellectual value of Tess's suffering has a radically egalitarian significance. The suggestion that Tess's history has endowed her with an at once poetic and philosophical consciousness goes far beyond the stock Victorian sentimentalisation of the fallen woman. It creates what Rancière calls a new 'partition of the sensible': that is, it challenges the hierarchical ordering of roles, bodies, and capacities that divides up common reality and determines what can be perceived and who is recognised as an intelligent being.[95] According to Rancière, literature exercises its political power – what he calls 'literary dissensus'[96] – by making 'audible as speaking beings' those who were previously heard only as 'noisy animals', expressing their needs. What could be dismissed as a merely subjective cry of pleasure or pain is rendered intelligible as a 'shared' understanding of the 'just and unjust', a claim on a common world.[97] When speaking to Angel during their courtship, Tess repeatedly extrapolates from her own suffering to interrogate the meaning of life in general, and she speaks with such incisive bleakness that Angel perceives how far her intelligence wanders beyond the boundaries of her social position. More, Angel intuits in these moments that Tess is his mental equal, as capable as he is of experiencing the 'ache of modernism'; the reader, who knows more of Tess's history than Angel does, realises that his perception of their intellectual equality is actually grounded in her knowledge of class domination, sex, and motherhood. In this way, *Tess* radicalises the critique of mind–body dualism present in *The Woodlanders* and challenges the distinctions between masculine intellectuality and female bodily experience, education and 'dumb' peasant suffering. The novel's pessimism has an egalitarian core: if, as Angel suggests, modern philosophy affirms that it is a 'mishap'[98] to be alive (Hardy is here surely thinking of Schopenhauer, whom he invokes elsewhere in the narrative[99]), then the downtrodden have the most direct access to enlightenment. The scandal or dissensual power of *Tess* is not that it offers a sympathetic view of an 'impure woman' – enough Victorian literature had dedicated itself to that cause for it to be a relatively palatable cliché – but lies in its insistence that the perceptions of a 'ruined' peasant girl count as philosophy.

Superficially, Hardy's relativisation of the concepts of education and philosophy in *Tess* may seem like the familiar, teleological logic of a *Bildungsroman*, wherein life is figured as a kind of school or university and difficult experiences imagined as enriching lessons. Yet while Hardy insists that Tess's dark experiences have intellectual value, he simultaneously emphasises their futility. Tess cannot put what she has learned to any kind of moral or practical use. The novel's hostility to the basic premise of the *Bildungsroman* form – that one may redeem bad experience by affirming it as education – is distilled in the narrator's quotation from Roger Ascham: 'By experience we find out a short way by a long wandering.' The narrator then remarks, 'Not seldom that long wandering unfits us for further travel, and of what use is our experience to us then?'[100] Although Tess's suffering does seem to bestow a keen consciousness of the suffering of others, particularly of animals, it does not in any straightforward sense prove morally edifying: after all, it leads her to commit murder.[101] What, then, does her 'mental harvest' consist of? Tess's experience of Alec d'Urberville teaches her what Rancière calls the 'devil's lesson': that 'life is without rhyme or reason'.[102] Anticipating the Job-like questioning of Jude, Tess claims that the only thing she would like to learn is 'why the sun do shine on the just and the unjust alike'.[103] At first glance, this suggests that Tess has no curiosity about books because she believes that no book can satisfactorily address the enigma of cosmic injustice, the traditional problem of theodicy. But throughout this scene, we know that Tess is ruminating on her own victimisation at the hands of Alec and her inability to tell Angel her story: she confesses evasively that she is 'woebegone [. . .] about my own self'.[104] Her construction – 'that's what books won't tell me' – hints the writers actually know but refuse to tell the truth about injustice; she will not read books because she suspects that they are mere apologies for the social order. Tess is peeling buds called 'lords and ladies' throughout this conversation and mournfully notes she keeps finding more 'ladies' than lords, which somewhat heavy-handedly symbolises that she is thinking specifically of class and sexual injustice.[105] Tess also asserts she has no interest in education because it can teach her only that she is 'one of a long row only' and that her life is preordained to be 'just like thousands and thousands'.[106] Tess's indifference to education could seem like philistinism, but paradoxically, Angel understands it as a sign of an iconoclastic intelligence, and Hardy prompts us to understand it this way, too. In this, Hardy subverts the long novelistic tradition in which a heroine's appetite for books is proof of her imaginative, potentially rebellious inner life.[107] Here the reverse is true: we are meant to recognise that Tess's antipathy to books is an astute refusal to be appeased by any religious or social justification for her woe. More, it is a refusal to be reconciled to a social hierarchy which consigns her to anonymous toil: the image of a long row evokes agricultural labour. It also evokes the classroom: we learn elsewhere that Tess is a product of the Revised Code of 1862.[108] As noted in the Introduction, the Code notoriously attempted to make mass elementary education cheap and efficient through standardised examinations and paying teachers according to exam results, which in turn led to a culture of rote learning and over-pressure. Tess's dismal view of learning resonates in part as a kind of Romantic reaction against the homogenising, utilitarian character of the Revised Code. However, Tess's rejection of learning is clearly more radical than an aversion to the existing educational system: she rejects education as such, including the informal kind Angel proposes, since it can teach her only the lesson she already knows too well, the fact of her social subordination. 'When I see what you know, what you have read, and seen, and thought, I feel what a nothing I am!' she laments to Angel.[109] And yet if Tess thinks that books can be only stultifying lessons in her own mental inferiority, there is a kind of redemptive irony in the fact that we are reading the book that values her intelligence. Like the vindication of Giles's and Marty's intellectual labour in *The Woodlanders*, the narrative of *Tess* seeks to redress the fact that its heroine's intelligence is largely indiscernible within the late Victorian social order; Angel perceives it during their courtship, but later reinterprets it as the taint of sexual knowledge and stigmatises it. *Tess*'s redistribution of the sensible demands that her intelligence be respected in its impurity – that is, in its inextricable connection to the history of her body and her experiences of oppression and despair.

Jude the Obscure: 'I have understanding as well as you'

The title of *Jude the Obscure* when it first appeared in serial form was *The Simpletons*, but Hardy changed it when someone pointed out the similarity to Charles Read's 1874 novel *The Simpleton*.[110] At first glance, the original title evokes the thread of the novel which romanticises Jude Fawley and Sue Bridehead as visionary innocents, too idealistic to adapt themselves to the cruelties of society or nature. However, it also points to the novel's iconoclastic stance toward late Victorian concepts of intelligence and intellectual value. That Hardy meant 'simpleton' to carry a dissident charge is also indicated by his subsequent choices of title: *Hearts Insurgent* and *The Recalcitrants*.[111] By the fin de siècle, there was a deepening tendency to biologise the problems of poverty and criminality, and a related preoccupation with the supposed prevalence of feeble-mindedness among the poor; as noted in the Introduction, concern focused with particular intensity upon the lower-class children newly in receipt of state education.[112] In this context, Hardy's sense that his protagonists may be classified fluidly – if ironically – as 'simpletons', 'insurgents', or 'recalcitrants' is suggestive: it reflects his desire to position his novel as an incendiary, if in some ways ambiguous, intervention in the contemporary politics of intellectual ability.

Although Marjorie Garber suggests that Jude is doomed by his 'logocentric wistfulness' and fetishisation of literature, he initially shares Tess's antipathy toward books.[113] It is a book's power to inculcate a sense of mental inferiority that first provokes explicitly suicidal feelings in the child Jude. Despairing of his capacity to teach himself Greek and Latin from an old grammar book, he concludes:

> There were no brains in his head equal to this business; and [. . .] he wished he had never seen a book, that he might never see another, that he had never been born. Somebody might have come along that way who [. . .] might have cheered him by saying that his notions were further advanced than those of his grammarian. But nobody did come, because nobody does; and under the crushing recognition of his gigantic error Jude continued to wish himself out of the world.[114]

Jude's contradictory status as at once the 'quintessential biopolitical novel' and as a lacerating critique of the late Victorian biopolitics of intelligence is submerged in this passage.[115] On the one hand, the novel invites us to interpret the young Jude's suicide ideation as a symptom of his degeneracy and 'unfitness' for the disciplines of education and social advancement, a degeneracy which is inherited by Father Time, his suicidal/fratricidal son.[116] On the other, Jude's despair is also inseparable from the novel's political rage, which is directed at the class and religious ideologies which convince Jude of the inferiority of his brains. The novel bears witness to the truth of Rancière's assertion that 'what stultifies the common people is not their lack of instruction, but the belief in the inferiority of their intelligence'.[117] Like *The Woodlanders* and *Tess*, *Jude* assails the idea that there are 'two humanities' or 'two levels of intelligence', but in *Jude* this is, above all, an indictment of what we are encouraged to understand as the Victorian class theology of intelligence, the division of the world into 'thoughtful and mentally shining ones' and the 'despairing worthless'.[118]

Rancière observes that the transformative encounter with a book is a stock novelistic trope which assumed a special place in nineteenth-century worker's literature. In such literature, the encounter with a book serves to allegorise how a child of the labouring classes is initiated into literacy and thereby into 'another destiny'.[119] Rancière notes that the same *topos* also surfaces in reactionary form in novels produced by nineteenth-century *littérateurs* alarmed by 'the invasion of the temple of art'.[120] In the reactionary version, the working-class child's encounter with a book is the 'work of death': the child is infected with impossible fantasies of social mobility and ultimately succumbs to criminality or despair, thus illustrating the fatality of mass literacy.[121] Jude's suicidal misery over the grammar book is open to being read in this way: the discovery of the world of learning is, for him, not the start of a process of self-development but the seeds of self-destruction. However, Hardy's eagerness to demystify the labour involved in literacy circumvents the conservative cautionary-tale reading of Jude's intellectual ambition. The initiation scene does not drama-tise Jude's unfitness for education but clarifies how easily and early the intellect of a child may be stultified. The young Jude under-stands learning in quasi-supernatural terms, as a form of alchemy: in his 'innocence', he fancies that there is a 'law of transmutation' which enables Latin and Greek to be converted into English, and is demoralised when he realises that languages must be acquired at the cost of 'years of plodding'.[122] Jude takes the discovery that education is a form of labour as a symptom of his personal unwor-thiness, a reflection of his status as a member of the labouring classes.[123] As the rest of the novel makes clear, however, this con-ception of education as a magical transmutation is far from being an innocent child's fancy; it is an ideology by which Victorian class inequality is maintained and Jude remains enthralled by it as an adult. Jude imagines Oxford (called Christminster in the novel) as a city of celestial luminosity, and those who attend it as ethereal beings, 'mentally shining ones'; although he becomes a conscientious autodidact, he remains tantalised by the notion that learning ought to be experienced as pure transcendence, not merely leisured but disembodied and out of time. Jude does come to recognise how his own labour, both imaginative and physical (he finds employment in Oxford as a stonemason), has served to fortify the illusion of a city devoted to pure spirit – an insight that the narrator ratifies as a 'true illumination'.[124] But this enlighten-ment is only 'moment[ary]'; Jude continues to 'love' Oxford even when he recognises that it 'hates all men like me' and despises the 'laboured acquisitions' of the 'self-taught'.[125] The real lesson of the grammar book – that all 'acquisitions' are 'laboured' – is never truly learned by Jude, though the narrator insistently foregrounds it for the reader.[126]

As Jonathan Memel has shown, Hardy's Jude has been an abiding touchstone in modern debates about class and education in England, his name invoked to convey the pathos of the bright working-class boy denied opportunity.[127] Yet this cultural myth of Jude falsifies the novel in crucial respects. The book is actu-ally an attack on the archetype of the poor boy of promise, the exceptional child who is entitled to climb the scholarship ladder from obscurity to the 'paradise of the learned'.[128] Critics routinely characterise Jude as 'bright', 'talented', or 'intelligent', but the narrator never passes judgement on Jude's intellectual ability and no other character in the novel credits him with particular intel-lectual gifts; Sue believes he ought to be admitted to Oxford on the grounds of his 'passion for learning', not because of any kind of innate intelligence.[129] Jude himself doubts that has sufficient 'brillian[ce]' and 'natural ability' to win a scholarship.[130] In Tess, Hardy freely availed himself of contemporary discourses of innate intelligence to vindicate the worth of his heroine; the fact that he refrains from doing the same for Jude is vital. After all, if Jude were presented as an unequivocally gifted young man, this would presumably serve to intensify the sense of injustice that attaches to his exclusion from university. Instead, however, the novel is a thornier provocation: it is the tragedy of an unexceptional poor boy who desperately wants to go to Oxford; more, it is the tragedy of a poor boy who becomes obsessed with the dream of Oxford precisely because he does not believe he has the 'brains' to go.

In a review of Jude, Edmund Gosse derided Hardy's apparent implication that Jude had the right to an Oxford fellowship and diagnosed Jude with 'degeneracy' and 'megalomania', although he is also decided that Jude showed 'brightness' and might have 'become fairly distinguished as a scholar'.[131] Gosse's review illuminates the extent to which medical and pedagogical judgements had begun to shade into one another at the fin de siècle. Gosse responds to the novel as if it were a kind of psychometric test, inviting us to scrutinise Jude's mental fitness and thereby determine his eligibility for a scholarship. As Shuman has suggested, nineteenth-century novelists were often self-conscious about the analogy between the realist novel and the examination: both forms purported to make nebulous mental qualities available for just evaluation.[132] Although modern readers tend to appraise Jude more sympathetically than Gosse does, they nevertheless often share his impulse to assess Jude's worth as a university candidate.[133] The novel's intervention in the late Victorian politics of education is both more radical and more ambiguous than such readings register. *Jude* is a kind of anti-scholarship examination, laying bare all social and psychological forces which conspire to make Jude's latent intellectual capacities unknowable and his desire to go to Oxford masochistic. In this, Hardy contests the idea that the 'natural ability' of a poor boy like Jude is discoverable, whether by competitive examination, social judgement, or even by the omniscience of a realist novelist.

Jude highlights the extent to which the sentimental myth of the poor boy of talent was a subset of the larger political distinction between the deserving and undeserving poor. This ancient distinction, concretised in Victorian culture by the New Poor Law of 1834 and implicit in much Victorian philanthropy, divided the poor into innocent victims entitled to charity and malefactors who required moral discipline or were simply beyond redemption.[134] As Gosse's confused assessment of Jude's mental worth registers, his character is precisely constructed to confound this distinction. To a marked degree, Jude is the delinquent twin of the deserving scholarship boy: not only does he lack the requisite 'brilliance', but he drinks too much, cannot contain his sexuality, and is given to bouts of iconoclastic rage. He also shows symptoms of hereditary degeneracy, though, as in *Tess*, heredity is treated more as a matter of folk superstition and class prejudice than of hard biological reality in *Jude*.[135] On the other hand, Jude is a paragon of the 'respectable' poor insofar as he embodies the earnest commitment to hard work associated with Smiles and the mid-Victorian culture of self-help. However, Hardy ensures that Jude's commitment to his ambition registers not as virtuous Smilesian persistence but as a disturbing form of perseveration: in effect, Jude compulsively re-enacts the childhood trauma of his encounter with the grammar book and the annihilating sense of inferiority it induced. For this reason, the novel has been rightly understood as an indictment of the Smilesian model of social mobility, with the case of Jude demonstrating that no amount of individual striving suffices to overcome systemic oppression.[136] Yet it is more accurate to say that the novel captures how the mid-Victorian model of self-help could produce a devastating kind of cognitive dissonance when it became entangled with fin de siècle scientific determinism about intelligence. Despite their obvious incompatibility, Jude is the victim of both ideologies, afflicted on the one hand by the egalitarian promise of agency and moral reward held out by the Smilesian ideal and by the sense of fatalism purveyed by late Victorian discourses about heredity and brains.

Where, in *Tess*, Hardy finesses the distinction between the exceptional and the ordinary in order to aggrandise and to universalise by turn his heroine's tragedy, in *Jude*, there is a more leaden emphasis upon the hero's ordinariness. As Emily Steinlight observes, Jude is always glimpsing himself 'in the mirror of statistics': he is dispirited by the thought that there are 'thousands of young men on the same self-seeking track' as himself.[137] Interestingly, Sue, who does not conflate intellectual self-worth and social distinction as Jude does, is nonetheless haunted by the same sense that she is nothing special: she can take no pleasure in being considered 'a clever girl' because 'there are too many of that sort now'.[138] This consciousness of one's statistical mediocrity, of there being 'too many' other people of the same average type as oneself, lies at the core of the novel's tragedy. Steinlight focuses primarily on the Malthusian dimensions of the novel's statistical thinking, grimly captured in Father Time's suicide note: 'done because we are too menny'.[139] But the problem of 'too many' is not just a matter of over-population and the supposedly excessive fertility of the poor. It is an effect of mass education and the logic of the scholarship ladder. As is often noted, education is often imagined as a positional or competitive good: that is, it is a good whose value depends on its social distribution.[140] As Jude's fantasies of Christminster make vivid, university education derived its quasi-sacral, quasi-aristocratic mystique in the Victorian age from its relative social scarcity. Toward the end of the novel, Jude laments that he could not benefit from new schemes to render university less 'exclusive', but the exclusivity of Oxford is the essence of its attraction for him.[141] Indeed, increased social mobility and mass education pose a threat to Jude's fantasy life, crowding it with a horde of anonymous men with the same aspirations: 'He sometimes felt that by caring for books he was not escaping common-place nor gaining rare ideas, every working-man being of that taste now.'[142] Although Jude espouses 'equality of opportunity', he does not, in fact, want a more egalitarian education system, but to enjoy the sense of spiritual 'election' possible within the existing elitist one.[143] At the same time, Jude has no faith that he is exceptional. As he feels keenly, it is not enough that he be extremely diligent or passionate about books; in order to be a poor boy deemed worthy of Oxford, he must be a statistical and biological outlier, in possession of rare 'natural ability'. Jude's ambition is thus perfectly self-defeating, or a form of cruel optimism, in Berlant's phrase. It is not simply that he has an unrealistic dream of attending an elite institution; his own exclusion is constitutive of what he desires, insofar as the glamour of Oxford inheres in the fact that it is a 'castle manned by scholarship and religion' against the 'too many', the democratic mass from which he has no means of distinguishing himself.[144]

Jude falls in love with Sue because she appears to embody his contradictory intellectual ideals. First, he fancies that she incarnates the kind of 'disinterested', 'ethereal' brilliance that he identifies with Oxford.[145] Indeed, he imagines her intelligence just as he imagines the university, as a radiant fact of nature: he says that her intellect 'scintillates like a star' or plays like 'lambent lightning' (this is a perception of Sue shared by Jude's rival, the schoolteacher Mr Phillotson: he remarks that Sue's intellect 'sparkles like diamonds, while mine smoulders like brown paper').[146] Second, Sue is also the meritocratic success story that Jude is not, even if her aspirations are more modest than his: she expects to 'pass high' in her examinations and duly wins a Queen's scholarship to attend teacher training college.[147] Third, where Jude seems to experience only the alienation and 'plodding' of autodidacticism, Sue exemplifies what an intellect can achieve by working outside of 'ordained lines': when Jude first encounters her, he is startled by her intellectual audacity, and she introduces him to the possibility that education might be experienced not as Christian transcendence but as a pagan pleasure and liberation, an idea captured in her penchant for quoting A. C. Swinburne's poetry.[148] Sue seems empowered by her very oppression: her gender means she is not prey to the same illusions about Oxford as Jude, and her mind is thus freer to 'play' among 'conventions and formalities'.[149] In contrast to him, she flippantly asserts her own mastery of Latin and Greek grammar and her wide reading of classical authors in translation, announcing that she has no 'fear of men as such, nor of their books'.[150] If Jude suggests the extent to which the auto-didactic intellect may be entrammelled by a sense of inferiority, then Sue at least initially seems to exemplify what an emancipated intellect might look like: in Rancière's terms, she suggests 'what an intelligence can do when it considers itself equal to any other and considers any other equal to itself'.[151]

Hardy's representation of Sue's intelligence condenses the same political ambiguities as his depiction of Jude's insofar as we are invited to interpret it by turn as a product of education and as an effect of biological determinism. On the one hand, the narrative highlights that Sue's intellectualism is impressive because it is largely her own creation: it is a product of her adventurous reading programme, which has in turn fed her 'Voltairean' scepticism in the face of social orthodoxies.[152] To this extent, Sue's intellect *is* her 'advanced' theories, her feminism and atheism.[153] On the other, Sue's intellect is biologised insofar as she is persistently characterised as neurasthenic. Both before and after the calamity of her children's deaths she is defined by her 'tight-strained nerves', and this pathologising discourse has multiple significations.[154] Neurasthenia, or nervous exhaustion, was considered a typically feminine malady and sometimes linked specifically to the cultural stereotype of New Woman, particularly in her incarnation as the 'exam girl' who had depleted her mental capacities through excessive 'cramming'.[155] But neurasthenia also carried a distinct intellectual prestige insofar as it was understood as an illness of modernity and a mark of high intelligence. The Romantic identification of madness with creative genius gained scientific authority at the fin de siècle, with a flurry of books claiming that modern brain science confirmed the poetic archetype.[156] Whether the novel's emphasis upon Sue's 'nerves' amounts to a sexist denigration of her intellect or serves to lend her some of the quasi-medical glamour of fin de siècle genius is open to dispute: Hardy's construction of her readily evokes both clichés. Hardy also leaves open the question of whether Sue's neurasthenia is a cause or effect of her intellectual rebelliousness, and thus the question of whether the pathology resides primarily in her or in the social order she rebels against. However, it is Sue's gender, or rather her departure from the norms of her gender, that inspires the novel's most categorical affirmation of biological determinism. It appears when the narrator describes the other women at Sue's teacher training college:

> they all lay in their cubicles, their tender feminine faces upturned [. . .] down the long dormitories, every face bearing the legend 'The Weaker' upon it, as the penalty of the sex wherein they were moulded, which by no possible exertion of their willing hearts and abilities could be made strong while the inexorable laws of nature remain what they are [. . .] Amid the storms and strains of after-years, with their injustice, loneliness, child-bearing and bereavement, their minds would revert to this experience as to something which had been allowed to slip past them insufficiently regarded.[157]

It is significant that Hardy invokes the 'inexorable laws of nature' in relation to a group of trainee teachers: it is the hopes these women have invested in the transformative power of education that makes the biological limits of their 'abilities' so pathetically stark. The pathos of their bondage is somewhat crudely amplified by the narrator's abrupt prolepsis: their education will be ineffectual, a faintly felt interlude in lives made predictable and homogeneous by biology. Yet part of the purpose of this passage is to highlight the rebellious individualism of Sue, who has escaped from the dormitory to visit Jude and, the narrator implies, is simultaneously attempting to escape from her biological destiny. If Sue does not, in fact, manage to avoid the stock fate of women, the text never attributes this to any weakness of her mental abilities; Jude's sense of awe at Sue's intellect, even in its ruined state, is never contradicted or undercut by the narrator.

The character of Arabella Donn is the most fraught expression of the novel's ambivalence toward the late Victorian biopolitics of mental capacity. Superficially, she is a grotesque manifestation of the Social Darwinist model of intelligence: a pig farmer's daughter who is herself depicted as bestial throughout the novel, her 'clever[ness]' is all animal instinct and ruthless self-interest.[158] At the level of plot, Arabella is the principle of plebeian carnality which continually disrupts Jude's *Bildungsroman* and spoils his rarefied ideals, whether she is hurling a pig's penis at him by way of seduction or wiping lard on his books. Within the terms of the novel's bleak transvaluation of Social Darwinism, Arabella is unredeemable because of her resilience and *joie de vivre*; as epitomised by her callousness in the wake of Jude's death, the will to survive and be happy can come only at the price of one's humanity in the moral universe of this novel. By the same logic, Jude's and Sue's despair of life proves that they are Arabella's moral and intellectual superiors: their failure to flourish in the world – what Galton or Maudsley might identify as their 'degeneracy' – confirms their finer humanity, their shared status as beautiful souls. Yet this reading overlooks the extent to which the novel is of Arabella's party. Arabella's contempt for Jude's 'higher' aspirations accords with the novel's wider attack on economic and educational inequality. In her unashamed vulgarity, Arabella actually lives out Jude and Sue's radical political ideals: she demonstrates the indifference to religion, sexual propriety, and class distinctions that they theoretically associate with enlightenment. More, she enacts the hedonistic naturalism that Sue can only theorise and yearn for: 'Nature's intention, Nature's law and *raison d'être* [is] that we should be joyful in what instincts she afforded us.'[159] Readers who experience an 'illicit' sympathy with Arabella are not reading against the grain of the novel, but registering the extent to which she is allied with its politics, specifically its desire to vindicate the claims of the poor and the material realities of the body.[160]

Hardy's critique of late Victorian hierarchies of the mind is distilled in the graffiti that Jude scrawls in chalk on a wall in Oxford, a quotation from the Book of Job: 'I have understanding as well as you; I am not inferior to you: yea, who knoweth not such things as these?' (Job 12: 3).[161] Jude is reacting to a patronising rebuff from the 'Master of Biblioll College' and the walls of Oxford at this moment symbolise the impassable barriers to his intellectual aspirations.[162] The fact that Jude derives this assertion of the equality of human intelligence from the Book of Job is rich with significance. The Book of Job has often been understood as the subversive book of the Hebrew Bible: Job's despairing interrogation of the nature of God's justice is open to being read as an archetype of religious doubt or political insubordination.[163] Jude clearly invokes Job as a biblical exemplar of a type of despair which radicalises the intellect and arouses righteous protest; in effect, he is countering the Oxford conflation of learning, religion, and privilege with his own identification of intellectual value with scepticism and suffering. However, the choice of quotation simultaneously undercuts the suggestion that suffering produces special insight. Jude's wisdom, like Job's, is both the privilege of his victimhood and banal, anybody's knowledge: 'who knoweth not such things as these?' In this way, *Jude* repeats the double gesture of *Tess*, grounding intellectual value in tragic suffering while also emphasising tragedy's egalitarianism.[164] The fact that Jude finds authorisation for his act of iconoclasm in the Bible means that the graffiti are also a pithy immanent critique of Oxford, which, as a Christian institution, purported to recognise the moral claims of the poor and outcast. In context, Jude's appropriation of Job's question accuses Oxford of possessing no recondite wisdom, of being founded upon the banality of social inequality – a truth that can be discerned as readily from outside its walls as from within them.

Notes

1 Thomas Hardy, *A Pair of Blue Eyes*, ed. Alan Manford (Oxford: Oxford University Press), 1985, p. 209.

2 Ibid.

3 Ibid.

4 Ibid., p. 212.

5 Ibid., p. 209.

6 Gillian Beer identifies 'the problem of finding a scale for the human' in relation to Darwinian evolution as the 'besetting preoccupation' of Hardy's work. See Beer, *Darwin's Plots: Evolutionary Narrative in Darwin, George Eliot, and Thomas Hardy* (Cambridge: Cambridge University Press, 2000), p. 233.

7 Hardy, *Pair of Blue Eyes*, p. 209.

8 For the strongest articulation of the case, see Peter Morton, *The Vital Science: Biology and the Literary Imagination 1860–1900* (London: George Allen & Unwin, 1984), pp. 194–211; for a more recent version of this argument, see Shuttleworth, *The Mind of the Child*, pp. 335–52. Suzanne Keen provides an extremely useful map of Hardy's reading of contemporary science and psychology. See Keen, *Thomas Hardy's Brains: Psychology, Neurology, and Hardy's Imagination* (Athens: University of Ohio Press, 2014), pp. 17–52.

9 Thomas Hardy, *The Woodlanders*, ed. Dale Kramer (Oxford: Oxford University Press, 1981), p. 46.

10 Ibid., p. 109.

11 As noted in the Introduction, Galton first attempts to delineate the distinction between 'nature' and 'nurture' in *English Men of Science: Their Nature and Their Nurture* (1874). Initially a heuristic distinction, even for him, the phrase rapidly comes to imply, both in his work and in the wider culture, that 'nature' and 'nurture' represent 'separate ontological realms', as Meloni writes. See Meroni, p. 43.

12 See Gould, pp. 62–173.

13 Ibid., pp. 127–41.

14 See Jane L. Bownas, *Thomas Hardy and Empire: The Representation of Imperial Themes in the Work of Thomas Hardy* (London: Routledge, 2016), p. 5 and pp. 105–12; and Foucault, *Society Must be Defended*, p. 103.

15 Hardy, *Woodlanders*, p. 93 and p. 46.

16 Ibid., p. 118.

17 Ibid., p. 45.

18 Ibid.

19 Ibid., p. 118.

20 Rancière, *Ignorant Schoolmaster*, p. 48.

21 Hardy, *Woodlanders*, p. 161.

22 Ibid., pp. 161–2.

23 Rancière, *Aesthetics and its Discontents*, trans. Stephen Corcoran (Cambridge: Polity Press, 2009), pp. 31–2.

24 Hardy, *Woodlanders*, p. 70 and p. 140.

25 See Andrew Wilson, 'The Old Phrenology and the New', *The Gentleman's Magazine* 244 (1879), pp. 68–85.

26 Hardy, *Woodlanders*, p. 70.

27 Ibid., p. 162 and p. 140.

28 Ibid., p. 186.

29 Ibid., p. 309.

30 Qtd in Shanta Dutta, *Ambivalence in Hardy: A Study of His Attitude to Women* (Basingstoke: Macmillan, 2000), p. 88.

31 Ibid., p. 301.

32 Daston, p. 212.

33 Hardy, *Woodlanders*, p. 119.

34 Ibid., p. 282.

35 Ibid., p. 297.

36 Ibid., p. 10.

37 Spencer, *Principles of Psychology*, p. 454.

38 Darwin, pp. 37–70.

39 See discussions of Darwin and Spencer in the Introduction, pp. 4–5 and 9–12.

40 Rancière, *Ignorant Schoolmaster*, p. 37.

41 Ibid., pp. 36–7.

42 Hardy, *Woodlanders*, p. 9.

43 Ibid., pp. 297–8.

44 See John Heaney, 'Arthur Schopenhauer, Evolution, and Ecology in Thomas Hardy's *The Woodlanders*', *Nineteenth Century Literature* 71.4 (2017), pp. 516–45.

45 William Cohen, 'Arborealities: The Tactile Ecology of Hardy's *Woodlanders*', *19: Interdisciplinary Studies in the Long Nineteenth Century* 19 (2014), 1–22, p. 9. Available at: <https://www.19.bbk.ac.uk/articles/10.16995/ntn.690/> (last accessed 28 November 2021).

46 See especially the often quoted passage which emphasises the violence of the struggle for existence among trees: Hardy, *Woodlanders*, p. 48.

47 Cohen, p. 17.

48 Hardy, *Woodlanders*, p. 58.

49 John Stuart Mill, *On Liberty and Other Essays*, ed. John Gray (Oxford: Oxford University Press, 1991), p. 66; and Fred Reid, *Thomas Hardy and History* (Basingstoke: Palgrave Macmillan, 2017), p. 190.

50 Hardy, *Woodlanders*, p. 40.

51 Mary Jacobus, 'Tree and Machine: *The Woodlanders*', in *Critical Approaches to the Fiction of Thomas Hardy*, ed. Dale Kramer (Basingstoke: Palgrave Macmillan, 1979), 116–34, p. 117.

52 Thomas Hardy, *Tess of the d'Urbervilles*, ed. John Paul Riquelme (Boston: Bedford St. Martin's, 1998), p. 185 and p. 210.

53 Ibid., p. 114.

54 Hardy 'dipped into' Weismann's book in 1890. See Angelique Richardson, 'Heredity', in *Thomas Hardy in Context*, ed. Philip Mallet (Cambridge: Cambridge University Press, 2013), 328–38, p. 333. On the growing authority of hard hereditarian theories at the fin de siècle, see Introduction, pp. 42–3.

55 Hardy, *Tess*, p. 109.

56 Greenslade, pp. 158–63.

57 For an analysis of the fin de siècle theory that genius is a form of deviance or degeneration, see Introduction, p. 41; for an analysis

of the public concern with mental deficiency, particularly the new category of 'feeble-mindedness', see Introduction, pp. 39–42 and Chapter 4, pp. 211–17.

58 Hardy, *Tess*, p. 109; and Dale Kramer, *Hardy: Tess of the d'Urbervilles* (Cambridge: Cambridge University Press, 1991), p. 80.

59 Hardy, *Tess*, p. 196.

60 Rancière, *Ignorant Schoolmaster*, p. 49.

61 Ruth, p. 5 and p. 63.

62 The 'pupil-teacher' system, established in 1846 and remaining the main form of teacher training until 1902, provided scholarships for 'promising' lower-class students to serve as apprentice teachers while completing their own educations.

63 Hardy, *Tess*, p. 142.

64 Ibid., p. 273.

65 On the salience of class distinctions in Victorian discourses surrounding heredity and eugenics, see Mazumdar.

66 Hardy, *Tess*, pp. 134–5.

67 Ibid., p. 323. For an analysis of Hardy's ethics of altruism, see Caroline Sumpter's 'On Suffering and Sympathy: *Jude the Obscure*, Evolution and Ethics', *Victorian Studies* 53.4 (2011), pp. 665–87. Although her argument focuses on *Jude*, many of her insights are applicable to *Tess*.

68 For an excellent reading of *Jane Eyre* and *David Copperfield* as *Bildungsromane* of meritocratic 'empowerment', see Julia Prewitt-Browne, 'The Moral Scope of the English *Bildungsroman*', in *Oxford Handbook of the Victorian Novel*, ed. Lisa Rodensky (Oxford: Oxford University Press, 2013), 664–77.

69 Hardy, *Tess*, p. 161 and p. 160.

70 Ibid., p. 161 and p. 41.

71 For nineteenth-century scientific debates on women's intellectual capacities, see Russett, *Sexual Science*, and Daston.

72 Rachel Malane, *Sex in Mind: The Gendered Brain in Nineteenth-century Literature and Mental Sciences* (Oxford: Peter Lang, 2005), pp. 157–89.

73 Ibid., p. 186; and Hardy, *Tess*, p. 181.

74 Qtd in Harold Orel, ed., *Thomas Hardy's Personal Writings* (London: Macmillan, 1967), p. 127.

75 Keen, p. 57.

76 For an analysis of the narrator's erotic investment in Tess's victimhood, see Kaja Silverman, 'History, Figuration, and Female

Subjectivity in *Tess of the d'Urbervilles'*, *Novel: A Forum on Fiction* 18.1 (1984), pp. 5–28.

77 Hardy, *Tess*, p. 245.

78 See Introduction, p. 45.

79 Hardy, *Tess*, p. 185.

80 Darwin, pp. 236–7.

81 Hardy, *Tess*, p. 185.

82 Walter Pater, *Studies in the History of the Renaissance*, ed. Matthew Beaumont (Oxford: Oxford University Press, 2010), p. 181. On the centrality of an ideal of creative receptivity to Pater's work and aestheticism more generally, see Jesse Matz, *Literary Impressionism and Modernist Aesthetics* (Cambridge: Cambridge University Press, 2004), pp. 66–78. On the decadent identification of artistic genius with acute sensory capacities, see David Weir, *Decadence and the Making of Modernism* (Amherst: University of Massachusetts Press, 1995), pp. 47–50.

83 Hardy, *Tess*, p. 166.

84 Ibid.

85 Ibid., p. 166.

86 Rancière, *The Lost Thread*, p. 15.

87 Hardy, *Tess*, p. 140.

88 Ibid.

89 Ibid.

90 As Peter Garratt shows, Victorian philosophers and writers in the empiricist tradition were often anxious to defuse accusations of thoroughgoing materialism. See Garratt, *Victorian Empiricism: Self, Knowledge, and Reality in Ruskin, Bain, Lewes, Spencer, and George Eliot* (Cranbury: Farleigh Dickinson University Press, 2010), p. 46, pp. 57–8, p. 246, and p. 152.

91 The narrator's characterisation of Tess's child, Sorrow, as a 'corporeal blight' also epitomises the anti-natalist sentiment that Aaron Matz locates in Hardy's work. Distinct from eugenics, anti-natalism is a radical negativity toward all procreation, grounded in the philosophical view that it is better not to be born. See Aaron Matz, 'Hardy and the Vanity of Procreation', *Victorian Studies* 57.1 (2014), pp. 7–29.

92 Hardy, *Tess*, p. 197.

93 Ibid., p. 193.

94 Ibid., p. 117.

95 Jacques Rancière, *Dissensus: On Politics and Aesthetics*, trans. Stephen Corcoran (London: Bloomsbury, 2015), pp. 44–5.

96 Rancière, *Politics of Literature*, p. 43.

97 Ibid., p. 4.

98 Hardy, *Tess,* p. 140.

99 Ibid., p. 169.

100 Ibid., p. 116.

101 On Tess's sensitivity to animal suffering, see Anna West, *Thomas Hardy and Animals* (Cambridge: Cambridge University Press, 2017), pp. 148–50.

102 Rancière, *Politics of Literature*, p. 62.

103 Hardy, *Tess,* p. 142.

104 Ibid., p. 142.

105 Ibid.

106 Ibid.

107 See Kate Flint, *The Woman Reader, 1837–1914* (Oxford: Clarendon Press, 1993).

108 Hardy, *Tess,* p. 46.

109 Ibid., p. 141.

110 See Francesco Marroni, *Victorian Disharmonies: A Reconsideration of Nineteenth-century English Fiction* (Newark: University of Delaware Press, 2010), p. 163.

111 Ibid.

112 See Introduction, pp. 33–5.

113 Marjorie Garber, *Hardy's Fables of Integrity: Woman, Body, Text* (Oxford: Oxford University Press, 1991), p. 154.

114 Thomas Hardy, *Jude the Obscure*, ed. Dennis Taylor (Oxford: Oxford University Press, 1998), p. 33.

115 This phrase is Anna Kornbluh's, though she discusses the novel's biopolitical imagination only in passing. See Kornbluh, 'Obscure Forms: The Letter, the Law, and the Line in Hardy's Social Geometry', *Novel: A Forum on Fiction* 48.1 (2015), 1–17, p. 2.

116 Shuttleworth reads Jude's tragedy in the light of Victorian psychiatry and hereditarian discourses. See Shuttleworth, *The Mind of the Child*, pp. 335–52.

117 Rancière, *Ignorant Schoolmaster*, p. 49.

118 Hardy, *Jude*, p. 22 and p. 71.

119 Rancière, *Mute Speech, Literature, Critical Theory, and Politics*, trans. James Swenson (Columbia: New York University Press, 1998), p. 90.

120 Ibid.

121 Ibid.

122 Hardy, *Jude*, p. 30.

123 Ibid.

124 Ibid., p. 84.

125 Ibid., p. 320.

126 For an illuminating account of how Hardy's narrator clarifies the oppressive effects of Jude's tendency to repress or despise his own labour, see Andrew Cooper, 'Voicing the Language of Literature: Jude's Obscured Labour', *Victorian Literature and Culture* 28.2 (2000), pp. 391–410.

127 See Jonathan Memel, '"Making the University Less Exclusive": The Legacy of *Jude the Obscure*', *Neo-Victorian Studies* 10.1 (2017), pp. 64–82.

128 Hardy, *Jude*, p. 113.

129 Ibid., p. 151. For instance, the *Oxford Companion to English Literature* characterises Jude as a young villager of 'exceptional intellectual promise'; see Dinah Birch, ed., *The Oxford Companion to English Literature*, 7th edition (Oxford: Oxford University Press, 2009). Jane Mattisson refers to his 'obvious talents' and 'intelligence'; see Mattisson, *Knowledge and Survival in the Novels of Thomas Hardy* (Lund: Lund University Press, 2002), p. 274. Richardson suggests he is 'far more gifted naturally than the men who are born to privilege'; see Richardson, 'Hardy and Biology', in *Thomas Hardy: Texts and Contexts*, ed. Philip Mallet (Basingstoke: Palgrave Macmillan, 2002), p. 171. Memel also shows how frequently the novel has been read as 'the first great literary treatment of the idea that talent can be wasted by exclusion from university', in the words of Boris Johnson. See Memel, p. 4.

130 Hardy, *Jude*, p. 115.

131 Edmund Gosse, 'Mr. Hardy's New Novel', *Cosmopolis* (1896), pp. 60–9.

132 Shuman, pp. 88–9.

133 See Memel.

134 Serena Romano, *Moralising Poverty: The 'Undeserving' Poor in the Public Gaze* (London: Routledge, 2017), pp. 13–29.

135 For an excellent analysis of the ambiguous and ironic dimensions of Hardy's use of degeneration theory in *Jude*, see Emily Steinlight, 'Hardy's Unnecessary Lives: The Novel as Surplus', *Novel: A Forum on Fiction* 47.2 (2014), 224–41, pp. 229–31.

136 See Patricia Ingham, *The Language of Gender and Class: Transformation in the Victorian Novel* (London: Routledge, 1996), pp. 170–4.

137 Steinlight, 'Hardy's Unnecessary Lives', p. 228; and Hardy, *Jude*, p. 129.
138 Hardy, *Jude*, p. 107.
139 Ibid., p. 336.
140 Charles Howell, 'Education as Positional Good Reconsidered', *Journal of the Philosophical Study of Education* 1 (2011), 19–36, p. 19.
141 Hardy, *Jude*, p. 399.
142 Ibid., p. 66.
143 Ibid., p. 304 and p. 113.
144 Ibid., p. 26.
145 Ibid., p. 187.
146 Ibid., p. 342, p. 344, and p. 229.
147 Ibid., p. 133.
148 Ibid., p. 115 and p. 150.
149 Ibid., p. 344.
150 Ibid., p. 147.
151 Rancière, *Ignorant Schoolmaster*, p. 39.
152 Hardy, *Jude*, p. 152.
153 Ibid., p. 166.
154 Ibid., p. 110.
155 See Introduction, p. 37.
156 See also Introduction, p. 41.
157 Hardy, *Jude*, pp. 140–1.
158 Ibid., p. 401.
159 Ibid., p. 33.
160 On Arabella as an object of 'rebellious' readerly identification, see Lesley Goodman, 'Rebellious Identification, or, How I Learned to Stop Worrying and Love Arabella', *Narrative* 18.2 (2010), pp. 163–77.
161 Hardy, *Jude*, p. 118.
162 Ibid., p. 117.
163 See Katherine Julia Dell, *The Book of Job as Sceptical Literature* (Berlin: Walter de Gruyter), 1991.
164 Eagleton observes that the aristocratic genre of tragedy is democratised in modern literature: the 'jealously patrolled frontiers between tragic registers and non-tragic victims' break down and 'anyone can be a tragic subject'. See Eagleton, p. 95.

3

Acting Clever in Henry James

In his 1913 autobiography, *A Small Boy and Others*, Henry James recalls how being bad at maths at school convinced him that he was stupid:

I recall strange neighbours and deskfellows who, not otherwise too objectionable, were uncanny and monstrous through their possession, cultivation, imitation of ledgers, daybooks, double-entry, tall pages of figures, interspaces streaked with oblique ruled lines that weirdly 'balanced', whatever that might mean, and other like horrors. Nothing in truth is more distinct to me than the tune to which they were, without exception, at their ease on such ground – unless it be my general dazzled, humiliated sense, through those years, of the common, the baffling, mastery, all round me [. . .] Everyone did things and had things – everyone knew how, [. . .], just as they kept in their heads such secrets for how to do sums [. . .] Those who surrounded me were all agog, to my vision, with the benefit of their knowledge. I see them, in this light, across the years, fairly grin and grimace with it; and the presumable vulgarity of some of them, certain scattered shades of baseness still discernible, comes to me as but one of the appearances of an abounding play of genius. Who was it I ever thought stupid? All of which, I should add, didn't in the least prevent my moving on the plane of the remarkable [. . .]; I was fairly gorged with wonders. [. . .] It was strange [that I was] so stupid without being more brutish and so perceptive without being more keen.[1]

It is easy to read this passage suspiciously. James's incapacity for calculation turns out to be a mark of election, a sign of a Romantic appetite for wonder that augurs his vocation as an artist. Where his classmates were presumably fit for a world of 'ledgers, daybooks, double-entry', of doing things and having things, he was a beautiful soul. James reassures us that his type of incapacity had no negative class connotations – he was in no way 'vulgar', 'brutish', or 'base' – and goes on to suggest that it was, in fact, so discreet that it escaped the attention of his teachers.[2] More subtly, the passage encourages us to recognise that if the twelve-year-old James was hopeless at maths, it was because he was a precocious philosopher; while his classmates calculated, he pondered the incalculability of other minds. But James's forms of self-aggrandisement here only reward so much suspicion: they are relatively overt, and predictable enough. Writing at the end of a long and distinguished career, James takes it for granted that the reader of his autobiography credits him with exceptional mental powers. More interesting is James's effort to convey that his celebrated perceptiveness had its origins in a hyperbolic childhood conviction of his stupidity. An acute sense of mental inferiority engenders a paranoid but perhaps also creative fascination with other people: it makes *all* other minds seem a store of troubling secrets, enviable knowledge, even when they are engaged in something as boring as schoolwork. James suggests that if his schoolboy self possessed any latent genius, it was because he never thought anyone stupid.

As Mark McGurl has observed, the critical tendency to focus on the epistemological dramas staged so obsessively by James's late fiction – who knows what, how they know it, and the value of their knowledge – has tended to obscure the extent to which James is interested in the evaluation of intelligence.[3] James's characters are typically preoccupied not just with the question of how and what other people know but how well they know; they are generally anxious to discover not just the contents but the calibre of other minds. For McGurl, this is because James is the master of the modernist art of making invidious distinctions: his formidably difficult late novels aspire to serve as an esoteric type of IQ test, sifting the 'intelligent from the stupid' at the level of both character and readership.[4] In McGurl's account, James's desire to adjudicate on the question of intelligence is his queasy reaction to a perceived blurring of social distinctions in the late nineteenth century; his anxieties about mass culture and social levelling inspire him to refigure and mystify volatile class distinctions as intellectual distinctions.[5]

Tellingly, however, McGurl's account dwells much more on the intimidating effects of James's representational strategies upon the reader than on how intelligence is represented through particular characters and conceptualised within James's fictional worlds. His claim that James is invested in 'distinguishing the stupid from the smart' appears as part of a brief discussion of James's 1896 novella, *The Spoils of Poynton*. McGurl suggests that this work illustrates James's tendency to equip certain characters with quasi-authorial insight – the characters James calls his 'centres of intelligence' – and to distinguish them from flat, dull-witted characters denied such authorial preferment.[6] Yet despite and sometimes because of this kind of authorial favouritism, it is extremely difficult to determine who passes for intelligent in James's fiction; rather than establishing a clear hierarchy of intellect with its own formal difficulties at the apex, he makes the vexed nature of judgements about intelligence one of the cardinal difficulties of reading his work. Take, for example, this brief passage from *The Spoils of Poynton*:

[Mrs. Gereth] had no imagination about anybody's life save on the side she bumped against. Fleda was quite aware that she would have otherwise been a rare creature; but a rare creature was originally just what she had struck her as being. Mrs. Gereth had really no perception of anybody's nature – had only one question about persons: were they clever or stupid? To be clever meant to know the marks.[7]

It is true that Fleda seems to be granted an authorial quasi-omniscience here. She is apparently so sensitive, so anxious to do imaginative justice to others, that she manages to take into account not just Mrs Gereth's actually existing complexities, but, circularly, the kinds of complexities Mrs Gereth might have possessed, had she exercised the same kind of moral imagination. Crucially, Mrs Gereth's preoccupation with the question of whether other people are clever or stupid is not only a moral but an intellectual limitation, depriving her of the apparently more enlightened perspective of Fleda; James implies that to ask 'is this person clever or stupid?' is to ask a stupid question, at least if it is your primary question. 'Marks' here perhaps carries the connotation of a student's test results – a meaning the word acquired in the early nineteenth century (*Oxford English Dictionary*) – but the primary reference is to manufacturer's marks: the phrase underscores Mrs Gereth's tendency to assess other people as if they were furniture and had a value determinable by aesthetic connoisseurship. The novella centres on Mrs Gereth's obsession with her family's antique furniture – the 'spoils' of the title – and her low opinion of the intelligence of her son, Owen, whom she fears will marry a 'stupid' girl, Mona Brigstock.[8] Although James does not falsify Mrs Gereth's estimate of her son in an obvious way – that is, by revealing that he has unsuspected depths of intelligence – he uses Fleda to underscore that Mrs Gereth's intelligence index is itself stupid, a self-ratifying epistemological circle. As Fleda observes, Mrs Gereth thinks the meaning of other people is exhausted by whatever obtrusive part of them her imagination happens to 'bump' against; and as the phrase implies, her imagination mostly bumps against the question of material possessions. However, Fleda's assessment of Mrs Gereth's intelligence mirrors rather than transcends Mrs Gereth's presumption of intellectual sovereignty; rather than simply bestowing authorial omniscience on Fleda, James ironises Fleda's aspiration toward it. Like Mrs Gereth, Fleda flatters herself that she 'knows the marks of cleverness', and fetishises Owen's 'beautiful dense[ness]' as if his mental capacity were as palpably material as an item of furniture: she desires him precisely because she thinks him a 'blockhead' and would like to 'contribute all the cleverness' to a marriage.[9]

Pursuing this line of interpretation seems to lead to the conclusion that Fleda's and Mrs Gereth's 'cleverness' is an immoral exercise of social power, and that Owen is the victim of their 'reifying aestheticism', to borrow Jonathan Freedman's phrase.[10] However, there is no simple equation between 'cleverness' and social power in *The Spoils of Poynton*. The novella as a whole can be read as either a satire on or a tragedy about the way two women draw upon discourses of aesthetics to construct a compensatory fiction of their 'superior acuteness', one that enables them to conceal from themselves their abjectness in relation to patriarchy.[11] The plot turns on Mrs Gereth's elaborate efforts to outwit the custom of primogeniture, by which she stands to be dispossessed of her house and furniture collection as soon as her son marries. Throughout, Owen's alleged 'stupidity' can be read as a sign not of his victimhood but of his complacent power. In effect, patriarchal custom does his thinking for him and spares him what appears to be the exhausting, feminised labour of 'cleverness' in this novella; he can afford to be ignorant of the women's baroque mental lives.

So far I have been echoing the novella's brutal binary of 'clever' versus 'stupid'. This binary is, in fact, pervasive in James's writing, and it is operative from the start: it is discernible in his first novel, *Roderick Hudson* (1875).[12] James's characters often favour the word 'clever' over 'intelligent' or any other synonym for intellectual ability; and the concomitant ubiquity of the word 'stupid' in his fiction tends to conjure a terrifying social world regulated by a stark distinction between cleverness and stupidity. On the face of it, this is surprising; why does James, celebrated for his attentiveness to the nuances of consciousness and of social life, revert to such a crude, even childish, vocabulary when capturing people's intellectual worth? Put another way, why does he persistently construct characters who, though often defined by their sensitivity and sophistication, have such an impoverished vocabulary for assessing the intelligence of others? These observations seem to support McGurl's argument that James sought to make the novel form the arbiter of a new kind of intellectual hierarchy. Yet, this chapter argues, at least in relation to James's 1890 novel, *The Tragic Muse*, that just the opposite is the case. In this comedy of English manners and of the theatre, the clever/stupid binary is invoked and worried over so incessantly by the characters that the terms acquire a dizzying range of implications and a deconstructive force. James's somewhat claustrophobic focus upon the meanings of 'cleverness' in upper-class English life in *The Tragic Muse* enables him to unravel the contradictions and anachronisms embedded in apparently modern conceptions of intelligence, professionalism, and merit. In particular, the novel's comedy persistently exposes the problematic aspects of the modern impetus to reify 'intelligence' as a unitary, objectively assessable phenomenon.

Although James was born and educated in the United States, he first settled in London in 1869, at the age of twenty-five, and spent the rest of his life living mainly in England, albeit with extended periods living on the Continent. *The Tragic Muse* is the first of a series of novels he published in the 1890s – *The Spoils of Poynton*, *What Maisie Knew* (1897), *The Turn of the Screw* (1898), and *The Awkward Age* (1899) – which focus on English society and do not include his famous 'international theme' (that is, his preoccupation with the experiences of Americans living in Europe and trying to make sense of European culture). Although I here treat James as an honorary English novelist and interpreter of English culture, his acute sensitivity to the anti-egalitarian and quasi-aristocratic assumptions at the heart of nineteenth-century English meritocracy and ideals of intelligence and professionalism is surely due at least in part to his Americanness.[13]

Unlike Eliot and Hardy, James tends to avoid direct engagement with the implications of the nineteenth-century biologisation of the intellect. He was nevertheless conscious of those implications, at least in part because of his familiarity with the work of his psychologist brother, William James. In the 1880s, William James had engaged in a transatlantic debate about the significance of Spencerian and Galtonian conceptions of human intelligence with Grant Allen and the American philosopher John Fiske.[14] The biological and evolutionary nature of intelligence was not in dispute in this debate; at stake was what an evolutionary understanding of intelligence meant for ideas of individual greatness, human difference (especially racial difference in the case of Allen), the nature of 'average' intelligence (especially in the case of Fiske), and the effects of environment and education in shaping character.[15] William James's contribution to this debate, 'Great Men, Great Thoughts, and the Environment' (1880), is a critique of what he takes to be the excessively deterministic interpretation of evolution underpinning the modern scientific conception of the mind and its capacities. As his title indicates, James's critique was primarily aimed at the environmentalist, or Lamarckian, hereditarianism of Spencer rather than the hard hereditarianism of Galton: further proof of the fact that Spencer's Lamarckianism could seem as disturbing as Galtonian hard heredity to those who wished to preserve belief in the power of 'individual initiative'.[16] James attempts to demonstrate that a belief in the reality of individual agency, creativity, and greatness is compatible with a Darwinian worldview. Henry James wrote to his brother that he 'greatly appreciated' this essay and, at William's urging, promised to read Allen's and Fiske's responses as well (though he loyally vowed that he would not be persuaded by their counter-arguments).[17]

Despite Henry James's sympathy with his brother's philosophical project, *A Tragic Muse* is not an attempt to rescue an ideal of individual genius from contemporary scientific determinism. Instead, the novel finds comedy in the banal and disenchanted nature of genius at the fin de siècle – its reduction to mere commodifiable 'cleverness' – and gestures insistently at the idea that it is not possible to dignify the struggle merely to be clever with the grandeur of tragedy. Yet as the novel also suggests, the banality of modern intelligence does not diminish its social and psychological power: its characters are all obsessed with cleverness, and they turn cleverness into a contestable phantom in their very efforts to fix it as a self-evident, measurable essence.

Acting clever

Being called 'clever' can be a backhanded compliment. This is firstly because, like most terms associated with the intellect, it can have a negative moral valence, and James's fiction often puts into play the traditional, Christian identifications of cleverness with corruption and ignorance with grace. Such identifications are ambiguously present in the *Spoils of Poynton*, for instance: Owen can be read as one of James's holy fools; both Mrs Gereth and Fleda can be understood as 'monster[s] of cleverness', to borrow Fleda's own phrase.[18] As Matthew Sussman has argued, James's late fiction often spiritualises 'stupidity' in quasi-Christian terms, constructing it as a 'palpable attitude toward experience, a positive expression of moral purity associated with self- or other-protecting ignorance'.[19] Although the sacred ignorance theme is crucial to how James problematises the modern investment in evaluating 'intelligence' in his late fiction, there is another, more secular, reason why 'clever' can be an insult. 'Cleverness' implies skilfulness – etymologically, it means to be nimble or dexterous with claws or hands, expert at seizing things (*OED*) – and so to call someone 'clever' without specifying what the person is clever *at* can have the effect of implying that his or her whole being is defined by or limited to his or her mastery of a particular skill or stratagem. At the very least, the adjective prompts the question: clever how? Applied to a person, the term elides distinctions between mental and physical acts, being and doing: how it is possible simply to *be* clever, abstracted from any particular skill or activity?

The perplexing and potentially insidious effects of being judged 'clever' are central to *The Tragic Muse*. As Freedman has remarked, this novel is James's 'most thorough treatment of the problem of vocation'.[20] The novel is essentially two *Bildungsromane* braided together. Both of these vocation narratives focus upon the confusions that attend trying to 'tak[e] the measure of aptitude', to borrow a phrase from the novel itself.[21] One is the story of Nick Dormer, the second son of an aristocratic family expected to follow his father into a career as a Liberal member of parliament. Nick is, however, more attracted to the idea of being a portrait painter, and for much of the novel, he agonises over whether he has sufficient talent to justify breaking with family tradition for the sake of art. The other is the story of Miriam Rooth, an aspiring actress who lives in genteel poverty with her mother. Miriam is apparently less conflicted in her ambition than Nick but, unlike him, must overcome other people's scepticism about her talent. Miriam is only 'apparently' less conflicted since, although she is the heroine of the novel, James never grants us access to her interior life. He here experiments with a strategy he uses much more extensively in *The Awkward Age* (1899): in James's own, somewhat disconcerting, theatrical metaphor in his 1908 Preface to the novel, he declines to 'go behind' Miriam, so we can judge her only by her words and actions, and by the impressions she makes on others.[22] This enables James to pose the question 'how does a person tell if he or she has talent?' in two obviously incommensurable ways: in the case of Nick, it is experienced primarily as an existential riddle, one that he attempts to solve mostly in private and by introspection; in the case of Miriam, it is presented as a matter of public performance and social judgement. Miriam's narrative concerns her effort to convince an audience of her talent; Nick's concerns his effort to convince himself of his. The juxtaposed vocation narratives enable James to raise a series of questions about the validity of aesthetic judgements; the distinctions between art forms; the relationship between public and private life; and the value of success in the marketplace. Crucially, however, talent is not a vexed question in the novel because the characters or the narrator treat it as an ineffable mystery. Although Romantic ideas about genius and inspiration vaguely haunt the characters, artistic talent is persistently framed in terms of a much more worldly, disenchanted, and categorical discourse, shared by all the major characters, of cleverness versus stupidity.[23] While many of the characters clearly wish to give this discourse an absolute, essentialist force, the novel does not naturalise it; on the contrary, James continually calls attention to its jarring effects, and its tendency to proliferate contradictory meanings. Miriam's alleged stupidity registers in part as stock prejudice against the theatre in general and against actresses in particular – prejudices that James's novel interrogates. The idea that Miriam is stupid is first put into circulation by Gabriel, an elusive trickster–aesthete figure generally acknowledged to be modelled on

Oscar Wilde, though his avowed philosophical positions are in some respects closer to Walter Pater's than to Wilde's.[24] Nash asserts that Miriam has no acting talent because she is 'splendidly stupid', and then challenges the other characters to 'judge' her stupidity for themselves.[25] Like Wilde, Nash is given to at once dogmatic and paradoxical pronouncements, and his verdict on Miriam is unstable, blending contempt with aesthetic appreciation; it incites other characters to become invested in the question of Miriam's intelligence rather than to dismiss her out of hand. Nash does not deign to justify his logic explicitly, but to the extent that it is manifest, it is obviously idiosyncratic: he seems to think Miriam is 'stupid' because she is an aspiring actress rather than an established one. And indeed, it becomes clear that Nash despises professional ambition as such. As Richard Salmon has noted in relation to *The Tragic Muse*, nineteenth-century aestheticism, as developed by Pater and Wilde, centred on a polemical, and quasi-aristocratic, valorisation of being over doing; for instance, Pater claimed that 'the end of life is not action but contemplation – *being* as distinct from *doing* – a certain disposition of mind'.[26] Nash considers Miriam's professional ambition stupid because it necessarily defers her desired identity to an uncertain future date and condemns her in the meantime to an undignified, subjunctive labour: trying to be. For instance, he sneers at the fact that she has adopted a stage name prior to having established herself as an actress: '[she] desires to be known by some *nom de guerre* before she has even been able to enlist'.[27] Nash's aristocratic logic, or illogic – Miriam lacks the talent to be an actress because she is not a successful actress already; to aspire is to have failed – captures the key paradox of professional identity that the novel is interested in probing. As Ruth has argued, the Victorian novel often dramatises the confused temporality of professional ambition, itself born of a wider cultural confusion about the status of the professional and the nature of his or her labour:

If the professional suffers from contradictory class *locations* – neither in the capitalist nor the labourer's camps and yet both a (mental) capitalist and an (intellectual) labourer – then he is also subject to ambiguous [. . .] *temporalities* – neither born a professional, as the gentry is born gentry, nor self-made, like the Smilesian businessman, and yet both born (with certain aptitudes) and made (through mental effort). With a simultaneously pregnant and collapsed relationship to time, the professional putatively boasts mental 'gifts' that anticipate his future (pregnant) but he simply becomes what he was always meant to be (collapsed).[28]

Such paradoxes mean that Miriam is continually subject to confounding judgements. Early in the novel, Miriam solicits the professional opinion of Madame Carré, a renowned French actress who has retired from the stage and now gives lessons. A range of major and minor characters witness Miriam's audition, and are also eager to assess if she has what one of them, Peter Sherringham, thinks of as the 'mark of a vocation'.[29] Significantly, however, the audition is framed less as a test of Miriam's acting talent than a test of her general intelligence; Madame Carré asserts that if an actress has intelligence 'she has every gift'.[30] Miriam's intelligence test/acting audition is premised upon the idea that her ability can be objectively quantified: Madame Carré seeks to 'count' Miriam's 'properties' in order to 'measure' her 'histrionic nature'.[31] Perhaps predictably, however, her judgements about intelligence and its relation to acting talent are at once peremptory and incoherent. On the one hand, she dismisses the idea that acting ability is a matter of 'education'; when Miriam's mother brags that her daughter can speak many languages, Madame Carré retorts that Miriam ought then to be a governess – 'there is no education that matters'.[32] Yet she is equally disdainful of the idea of 'natural endowments' and claims that real acting ability is a matter of 'unremitting and ferocious work'; she prizes 'the effects the actor had worked hard for, had dug out of the mine by unwearied study'.[33] In the context, this is a bewildering position. The purpose of Madame Carré passing judgement on Miriam is that her long experience should give her an eye for spotting potential; if Miriam already possessed Madame Carré's own sedimented knowledge – the achievement of a long career as an actress – she would not need to submit herself to Madame Carré's examination. In effect, Miriam is judged 'stupid' because she does not yet possess the experience she is trying to prove her capacity to acquire. However, no less than Miriam, Madame Carré is caught in a bind produced by tensions that inhere in the ideal of the professional. As a venerable expert, Madame Carré predictably values accumulated experience over the idea of natural gifts; but her expertise is being called upon to adjudicate on the question of whether Miriam has natural gifts, or at least whether she has latent capacity to acquire the same type of expertise. She cannot declare that Miriam simply has 'talent' without undercutting the authority by which she makes the statement.[34]

James encourages us to perceive that the verdicts about Miriam's mental capacity are sieved through an array of prejudices. First, he opens up the possibility that Miriam is merely suffering from stage-fright, both in relation to the acting audition/intelligence test and in relation to the complex theatricality of the upper-class social milieu she is trying to negotiate. Certainly, Nick responds to Miriam's audition as a spectacle of class sadism: he grows distressed watching 'a poor working-girl's struggle with timidity'.[35] Yet the other characters persistently find Miriam 'crude', 'vulgar', and 'coarse'.[36] Her alleged 'stupidity' is clearly, at least in part, a judgement about the spectacle of a *déclassé* woman whose need to establish a career makes her appear gratingly self-assertive to many of the novel's upper-class characters, despite the fact that several of them are also professionals. Later in the novel, Nash reflects that it was Miriam's ambition that initially made her appear stupid to him: she was so 'hungry to adopt an overrated profession that he had not imputed to her the normal measure of intelligence'.[37] Similarly, it is later clarified that Peter Sherringham's perception that Miriam is stupid is partly produced by his suspicion that the acting profession demands a 'vulgar [. . .] conscience'.[38] In a play upon the word 'acting' typical of the novel, however, James also highlights that Peter's prejudice is not actually specific to the acting profession, but is an aristocratic distaste for all professions, all 'acting' or doing in the world: Peter reflects that any effort to convert ideas into action is necessarily a 'vulgarisation' of the self.[39]

Madame Carré's low opinion of Miriam's talent is explicitly a Gallic disdain for the English character, which she regards as too bourgeois and puritan to be compatible with the artistic life.[40] This judgement is also confusing, since the novel's English characters generally fail to recognise Miriam as English; by them, she is classified as a cosmopolitan Jew, though the novel repeatedly specifies that she is only part-Jewish and we later learn that she considers herself English, or at least that her mother considers her so.[41] The general perception that there is something 'vulgar' or 'coarse' in Miriam's ambition savours not only of class prejudice but of anti-Semitism.[42] It is also Miriam's Jewish ancestry that first leads Peter to suspect that she may, in fact, be 'clever'. Prior to having met her, he challenges Gabriel's assertion that she is stupid on the grounds that Jews are known to be of superior intelligence; Peter remarks that if Miriam turns out to be stupid, she will be the first known Jewish case.[43] In the 1880s, the often anti-Semitic stereotype of the 'clever Jew' was reframed in the light of the new scientific conception of intelligence as an evolutionary, hereditary characteristic.[44] Some Jewish intellectuals attempted to wield the new scientific understanding of intelligence as a weapon against anti-Semitism. In 1884, the anthropologist Lucien Wolf published a long article in *The Fortnightly Review* which estimated that the 'notorious intellectual superiority' of Jews to other races and religions could be put at between 30 and 40 per cent.[45] Wolf suggested that this superiority was a Lamarckian evolutionary effect of Jewish traditions and education.[46] In 1886, the psychologist and literary critic Jacobs – whose intelligence tests I discussed in the Introduction – applied Galtonian methods of analysis to the distribution of Jewish intellectual ability and arrived at the conclusion that 'the average Jew has 4 per cent more ability than the average Englishman'.[47] Jacobs's analysis was not strictly Galtonian insofar as he was interested in how Jewish intellectual 'eminence' was shaped by education and tradition as well as by poverty and persecution.[48] Peter's confidence that he can judge Miriam's intellectual capacities in advance of having met her because she is 'half-Jewish' is suggestive not only of the popular currency of the fraught stereotype of the 'clever Jew', but the extent to which racialised judgements about intelligence were themselves deployed as a social sign of intelligence, or at least of superior knowingness: Peter clearly enjoys his capacity to judge Miriam's mind in advance as an exercise of his own sophistication.

While other characters' judgements about Miriam's mental capacity tend to be issued with dogmatic certitude, the fact that the subject provokes so much fascinated speculation and is analysed through a confusing kaleidoscope of clichés and stereotypes paradoxically serves to render it enigmatic and posit it as that which standard frames of social judgement are inadequate to capture. Moreover, the fact that other characters are assessing Miriam's intelligence by assessing her acting ability underscores the extent to which they conceptualise intelligence as a form of theatrical display. In her study of the rise of examination culture in nineteenth-century England, Shuman emphasises the theatrical dimensions of the examination scene, its 'sense of disaster and drama'.[49] Yet, as noted in the previous chapter, Shuman suggests the underlying assumptions of nineteenth-century exam are aligned not with the theatre but with novelistic realism: the exam and the realistic novel both claim to fathom depths and to make interior worth available for fair evaluation.[50] It is often observed that James's fiction foregrounds the theatricality of everyday life, and, as one might expect, this is especially true of *The Tragic Muse*, his novel about the theatre.[51] More surprising is how the novel highlights the extent to which modern social life has the quality of a formal examination; or, more precisely, that it combines theatricality with the exam's promise to make interior worth justly assessable. The novel's imaginative conflation of the stage and the exam is clarified through the minor character of Basil Dashwood, an actor and ultimately Miriam's husband. Basil is said to have 'gone on the stage' because he 'tried for the diplomatic service' but failed to 'dazzle his examiners'.[52] In this, Basil stands in chiastic relation to Peter, the rival for Miriam's hand, who is said to have been highly successful in the same Civil Service exam but who is also a theatre aficionado.[53] Throughout the novel, we are encouraged to perceive an underlying equivalence between the theatre and the diplomatic service, and Basil's and Peter's contrasting experiences of the Civil Service exam and subsequent career paths highlight the nexus between acting ability and the performance of class identity. James keeps the social origins of Basil obscure; other characters question both his intelligence and his status as a gentleman, though it is not clear if this is simply another manifestation of prejudice against the theatre.[54] By contrast, James emphasises that Peter performed brilliantly in the Civil Service exam because there were 'flattering prejudices in his favor'; the exam tested not his intellectual abilities but his class privileges and the aura of natural authority that they conferred upon him.[55] As discussed in the Introduction, the home Civil Service began recruiting through open, competitive examinations in 1870 – a reform that was widely touted as the eradication of an ancient culture of patronage and the enshrinement of a new principle of meritocratic transparency. However, as James's characterisation of Peter's exam experience registers, meritocratic recruitment overwhelmingly favoured young men from the ancient public schools and universities. Here as throughout the novel, James emphasises the extent to which a courtly ideal of *sprezzatura* – that is, the courtier's obligation to

maintain a mask of nonchalance and convey effortless superiority
– haunts apparently modern ideals of merit and intelligence.[56]

One important exchange between Basil and Peter blurs the distinctions between theatrical technique and social performance.
More important for my purposes, it highlights how the association
of intelligence with aristocratic ideals of cultivated nonchalance
and inscrutability has the effect of blurring the distinction between
displaying cleverness and acting dumb:

> '*Ars celare artem*', Basil Dashwood jocosely dropped.
> 'You must first have the art to hide', said Sherringham, wondering a
>   little why Miriam didn't introduce her young friend to him [. . .].
> 'If you haven't any art it's not quite the same as if you didn't hide it, is
>   it?' Basil Dashwood ingeniously threw out.
> 'That's right — say one of your clever things!' Miriam sweetly
>   responded.
> 'You're always acting', he declared in English and with a simple-
>   minded laugh, while Sherringham remained struck with his express-
>   ing just what he himself had felt weeks before.[57]

The classical maxim *ars celare artem* – it is art to conceal art; or,
true art conceals its artfulness – is often identified with the courtly
ideal of *sprezzatura*.[58] It is also the key paradox that undermines
the distinction between cleverness and stupidity in *The Tragic
Muse*. As Avital Ronnell observes, James tends to equate intelligence with reserve and with the capacity for concealment: 'unre-
served, stupidity exposes while intelligence hides'.[59] In other
words, Jamesian intelligence tends to manifest itself as an absence
or as something that is only faintly perceptible – 'subtlety' – and
the comedy of *The Tragic Muse* often hinges on the paradoxes
produced by this logic. As the dizzying exchange between Basil
and Peter dramatises, cleverness which conceals itself is always
at risk of being read as stupidity; any artfulness that succeeds
too well is in danger of seeming like artlessness. Basil's response
to Miriam, 'you're always acting', implies that he thinks that her
remark – 'say one of your clever things!' – is, in fact, insincere; she
is playing the ingénue, and implying that Basil is a fool. Peter certainly seems to consider Basil a fool – the impression that Basil's
laugh is 'simple-minded' is apparently focalised through Peter –
but the passage opens up the possibility that this is only Peter's
obtuseness, or at least a sign of his exclusion; Basil's and Miriam's

interchanges have so many tiers of acting-clever-by-playing-dumb that their real relationship is opaque to Peter (though perhaps not to the reader, who suspects that the play of irony between them discloses their deepening intimacy).

Miriam apparently succeeds as an actress because she masters the art-conceals-art paradox: Nick observes of her that she becomes the 'performer who could even produce the impression of not performing'.[60] By the second book of the novel, she seems to others to be 'always acting'; like the courtier who has perfected *sprezzatura,* she has disappeared into her mask.[61] Yet the ironic effect of her becoming a successful actress is the apparently widespread perception that she is not an actress at all, that her 'profession' entails no technique or mental labour but is simply her natural way of being in the world, or a matter of feminine instinct. For instance, Gabriel rhapsodises: 'you've stopped acting, you've reduced it to the least that will do, you simply are – you're just the visible image, the picture on the wall'.[62] Peter meanwhile seeks to demystify Miriam's acting ability in Darwinian terms. Echoing Darwin in *The Descent of Man,* Peter reflects that women's intelligence is essentially intuitive and imitative, akin to the intelligence of 'lower races' and inferior to the rational capacities of European men[63]:

> She had her ideas, or rather she had her instincts, which she defended and illustrated, with a vividness superior to argument, by a happy pictorial phrase or a snatch of mimicry; [. . .] she liked experiments and caught at them, and she was especially thankful when some one gave her a showy reason, a plausible formula, in a case where she only stood on an intuition. She pretended to despise reasons and to like and dislike at her sovereign pleasure; but she always honoured the exotic gift, [. . .] as if she had been a naked islander rejoicing in a present of crimson cloth.[64]

We are meant to recognise the compensatory structure of this colonial flight of fancy. James often implies that Peter's boorishness as a suitor – inseparable from his faith in his mental superiority and in the potency of his class privileges – means he is not much good as a diplomat, either. Peter lacks the finesse to conceal his will to mastery in his courtship of Miriam; he plainly imagines it as a civilising mission of an exotic primitive. The extended joke of this thread of the narrative is that Peter is a bad lover and a bad diplomat because, despite his fascination with the theatre, he is a bad actor:

his attempts at romantic diplomacy read all too transparently as acts of imperialism. As John Carlos Rowe has pointed out, Miriam proves herself sharply aware of the psychological link between Peter's efforts to woo her by treating her to an aesthetic education and his professional commitment to English imperial ambitions.[65] Later, seeking to convince Miriam to give up the stage in order to become an ambassador's wife, Peter announces: 'I shall be a great diplomatist [. . .] I'm infinitely cleverer than you have the least idea of, and you shall be a great diplomat's wife.'[66] When this ludicrously undiplomatic speech fails to persuade Miriam, he leaves Europe for an undistinguished diplomatic post in an unspecified 'little hot hole' in Central America – a phrase that once again underscores Peter's tendency to confuse sexuality and imperialism.

You must be as clever as we think you

As has been suggested, Nick's narrative is the mirror inverse of Miriam's: he is assumed to be 'clever' by virtue of his gender, class, and indubitable Englishness, and he comes to find his reputation for cleverness oppressive. On the most obvious level, this is because he associates it with the pressure to follow his father into politics when he would rather be an artist. However, the deeper logic of his narrative is that Nick has internalised the modern meritocratic ideal, and so recoils in disgust from the advantages conferred by his aristocratic status. Although Nick obviously has to win his seat as a Liberal member of parliament by campaigning, James emphasises that the process is only superficially democratic: Nick really takes his seat by hereditary privilege and through a network of patronage, and this sours his faith in the Liberal cause and democracy in general.[67] His reputation for a general, innate 'cleverness' engenders self-contempt as well as contempt for others — 'ah the idiotic clever! if he was clever, what fools other people were!'[68]

The insistence with which other characters refer to Nick as 'wonderfully clever' and 'immensely clever' comes to register as glib and hyperbolic.[69] It also often has a coercive dimension. For instance, Nick expresses qualms about marrying his patron, Lady Julia Dallow, to another of his patrons, Mr Carcenet, on the grounds that Julia 'thinks me cleverer than I am'. Mr Carcenet responds: 'You must be as clever as we think you. If you don't prove so – !'[70] The ambiguity of Mr Carcenet's statement – is it a declarative or an imperative? a reassurance or a threat? – epitomises how judgements about intelligence in the novel often manage to be both dogmatic and unstable. On the one hand, Mr Carcenet takes Nick's cleverness for granted because Nick is the son of an aristocratic politician; it requires no proof because it is a matter of his heredity and his upper-class enculturation. And yet the same logic that makes Nick's 'cleverness' self-evident also renders it apocryphal: Mr Carcenet casts doubt on it in the very act of conferring it by fiat. Put another way, Mr Carteret's statement typifies the unstable performativity of judgements about intelligence in this novel: Nick's 'cleverness' is not a fixed attribute of his that others acknowledge and that qualifies him for professional life so much as a reality that others conjure into being.[71] The novel's tendency to compare all professions to the theatre heightens our perception of the performativity of intelligence and professional merit. Like Miriam's status as a 'stupid' actress, Nick's status as a 'clever young man' registers as a stock role, a conventional form of make-believe that must be continually sustained by himself and others.[72] James also highlights the extent to which the attribution of talent is a financial speculation; Nick has to live up to his aristocratic essence – to borrow Pierre Bourdieu's phrase – and thereby make good on other people's investment in his being what they speculated he was.[73] Nick's angst is produced partly by his recognition that his being called clever is not really a 'compliment' because it is not freely bestowed; it is a form of credit or patronage that places him in the humiliating position of a debtor or client.[74]

In an early scene of *The Tragic Muse* set in the sculpture floor of the Paris Salon, the annual exhibition of contemporary art, Nick discusses the nature of artistic talent with his sister, Biddy, who is an aspiring sculptor. Nick and Biddy both appear certain that it is a matter of innate ability, but their dialogue reveals a shared, underlying confusion about the relationship between ability and effort, being and doing:

> 'Don't you think I've any capacity for ideas?' the girl continued ruefully.
> 'Lots of them, no doubt. But the capacity for applying them, for putting them into practice, how much of that do you have?'
> 'How can I tell until I try?'
> 'What do you mean by trying, Biddy dear?'
> 'Why you know — you've seen me'.
> 'Do you call that trying?' her brother amusedly demanded.[75]

On the one hand, Biddy protests that the question of her talent remains open because she has not yet tried in earnest to become an artist; on the other, she suggests that her brother should be able to judge if she has 'capacity' by having 'seen' her, but it is not clear if she means that he has seen her 'try' or that he might be able to judge the quality of her 'ideas' simply by judging how she looks. Nick picks up on this ambiguity and makes a joke of it – he implies both that she has not tried in earnest and that she is taxing him with judging her talent by her physical appearance. This minor joke adumbrates the tendency of novel's characters to render absolute judgements about mental worth on the basis of outward appearance, and in this sense, introduces one of the novel's key themes. As I emphasised in the Introduction, the notion that a person's mental qualities can be read off his or her physical characteristics recurred in various forms in the nineteenth century: it had been axiomatic to the discredited sciences of physiognomy and phrenology, but it persisted in the practice of craniometry and in the diverse types of intelligence test being pioneered by Galton, McKeen Cattell, Warner, and others. As this scene suggests, *A Tragic Muse* is particularly attentive to how judgements about mental ability are often entangled with the mystifying discourses of aesthetic judgement. For instance, Biddy is convinced of Nick's mental superiority because he is able to make aesthetic judgements more quickly and authoritatively than she can:

> His certainty of eye impressed her, and she felt what a difference there was yet between them – how much longer in every case she would have taken to discriminate. She was aware of how little she could judge of the value of a thing till she had looked at it ten minutes; indeed, modest little Biddy was compelled privately to add, 'And often not even then' [. . .] She was mystified – Nick was often mystifying – but one thing was definite: her brother had high ability. It was the consciousness of this that made her bring out at last: 'I don't much care whether or not I please mamma, if I please you'.
> 'Oh don't lean on me. I'm a wretched broken reed – I'm no use *really*!' he promptly admonished her.
> 'Do you mean you're a duffer?' Biddy asked in alarm.
> 'Frightful, frightful!'
> [. . .]
> 'A great talent – what's simpler than that?' [Biddy asked].

'One excellent thing, dear Biddy: no talent at all'.

'Well, yours is so real you can't help it'.

'We shall see, we shall see', said Nick.[76]

Tellingly, Biddy's suggestion that her brother's 'talent' is a self-evident reality prior to any specific achievement induces one of Nick's characteristic paroxysms of self-loathing. And he is perhaps right to distrust her judgement, since her faith in his 'high ability' turns out to be labile; he only has to articulate self-doubt for her to be alarmed by the possibility that he is, in fact, a 'duffer'. Biddy essentially takes her brother at his own estimation: when he condescends to her, she attributes 'high ability' to him; when he disparages himself, her faith in him wavers too. There is also a more interesting instability here. The siblings offer contrasting but equally categorical judgements about each other's innate mental capacities; but ironically, both Nick and Biddy suspend judgement and invoke the criteria of time and effort when assessing themselves.

Nick's *Bildung* entails his effort to escape the paralysing effects of a reified, hereditarian conception of his own intelligence and to embrace an ideal of creative labour. At certain points James encourages us to read Nick's renunciation of his political career for the sake of art as an act of sublime masochism, the choice of a noble ascetic vocation over worldly success. However, James deprives Nick's choice of any obvious grandeur in that the novel never clarifies whether Nick's paintings are any good. It remains pointedly agnostic on the question, but suggests that Nick might, in fact, be a mediocrity, precisely because other people are too ready to pronounce his work 'clever'. If there is dignity in Nick's choice, we are encouraged to feel that it is because he exposes himself to the risk of humiliation and failure:

There were moments when he felt almost angry, [. . .] when by the few persons who saw [the paintings] they were pronounced wonderfully clever. That they were wonderfully clever was just the detestable thing in them, so active had that cleverness been in making them seem better than they were [. . .] he thought he saw as in an ugly revelation that nature had cursed him with an odious facility and that the lesson of his life, the sternest and wholesomest, would be to keep out of the trap it had laid for him [. . .] He was at all events too clever by half, since this pernicious overflow had wrecked most of his attempts [. . .].[77]

Nick's 'cleverness' is here posited as a fact of nature akin to a sexual impulse that must be sublimated for the sake of moral decency. Freedman notes that Nick's adoption of an artistic career is constructed as an 'acceptance of the professional work ethic', but this implies that the prevailing late nineteenth-century model of professionalism enshrined an ideal of humiliating slog, when, in fact, it tended to posit the professional as a mysterious interaction of latent ability and accumulated expertise.[78] Nick is always insisting that his desire to be an artist is perverse: he wants to be one because he thinks he has 'no talent' at it, and it will therefore entail a properly radical form of self-mortification.[79] This logic is framed partly in terms of the novel's pervasive 'rhetoric of testing':[80]

> The greatest time to do one's work was when it didn't seem worth doing, for then one gave it a brilliant chance, that of resisting the stiffest test of all – the test of striking one as too bad. To do the most when there would be the least to be got by it was to be most in the spirit of high production [. . .] Art was *doing* – it came back to that – which politics in most cases weren't.[81]

This representation of art as strenuous, ascetic *doing* calls to mind James Eli Adam's claim that the professionalisation of literature in the Victorian period often prompted male writers to represent their own writing as a form of heroic self-discipline compatible with normative ideals of masculinity.[82] Yet it is difficult to read Nick's vision of art as a form of masochistic *doing* as a self-legitimating gesture on James's part; if it is, it is an extraordinarily oblique one. Nick forfeits not just the idea of worldly success, but any compensatory Romantic ideal of the artist as suffering genius; he labours on not just in spite but because of the possibility that he has no talent. Nick embraces art because it grants him the opportunity to feel stupid, and as if he were condemned to a life of obscure, futile toil: he affirms 'I must go and sit down in a corner and learn my alphabet'; and at the end of the novel, he fantasises not about success but of 'an eternity of grinding'.[83] 'Doing' art is simultaneously Nick's effort to escape what he experiences as the burden of hereditary intelligence. Nick half-facetiously tells Gabriel that he wants to be an artist in spite of the fact that it means divesting himself of hereditary advantage: he has checked his genealogy carefully and found no examples of artistic 'eminence'.[84] It is telling that Nick uses Galton's favoured term, 'eminence', in the context of his family tree, since it is the Galtonian model of hereditary eminence that haunts Nick and which makes the artistic vocation seem to him an emancipation from 'family, [. . .] blood, [. . .] heredity, [. . .] traditions'.[85]

The art of getting your experience fast

So far I have emphasised that Nick associates 'cleverness' with his own class origins and with the aristocratic valorisation of being over doing. However, the term 'clever' also acquires an antithetical range of connotations in the novel: it is associated with commercialism, publicity, and the temporality of modernity. As Ronnell observes, intelligence is often measured by a 'technostandard': we assume that it is aligned with

> quick-wittedness, speed of comprehension – in general, with the high velocity of mind of our modernity. The mind capable of quick comprehension may be a calculative mind, agile in performing mechanical operations that, however, are not interiorised or broken but smooth and unproblematic in terms of the results they yield.[86]

It is frequently suggested that both Miriam's 'genius' and Nick's 'cleverness' consist of a capacity for rapid assimilation that thwarts their development of deep, individualised interiority – the traditional *telos* of the *Bildungsroman* form – and makes them exploitable as slick commodities. (Both characters are extensively 'stage-managed' by a range of patrons, mentors, and family members, and their degree of agency in their own careers is always obscure.) In the tradition of the *Bildungsroman*, 'intelligence', 'genius', or 'talent' is often the characteristic that justifies a protagonist's status as an exemplary hero or heroine and is associated with his or her capacity to cultivate an especially rich inner life.[87] Yet in *The Tragic Muse*, the mental capacities of the two key protagonists are in apparent tension with the humanistic assumptions of the ideal of *Bildung*: in the cases of both Nick and Miriam, the attribute of 'cleverness' threatens to empty out any kind of private inner life or sense of meaningful vocation. Nick's 'talent for appearance', his 'damnable suppleness' and 'gift of immediate response', propel him to electoral success in an age of expanding democracy, despite his utter lack of conviction and patrician disdain for his constituency.[88] This is another source of Nick's self-contempt: he regards the political system as 'humbuggery, hypocrisy and cant' precisely because he manages to 'get on fast' in it.[89] The novel is structured to highlight the parallels between democratic politics and the theatre, and like Miriam's success on the stage, Nick's electoral victory entails 'becom[ing] a spectacle to the vulgar'.[90] Similarly, James often prompts us to wonder if Miriam's much-touted 'genius' is merely an aptitude for self-commodification. Other characters suggest that Miriam succeeds because she is a chameleon without any underlying character or substance, and is therefore a fitting muse for a shallow, distractible modernity. Peter reflects of Miriam: 'to hear her you might have thought there was no cleverness anywhere but in her own splendid impatience'; he later remarks of her, 'she learned so fast [. . .] Genius is only the art of getting your experience fast.'[91] Like Nick, Miriam suspects that her success is meretricious and worries that it will undermine her capacity to take herself seriously as an artist.[92] Although Miriam eventually triumphs in the role of Juliet, there is the repeated suggestion that she is essentially preoccupied with managing her celebrity and is more truly suited to 'do[ing]' comic roles; she regards the 'art of comedian' as the 'most distinguished thing in the world'.[93] This gives a bitterly ironic flavour to James's choice of title: James implies that, in an 'age of publicity', the idea of tragedy is an anachronism, or is at least likely to be subordinated to 'clever' comedies; there is little patience for high seriousness and no real nobility in suffering.[94] 'You can't suffer for art,' Peter observes to Nick at one point. 'That grand romance is over.'[95]

This brings us to Wilde's place in the novel. The fact that the word 'cleverness' in this novel does duty for old aristocratic ideals, on the one hand, and modern forms of self-commodification, on the other, has an intelligible logic when it is remembered that the personification of 'cleverness' in this novel, Gabriel, is a thinly veiled Wilde. In a novel about artistic vocations, Gabriel is the only character with a decidedly literary bent: he is said to have written a 'very clever' novel, but he claims to have renounced all literary ambition, and now appears to live as a kind of Socratic dandy who will dispense his aphorisms only *in propria persona*, as unscheduled, one-off performances.[96] Like Wilde in the 1880s, Gabriel is essentially a professional talker: he lives to dazzle and provoke by his stream of perfectly turned phrases which at once draw attention to the theatricality of his own persona and, as Peter Brooks

notes, the 'staginess' of other characters.[97] Shelley Salamensky has
suggested that James's famous antipathy to Wilde can be traced in
part to the fact that Wilde's repartee left him tongue-tied; James
felt humiliated by one of Wilde's quips upon their first meeting and
thereafter distrusted Wilde's hyper-fluent talk, dismissing him as
'fatuous fool, a tenth-rate cad'.[98] The fact that Gabriel is the only
literary figure in this novel about the arts and even he has repudi-
ated writing in favour of 'clever' talk – talk which entrances some
of the characters but which is found 'fatuous' by others[99] – seems
to encode James's fear that Wilde's career adumbrated the fate
of the modern writer: the reduction of literature to clever slogans
and of the writer to an amusing but marginal personality. The fact
that Nick's portrait of Gabriel seems to Nick to fade mysteriously
has been read as a sign of Gabriel's queer elusiveness, his capacity
to resist conventional representation and float free of the determinants of identity[100]; yet it may also be read in more pessimistic
terms, as a symbol of the attenuation of the novelist in a debased,
spectacle-driven culture.

At the end of the novel, Miriam, the poor, supposedly 'stupid'
actress, is fêted as a genius; Nick, the 'clever' aristocrat, has
embraced art because it enables him to feel like a 'poor clumsy
beginner' and to experience a kind of imaginary *déclassement*.[101]
The fact that James tells their vocation narratives according to
two incommensurable representational logics – one realist, one
theatrical – deprives us of stable grounds for interpreting these
ironic reversals; we cannot examine Miriam and Nick by a
common standard. James's refusal to arbitrate among the cacoph-
ony of judgements about Nick's and Miriam's mental worth and
to clarify if either of them have genuine talent for their chosen
vocations underscores the novel's wider project of interrogating
the complicity of aesthetic discourses in facile and potentially
oppressive measurements of intelligence and merit. In a novel in
which most of the characters are in a rush to deliver summary
judgements about the mental worth of others, it is a minor, apparently 'stupid' character, Mrs Rooth – Miriam's mother – who
articulates the perplexity that the reader reasonably feels, and
poses the question that we might wish to ask of James:

> 'Dear me, if he isn't clever you must tell us: we can't afford to be
> deceived!' Mrs. Rooth innocently wailed. 'What do we know – how
> can we judge?' she appealed.

[Peter] had a pause, his hand on the latch. 'Oh, I'll tell you frankly what I think of him!'[102]

As so often in this novel, the question of intelligence is a financially interested one here: Mrs Rooth cannot *afford* to be wrong in her speculations about it. Yet this apparently trivial moment is also charged with more complex implications. James prompts us to entertain the possibility that Mrs Rooth is herself a talented actress and not, in fact, the vacuous stage-mother she is generally taken for: she might be playing dumb here in order to trap Peter into exposing his overweening faith in his own intellect and thereby ensure that Miriam marries Basil, the person whose intelligence is in doubt. One way of reading the novel is that Mrs Rooth manages her daughter's career and love life with consummate artfulness. On this reading, Mrs Rooth only appears to be a peripheral, dim-witted character; she is, in fact, the ingenious architect of a substantial part of the plot. James gives us no good grounds for judging whether her stupidity is actually artful, except for the fact that Mrs Rooth is usually 'in the wings' of any scenes in which Miriam appears and that she gets what she appears to want. This epistemological wormhole is comic, a counter-narrative briefly opened up but not explored. It nonetheless reflects James's larger effort to keep the question of the intelligence of every character – even the apparently minor, foolish ones –in play.[103]

James, rather than seeking to make the novel form an instrument for adjudicating differences in intelligence, uses it as a means of staging the incalculable complexities embedded in such judgements. Although *The Tragic Muse* finds comedy in the hypocrisies and confusions generated by the modern preoccupation with evaluating mental ability, in James's late, major-phase novels, *The Wings of the Dove* (1902), *The Ambassadors* (1903), and *The Golden Bowl* (1904), the moral stakes of not thinking anyone stupid – of sustaining a paranoid agnosticism about everyone's intelligence – are much higher. James's interrogation of late nineteenth-century constructions of intelligence in *The Tragic Muse* is primarily a critique of the idea that true art conceals art – that is, that it conceals mental labour and projects easeful 'cleverness'. At the end of novel, it is far from clear that Nick will be able to sustain his ideal of art as a form of ascetic labour which resists not only the temptations of the marketplace but the temptations of 'cleverness': we learn that he has exhibited a 'noble' portrait of his former patron, Lady Julia Dallow, which perhaps indicates that his art has been co-opted by the political establishment he sought to escape.[104] Yet Nick's earlier model of art as masochistic, impotent *doing* in the absence not only of hope for success but of belief in his mental gifts is the novel's only gesture toward fulfilling the promise of 'tragedy' held out in the title.

Notes

1 Henry James, *Autobiography: A Small Boy and Others, Notes of a Son and Brother*, and *The Middle Years*, ed. Frederick W. Dupee (London: W. H. Allen, 1956), pp. 127–9.

2 Ibid., p. 129.

3 Mark McGurl, *The Novel Art: Elevations of American Fiction After Henry James* (Princeton, NJ: Princeton University Press, 2001), p. 75.

4 Ibid., p. 75.

5 Ibid., p. 65.

6 Ibid., p. 75.

7 Henry James, *The Spoils of Poynton* (London: Penguin, 1963), p. 126.

8 Ibid., p. 111.

9 Ibid., p. 186 and p. 40.

10 Jonathan Freedman, *Professions of Taste: Henry James, British Aestheticism and Commodity Culture* (Stanford, CA: Stanford University Press, 1993), p. 160.

11 James, *Spoils of Poynton*, p. 125.

12 The word 'clever' appears twenty-four times and 'stupid' ten times in *Roderick Hudson* (Oxford: Oxford University Press, 1980). As in *The Tragic Muse*, 'cleverness' is often used as a term for artistic talent in this novel, but also as an unspecific trait, detached from any particular skill or activity, though clearly associated with the glamour of wealth and refinement. For the former usage, see p. 157; for the latter, see p. 285.

13 For an account of the cultural politics of merit, talent, and intelligence in nineteenth- and early twentieth-century American culture, see Carson, *The Measure of Merit*.

14 Ibid., p. 166.

15 William James, 'Great Men, Great Thoughts, and the Environment', *Atlantic Monthly* 46 (1880), pp. 441–59; John Fiske, 'Sociology

and Hero-worship: An Evolutionist's Reply to Dr. James', *Atlantic Monthly* 47 (1881); and Grant Allen, 'The Genesis of Genius', *Atlantic Monthly* 47 (1881), pp. 371–81; Allen, 'Idiosyncrasy', *Popular Science Monthly* 24 (1884), pp. 387–403; and Allen, 'Genius and Talent', *Popular Science Monthly* 34 (1889), pp. 341–56.

16 William James, p. 459.

17 Henry James to William James, 13 November 1880, in *William and Henry James: Selected Letters*, ed. Ignas K. Skrupskelis and Elizabeth M. Berkeley (Charlottesville: University Press of Virginia, 1997), p. 128.

18 James, *Spoils of Poynton*, p. 111.

19 Matthew Sussman, 'Henry James and Stupidity', *Novel* 48 (2015), 45–62, p. 48.

20 Freedman, p. 182.

21 Henry James, *The Tragic Muse*, ed. Philip Horne (London: Penguin, 1995), p. 307.

22 Ibid., 'Preface', p. 9.

23 The word 'clever' appears 103 times and the word 'stupid' 31 times in *The Tragic Muse*.

24 As David Garrett Izzo suggests, James's Gabriel is 'Walter Pater as interpreted by Oscar Wilde'. See Garrett Izzo, 'A Pair of Afterwords', in *Henry James Against the Aesthetic Movement: Essays on the Middle and Late Fiction*, ed. Garrett Izzo and David T. O'Hara (Jefferson, NC: McFarland, 2006), 229–38, p. 229.

25 James, *Tragic Muse*, p. 49.

26 Walter Pater, *Appreciations* (London: Macmillan, 1889), p. 61; and Richard Salmon, 'Aestheticism in Translation: Henry James, Walter Pater, and Theodor Adorno', in *Translating Life: Studies in Transpositional Aesthetics*, ed. Shirley Chew and Alistair Stead (Liverpool: Liverpool University Press, 1999), 277–98, p. 289.

27 James, *Tragic Muse*, p. 49.

28 Ruth, pp. 4–5.

29 James, *Tragic Muse*, p. 93.

30 Ibid., p. 87.

31 Ibid., p. 93.

32 Ibid., p. 86.

33 Ibid., pp. 93–4.

34 The instability of Madame Carré's assertions is also produced by what Harold Perkin identifies as the essentially 'fiduciary' nature of professional expertise: 'the professional is [. . .] offering a service

that is [. . .] esoteric, evanescent, and fiduciary – beyond the lay-man's knowledge or judgment, impossible to pin down or fault even when it fails, and which must therefore be taken on trust'. See Perkin, *The Rise of Professional Society: England Since 1880* (London: Routledge, 1989), p. 117.

35 James, *Tragic Muse,* p. 86.

36 Ibid., p. 92, p. 110, p. 128, p. 129, p. 146, p. 147, p. 94, p. 127, and p. 150.

37 Ibid., p. 259.

38 Ibid., p. 147.

39 Ibid.

40 Ibid., p. 89.

41 Ibid., p. 139.

42 For an analysis of the unstable significations of Miriam's Jewishness, see Sara Blair, *Henry James and the Writing of Race and Nation* (Cambridge: Cambridge University Press, 1996), pp. 123–57.

43 Ibid., p. 49.

44 For an analysis of the nineteenth-century currency of the stereo-type of Jewish intellectual superiority, see Sander L. Gilman, *Smart Jews: The Construction of the Image of Jewish Superior Intelligence* (Lincoln: University of Nebraska Press, 1997).

45 Lucien Wolf, 'What is Judaism?: A Question of Today', *Fortnightly Review* (1884), 237–56, p. 241. Gilman's analysis drew my atten-tion to this article; see Gilman, p. 71.

46 Wolf, 'What is Judaism?

47 Joseph Jacobs, 'The Comparative Distribution of Jewish Ability', *Journal of the Anthropological Institute of Great Britain and Ireland* 15 (1886), 351–79, p. 361.

48 Ibid., p. 357 and pp. 365–6.

49 Shuman, p. 3.

50 Ibid., pp. 88–9.

51 For a recent discussion of James's preoccupation with the theat-ricality of social life, see Maya Higashi Wakana's *Performing the Everyday in Henry James's Late Novels* (Farnham: Ashgate, 2013).

52 James, *Tragic Muse,* p. 111.

53 Ibid., p. 66.

54 Ibid., p. 211, p. 215, and p. 307.

55 Ibid., p. 66.

56 For a discussion of how the courtly ideal of *sprezzatura* survived in the nineteenth- and early twentieth-century conceptions of gen-tlemanliness, see Christine Berberich, *The Image of the English*

Gentleman in Twentieth-Century Literature (Farnham: Ashgate, 2013), pp. 16–17.

57 James, *Tragic Muse*, pp. 218–19.

58 Though often attributed to Ovid or Horace, the origin of '*ars celare artem*' is unknown. For the link between the tag and the ideal of *sprezzatura*, see Heinrich F. Plett, *Rhetoric and Renaissance Culture* (Berlin: Walter de Gruyter, 2004), p. 424.

59 Avital Ronnell, *Stupidity* (Urbana and Chicago: University of Illinois Press, 2002), p. 10.

60 James, *Tragic Muse*, p. 265.

61 Ibid., p. 126 and p. 218.

62 Ibid., p. 269.

63 Darwin, pp. 236–7.

64 Ibid., p. 315.

65 John Carlos Rowe, *The Other Henry James* (Durham, NC: Duke University Press, 1998), pp. 84–5.

66 Ibid., p. 385.

67 Richard Dellamora's reading of the novel helpfully situates it in relation to the ideological fragmentation of the Liberal Party in the late nineteenth century. See Dellamora, *Friendship's Bonds: Democracy and the Novel in Victorian England* (Philadelphia: University of Pennsylvania Press, 2004), pp. 153–77.

68 James, *Tragic Muse*, p. 198.

69 Ibid., p. 155 and p. 101.

70 Ibid., p. 194.

71 The appositeness of J. L. Austin's concept of performatives, and of speech act theory more broadly (particularly as it was developed by Paul de Man, Jacques Derrida, and Judith Butler), to reading James's fiction has been established by Eve Kosofsky Sedgwick and J. Hillis Miller. See Sedgwick, *Touching Feeling: Affect, Pedagogy, Performativity* (Durham, NC: Duke University Press, 2002), pp. 35–66; and J. Hillis Miller, *Literature as Conduct: Speech Acts in Henry James* (New York: Fordham University Press, 2005).

72 Eve Kosofsky Sedgwick and Andrew Miller highlight the complex links between the concept of 'performatives' in speech act theory and performance in the theatrical sense in their editors' introduction to *Performativity and Performance* (London: Routledge, 1995), p. 8.

73 Bourdieu writes, 'Aristocracies are essentialist. [But] the same essentialism requires them to impose on themselves what their essence

imposes on them – noblesse oblige – to ask of themselves what no one else could ask, to "live up" to their own essence.' See Pierre Bourdieu, *Distinction: A Social Critique of the Judgment of Taste*, trans. Richard Nice (London: Routledge, 2000), p. 16.

74 I am indebted here to Ruth's analysis of the relationship between financial speculation and the emerging nineteenth-century conception of intelligence as an innate capacity that can be detected by written examinations. See Ruth, p. 63, pp. 68–70.

75 James, *Tragic Muse*, p. 25.

76 Ibid., p. 26.

77 Ibid., p. 450.

78 See Freedman, p. 186; and Ruth, pp. 3–5.

79 James, *Tragic Muse*, p. 182.

80 I borrow this phrase from Ronnell; see *Stupidity*, pp. 95–163.

81 James, *Tragic Muse*, p. 393.

82 James Eli Adams, *Dandies and Desert Saints: Styles of Victorian Masculinity* (Ithaca, NY: Cornell University Press, 1995). See especially pp. 107–48.

83 James, *Tragic Muse*, p. 398 and p. 468

84 Ibid., p. 122.

85 Ibid.

86 Ronnell, p. 300.

87 As Christiane Gannon observes, the protagonist of the *Bildungsroman* is often an artist or a genius who is capable of developing an exceptional kind of private interiority. See Gannon, 'Walter Besant's Democratic Bildungsroman', *Narrative* 22 (2014), 372–94, p. 377.

88 James, *Tragic Muse*, p. 450.

89 Ibid., p. 255 and p. 399.

90 Ibid., p. 169.

91 Ibid., p. 314 and p. 311.

92 Ibid., p. 466.

93 Ibid., p. 314 and p. 232.

94 Ibid., p. 346.

95 Ibid., p. 397.

96 Ibid., p. 31.

97 Peter Brooks, *Henry James Goes to Paris* (Princeton, NJ: Princeton University Press, 2008), p. 81.

98 Qtd in Shelley Salamensky, 'Henry James, Oscar Wilde, and "*Fin de Siècle* Talk": A Brief Reading', *Henry James Review* 20 (1999), 275–81, p. 275.

99 James, *Tragic Muse*, p. 113.

100 See Eric Haralson, *Henry James and Queer Modernity* (Cambridge: Cambridge University Press, 2003), pp. 74–6.

101 James, *Tragic Muse*, p. 420.

102 Ibid., pp. 211–12.

103 My thinking is influenced here by Woloch's theorisation of how the 'distribution' of attention among major and minor characters structures our experience of narrative. Woloch suggests that nineteenth-century realist novels often highlight the anti-democratic implications of their granting psychological depth to a particular protagonist at the cost of consigning other, perhaps equally worthy, protagonists to the status of 'minor', flat characters. See Woloch, pp. 30–2.

104 James, *Tragic Muse*, p. 491.

4

H. G. Wells's Very Ordinary Brains

In H. G. Wells's 1901 scientific romance, *The First Men in the Moon*, the Grand Lunar, the super-intelligent ruler of a race of moon aliens, is perplexed when he learns about the human institution of democracy. Do human beings really possess no means of distinguishing between superior and inferior minds, and organising their civilisation accordingly? The superiority of the Grand Lunar's own intellect to those of his subjects is incontrovertible: he has no skull, and so the many 'ghost[ly]' 'undulating' convolutions of his brain are visible.[1] As Anne Stiles has noted, Wells was here drawing upon the hypothesis that more numerous brain convolutions indicate higher intelligence.[2] Yet Cavor, the novel's scientist protagonist, has to confess that human intellectual inequality, however profound, has no obvious physical referent:

> 'It is all hidden in the brain', I said, 'but the difference was there. Perhaps if one could see the minds and souls of men they would be as varied and unequal as the Selenites [the race of aliens who inhabit the moon]. There were great men and small men, men who could reach out far and wide, and men who could go swiftly; noisy, trumpet-minded men, and men who could remember without thinking . . .'
> He interrupted me [. . .] 'But you said all men rule?'
> 'To a certain extent', I said, and made, I fear, a denser fog with my explanation.[3]

Throughout his writing career, Wells attempted to modernise Plato's dream of a beautiful city ruled by philosopher kings. In both his fiction and his sociological treatises, he fantasised about a World State devoted to the principles of socialism and scientific rationality and administered by a small, rigorously selected cognitive elite. Although Wells was only briefly a member of the Fabian Society, his faith in the 'coming predominance of the man of science, the trained professional expert' and in meritocratic elitism clearly accords with the thinking of Beatrice and Sidney Webb and with the spirit of Fabian socialism in general.[4] For Wells, abolishing democracy in favour of a kind of noocracy or geniocracy (government by the wise or intellectually gifted) followed logically from any honest reckoning with the starkness of natural human inequality, a notion which he took to be undeniable in the light of Darwinian science:

> As [Darwin's theory of natural selection] has been more and more thoroughly assimilated and understood by the general mind, it has destroyed, quietly but entirely, the belief in human equality which is implicit in all the 'Liberalizing' movements of the world [. . .] It has become apparent that whole masses of the human population are, as a whole, inferior in their claim upon the future, to other masses, that they cannot be given opportunities or trusted with power as the superior peoples are trusted, that their characteristic weaknesses are contagious and detrimental in the civilizing fabric, and that their range of incapacity tempts and demoralises the strong.[5]

This quotation is from Wells's bestselling treatise, *Anticipations*. This work of speculative sociology, published in the same year as *The First Men in the Moon* and marking his debut as a social commentator, is Wells at his most chillingly doctrinaire. It is the work which supplies John Carey with the most damning evidence for his thesis that Wells's imagination is pathologically elitist, fired by a hatred for ordinary humanity and the eugenicist's passion for 'getting rid of people'.[6] Yet Carey also highlights what he takes to be Wells's redeeming inconsistency: even as Wells divides humanity into superior and inferior types and entertains negative eugenics in his theoretical writings and scientific romances, his comic-realist novels of the fin de siècle and Edwardian period – *The Wheels of Chance* (1896), *Love and Mr. Lewisham* (1900), *Kipps* (1905), *Tono-Bungay* (1909), and *The History of Mr. Polly* (1910) – are grounded in a warm egalitarianism, or at least in a sense of affinity with the lower middle class into which Wells himself was born. Carey's split assessment of Wells's work (he deals with Wells across two dialectically opposed essays in his *Intellectuals and the Masses*) is a means of negotiating the fact that Wells, despite his commitment to logic and system-building, was a mercurial thinker who adopted contradictory positions not only over the course of his long career but often within given texts.[7] This chapter argues that the primary source of Wells's contradictions is actually the rigour with which he interrogated his primary obsession: human intelligence, and the extent to which it can be measured, ranked, and optimised.

Wells was not completely sure that he belonged to the caste of superior intellects that he deemed fit to rule the world. His 1935 autobiography was subtitled 'Discoveries and Conclusions of a Very Ordinary Brain (Since 1866)'. In it, Wells treats his own brain as an object of scientific enquiry and interprets his life as a series of experiments that tested its powers. Rather than reflecting upon the origins of his psychology or personality, as we might expect at the opening of an autobiography, Wells speculates about the quality of his brain anatomy and how his mental abilities might be judged in relation to population averages:

> The brain upon which my experiences have been written is not a particularly good one. If there were brain-shows, as there are cat and dog shows, I doubt if it would get even a third-class prize. Upon quite a number of points it would be marked below the average [. . .] In relation to everyday people with no claim to mental distinction I still find it at a disadvantage. All this indicates a loose rather inferior mental texture, inexact reception, bad storage and uncertain accessibility [. . .] I know practically nothing of brain structure and physiology, but it seems probable [. . .] the general shape and arrangement of my brain is better than the quality of its cells, fibres and blood-vessels [. . .].[8]

Wells evidently takes a perverse pleasure in assessing – and denigrating — himself from the estranging perspective of the biopolitics of intelligence. (Indeed, in his secret and more candid 'postscript' to his published autobiography, *H. G. Wells in Love*, Wells even turns the language of eugenics against himself as a way of articulating his 'conviction' of his own 'unworthiness': 'Sometimes I realise something in myself so silly, fitful, and entirely inadequate to opportunity, that I feel even by own my standards I am not fit to live.'[9]) Although – as we shall see – Wells was sceptical of Galton's eugenic proposals for raising the national level of intelligence, he thoroughly absorbed Galton's biopolitical premise: intelligence is a natural resource that societies must foster and manage, and an individual's mind derives its value from its relationship to a population average. Thus, when looking back over his life, Wells feels that the most compelling question is how his innate mental capacities compare to those of the average person; and thus the question at the centre of his sociological works is how the intelligence of the human species might be harnessed and improved. His most insistent answers to the latter question are socialism and education rather than eugenics, but – as Carey has shown – Wells's discussions of the utopian potential of education are shadowed by a pessimism about the educability of the masses, and sometimes by his attraction to eugenic solutions.[10] Wells always considered his own experience of meritocratic social mobility as a testament to the grandly transformative powers of education – he escaped the deprivations of his lower-middle-class origins and his miserable apprenticeship to a draper by winning a scholarship to study under Thomas Huxley at the Normal School of Science in South Kensington. However, Wells's comic-realist novels of the fin de siècle and Edwardian period interrogate the costs and the justice of the meritocratic ideal and are imaginatively allied with meritocracy's losers and others: the mediocre students; the badly educated; the lazy, pleasure-seeking, and feckless; and those classified as 'ineducable' and 'feeble-minded'.

Wells's insistence on the mediocrity of his brain in his *Autobiography* reveals the complexity of his investment in the biopolitical model of intelligence. The purpose of the autobiography of a famous writer is presumably to cast light on the origins and development of his or her creativity and accomplishments. But this is just the expectation that Wells is determined to disappoint: at every turn, he seeks to demystify, even to belittle, his own mental capacities. This is not, or at least not simply, due to modesty: in fact, Wells disclaims that he is at all modest, and insofar as he takes credit for his own success, he attributes it to his 'very obstinate self-conceit'.[11] It is more crucially a disorienting effect of Wells's effort to apply his political and scientific theories to the case of his own life. The socialist in Wells is determined not to cast his experience of social mobility as evidence of his exceptional merits. Wells despised the 'superstition that "genius will out" in spite of all discouragement'.[12] He writes:

The fact that great men have risen against crushing disadvantages proves nothing of the sort: this roll-call of survivors does no more than give the measure of the enormous waste of human possibility human stupidity has achieved.[13]

Accordingly, Wells attributes his success to 'chance and opportunity' rather than any kind of uncommon talent or virtue, and emphasises that his brothers and some of his schoolfriends possessed equal or superior intellectual potential to his but were not so lucky.[14] Equally, Wells is determined to avoid turning his life into a Smilesian fable about the fruits of hard work: although he acknowledges that he was a diligent student at certain points in his life, he also emphasises that he was inconsistent and prone to distraction and 'indolen[ce]'.[15] Instead, Wells highlights the importance of a leg injury he sustained has a child, which left him bed-bound for weeks and created the conditions for him to develop a love of reading.[16]

Wells's at once political and scientific commitment to foregrounding the contingencies of his career extends to his analysis of his mental aptitudes. He suggests that he owed his success in competitive examinations – the means of ascending the coveted rungs of the scholarship ladder – less to any kind of absolute mental gift but to what might be considered a fortuitous defect: he claims to have an innate 'coldness and flatness' in his sensory perceptions (attributable, he thinks, to his brain anatomy) that made it easy for him to grasp general ideas and to think systematically.[17] He goes so far as to assert that his aptitude at school actually reflects a kind of congenital dullness – 'I was easy to educate', he claims, because of a 'relative defect in my brightness of response'.[18]

Wells's emphasis upon the relative and contingent nature of his mental abilities partly reflects how scrupulously he had internalised Darwin's theory of evolution. He was critical of Galton's eugenics because he thought it was impossible to determine 'what points we ought to breed for and what points to breed out'; in the case of intellectual ability, he emphasised the instability and ambiguity of the qualities which come to be recognised as 'ability' in a given context.[19] Thus he suggests that his particular mental attributes turned out to constitute Darwinian fitness in the context of the 'queer discontinuous educational processes' of late Victorian England, but resists the idea that they amount to any kind of essential genius.[20]

Wells's will to demystify his own mental abilities in his *Autobiography* also reflects his suspicion of the influence of a quasi-aristocratic ideal of aesthetic sensibility upon modern conceptions of intelligence. His emphasis upon the mechanical, unglamorous nature of his own abilities is polemical: it is an effort to vindicate the value of scientific thinking over Romantic claims for the creative imagination or the aesthete's claims to refined perceptions; more particularly, it is an effort to assert that scientific minds like his own can make distinctive contributions to literature. In this way, Wells's autobiography of his brain is entangled in his long-running debates with Henry James and Joseph Conrad over the nature of art and the purpose of the novel. Wells attempts to make the terms of those aesthetic debates a matter of brain differences: he claims that while Conrad and James demonstrate the hyper-receptivity and unruliness of the artistic mind, he possesses the comparatively stolid type of mind that is easy to subject to the disciplines of education and scientific thought.[21] Although the autobiography was composed between 1932 and 1934, Wells is here reacting to the prominence of the category of 'sense-impressions' in late Victorian and Edwardian efforts to devise a scientific theory of intelligence. As noted in the previous chapter, the assumptions of the intelligence testing movement in the late Victorian period aligned with those of aestheticism and decadence in a crucial respect: both imagined that sensory acuity was correlated with, or actually was a form of, intelligence. Wells accepts this aesthetico-scientific model of intelligence and the aestheticist (and proto-modernist) ideal of art associated with it but seeks to offer a countervailing model, which he calls the 'educated' mind.

Wells's belief that his only special mental gift was the relatively 'ordinary' one of being 'easy to educate' reflects the extent to which his thinking was shaped by the distinction between the 'educable' and 'ineducable' that became culturally potent following the Education Act of 1870 and which, as I have noted, became charged with eugenicist implications in the 1880s and 1890s. Like Galton and his followers, as well as many later proponents of intelligence testing, Wells conceives of 'educability' as a 'mainly innate' biological trait.[22] Although Wells believed that most people's intellectual capacities were wasted or perverted by the world's political and education systems, he did not believe that an individual's level of intelligence was itself alterable: one is born with fixed mental capacities. More, like Galton and the intelligence testers, Wells believed that examinations could test not simply what one had learned but one's underlying ability to learn. In his 1905 treatise-novel, *A Modern Utopia*, the ruling 'Samurai' class – essentially a technocratic priesthood – are selected partly through a system of competitive examinations.[23] These examinations are not designed to capture intellectual brilliance but 'normal[cy]' and 'teachability': qualities aligned with the 'Kinetic' class, one of the two classes eligible to become Samurai.[24] In contrast to the 'Poietic' or creative class, the Kinetic class are 'clever' and 'capable' people with a 'restricted' and 'unoriginal' imagination.[25] As his *Autobiography* make clear, Wells prized examinations because he believed that they effectively tested a person's capacity to marshal and order information.[26] Wells's notion of the 'educated mind' is essentially a computational theory of the mind, though he posits it as an ideal type of mind rather than a general theory of how minds work: it is the type of brain which is efficient at information processing. Although he readily acknowledged that computation is not the only form of intelligence – *A Modern Utopia* also privileges the 'poietic' mind – he valorised it because he believed it was instrumental to his creation of a modern utopia: that is, a technocratic socialist World State. In his *Autobiography*, he even likens his own mind to a well-functioning government bureau: it is 'narrow, centralised, economical and exacting'.[27]

Wells's relentlessly unromantic portrait of his own brain – over the course of the autobiography, it is 'ordinary', 'narrow', 'feeble and inert', 'dull', 'slow' and 'wriggling', rather 'inferior in texture and anatomy' – precisely conforms to the modernist caricature of the petit bourgeois intellect that Carey anatomises so unsparingly.[28] Yet while Carey rightly acknowledges that Wells was torn between elitist and egalitarian impulses, he treats this as a simple contradiction or form of 'imaginative duplicity', and does not recognise the extent to which Wells mobilised his sense of identification with the lower middle classes to interrogate his own dreams of an intellectual elite.[29] All of the banality and intellectual limitations that Carey indicts modernist writers for ascribing to the suburban masses, to clerks, to 'cramming' lower-class scholarship students, and to 'half-educated' autodidacts, Wells embraces as his own in his autobiography. This might be interpreted as evidence of a strain of class-based shame or self-loathing in Wells, or at least indicate how far he had internalised the often snobbish critiques of his novels mounted by James, Conrad, and Woolf.[30] Yet Wells is also clearly undertaking a transvaluation of values: he believed that many of his apparently 'common' and 'inferior' mental characteristics would be recognised as marks of intellectual superiority, or at least considered eminently useful, in the scientific utopia to come. In this way, Wells's preoccupation with utopian futures injects an element of relativism into the biological determinism undergirding his model of human intelligence: what is considered a merely 'ordinary' brain in the present may be valued very differently in the near future. Further, Wells's acute sensitivity to the presence of class distinctions in modern ideas of talent and intellectual ability always destabilised his own dreams of a perfectly meritocratic society, and meant that he could not arrive at a definition of intelligence that satisfied him.

Wells's consciousness of the difficulties of disentangling the category of intelligence from class prejudices is apparent in his 1896 short story, 'A Slip under the Microscope'. Superficially, the story is a critique of the partial and dysfunctional nature of late Victorian meritocracy.[31] It concerns a working-class scholarship student at a college of science who we know only by his surname, Hill. (The college is clearly based on Wells's *alma mater*, the Normal School of Science.) Hill is engaged in at once intellectual and romantic rivalry with another student, the upper-class Wedderburn: they compete for academic honours as well as for the attentions of a female student, Miss Haysman. Initially, Hill's socialist convictions enable him to experience the rivalry as a form of class warfare in which he is the righteous underdog; Wedderburn's class privileges only reinforce Hill's burning sense of personal worth. Then Hill – perhaps inadvertently – gains an unfair advantage in a botany exam when he looks at the concealed section of a specimen on a slide that was intended to test the students' microscope skills. Hill subsequently beats Wedderburn in the exam, but the possibility that he did so only because he cheated haunts him and corrodes his self-respect. He confesses to a professor in the belief that he will simply have a mark deducted from his exam result, but instead he loses his scholarship and thus his chance at a scientific career. The professor expresses sympathy but also pontificates about the fact that Hill's expulsion from the college illustrates the blind justice of meritocracy. In a concluding twist, there is a heavy hint that Wedderburn also cheated in the exam but experienced no equivalent twinges of conscience.

On the most obvious level, 'A Slip under the Microscope' exposes the cruelly ironic effects of the meritocratic ideal when it is grafted on to systemic social inequalities: the cobbler's son, Hill, internalises the ideal with puritanical rigour and so ruins his chances, while the doctor's son, Wedderburn, apparently succeeds because he has no compunction about rigging the system in his favour. What appears to be an objective test of the two men's intellectual merits is confounded not simply by material inequalities but by those inscribed in the moral psychology of class. However, the fact that we do not know for certain if either or both Hill and Wedderburn cheated means that the story's social critique goes beyond the effort to expose the tendency of meritocracy to reinforce existing social hierarchies. Hill's uncertainty about whether he intentionally slipped the slide cover prompts us to wonder if Wedderburn's intentions and degree of moral agency would seem equally opaque if the story also granted us access to his mind. This aporia in the plot underscores that the effects of class reach too deeply into the imponderable realms of psychology to be detectable under the 'microscope' of meritocracy, to borrow the story's central metaphor. Wells encourages us to perceive the incommensurability of scientific and social experiments: the apparently meritocratic technology of the competitive examination cannot control for all the ambiguous and irrational effects of the class system.

It is notable that Wells's story only prompts us to consider the drama of meritocratic competition through the prism of class; although the science college's progressive ethos extends to admitting female students, the question of how gender inequalities might compromise the meritocratic ideal is beyond the story's ideological horizon. The college's female students, and Miss Haysman in particular, are not emancipated intellectuals but purveyors of retrograde class distinctions; their function in the story is to highlight that sexuality is another confounding variable in any meritocratic contest between lower- and upper-class men. Wells's narrator ironises Miss Haysman's fancy that 'men's activities are determined by women's attitudes', but it is, in fact, her bourgeois social pretensions that divert the two men's rivalry from the empirical realm of science exams into an insidious contest over cultural capital, a contest that Hill can only lose.[32] Although Hill is a rationalist with a proud contempt for metaphysics and all 'loose ideas', Miss Haysman renders him susceptible to the religion of art, and he embarks on a programme of poetry reading in an effort to impress her.[33] The narrator underscores the futility of Hill's bid at literary self-culture by clarifying the thoroughly material basis of Miss Haysman's aestheticism: 'Although [Miss Haysman] did not know it, [the aesthetic side of life] meant good wall paper and upholstery, pretty books, tasteful clothes, concerts and meals nicely cooked and respectfully served.'[34] She simultaneously undermines Hill's socialist convictions by suggesting that Wedderburn has inherited his aptitude for science from his doctor father, which in turn leads Hill to wonder if Wedderburn's class privileges are not arbitrary but proof of a natural superiority. Wells here captures the demoralising effects of the hard hereditarian discourses about intelligence. Miss Haysman's casual biological determinism makes a tautology of Hill's objections to hereditary privilege:

> She told Hill that she had met [Wedderburn] at the house of some people she knew, and 'he's inherited his cleverness; for his father, you know, is the great eye-specialist.
>
> 'My father is a cobbler,' said Hill, quite irrelevantly, and perceived the want of dignity even as he said it. [. . .] He suffered bitterly from a sense of Wedderburn's unfairness, and a realisation of his own handicap. Here was this Wedderburn who had picked up a prominent man for a father, and instead of losing so many marks on the score of that advantage, it was counted to him for righteousness![35]

The spectres of aestheticism and biological determinism raised by Miss Haysman appear to undermine Hill's belief in his intellectual ability and thereby to create the psychological conditions for him to cheat in the exam. Alternatively, perhaps Miss Haysman's logic leads Hill to experience his class position as a form of moral inferiority, which in turn prompts him to experience an excessive sense of guilt over an involuntary 'slip'. Either way, the story highlights how the late Victorian biologisation and moralisation of class renders intellectual ability a fugitive category, even within an apparently rigorous system of competitive examinations.

The sloughs of monotonous mediocrity: *Love and Mr. Lewisham*

'A Slip under the Microscope' formed the kernel of Wells's 1900 novel, *Love and Mr. Lewisham*. Like its precursor story, *Love and Mr. Lewisham* centres upon a lower-middle-class young man who gains and then loses a scholarship to study at the Normal School of Science and whose *Bildung* exemplifies the broken promises of late Victorian meritocracy. Disappointed that the novel was not another scientific romance but a realist *Bildungsroman*, the reviewer at the *Saturday Review* complained that it contains 'not the slightest deviation from the sloughs of monotonous mediocrity, never even the promise of a promise'.[36] This remark captures the novel's determination to disappoint not just the meritocratic hopes of its protagonist but the meritocratic hopes the narrative of an earnest scholarship boy inevitably inspires in the reader. As Simon James notes, *Love and Mr. Lewisham* is clearly Wells's homage to Hardy's *Jude the Obscure*.[37] When Wells reviewed *Jude the Obscure* in 1896, he celebrated it for capturing

[the almost intolerable difficulties that beset the ambitious man of the working class – the snares, the obstacles, the countless rejections and humiliations [. . .] The man of the lower class who aspires to knowledge can only escape frustration by ruthlessly suppressing affections and passions; it is a choice of one tragedy or another.[38]

Like *Jude the Obscure*, *Love and Mr. Lewisham* highlights the 'embittering' fact that lower-class men must sacrifice either their aspirations for upward mobility or their sexuality, since the latter leads inexorably to marriage and children and so to economic entrapment within their own class.[39] And like *Jude the Obscure*, *Love and Mr. Lewisham* uses this plot to critique the puritanical and disciplinary essence of meritocratic striving for lower-class men, which turns out to be not a fulfilment but an impoverishment of the self. However, *Love and Mr. Lewisham* repeats the history of *Jude the Obscure* not as tragedy but as farce, and its ultimate attitude to failure is more sanguine: Wells suggests that late Victorian meritocracy is so tainted and punitive that it may be a happier fate to 'fail hopelessly' than to succeed.[40]

At the start of the novel, Mr Lewisham is an eighteen-year-old pupil-teacher at a minor private school in Sussex, Whortley Proprietary School. As Jonathan Franklin points out, Lewisham has so thoroughly interiorised his professional identity that he is only ever 'Mr Lewisham': 'as with all good teachers, [Lewisham] maintains such an affective distance we never discover his first name'.[41] Yet this affective distance signals not so much a desire to hold himself aloof from others but the depth of his self-estrangement:

Mr Lewisham is an awkwardly formal teacher, even in private and in relation to himself. Lewisham is committed to an ascetic programme of self-education in addition to his teaching duties, and appears to have no friends, family, or meaningful relationships. His only company is his ego-ideal: the future, greater versions of Mr Lewisham he intends to educate into being. He has plotted out his 'career to Greatness' in what he calls his 'Schema': his plan for obtaining a scholarship, completing a BA at London University, and launching himself as a journalist or politician 'in the Liberal interest', worked out into a timetable in which every waking minute (including mealtimes) is turned to academic account.[42]

Lewisham's programme of study is partly redolent of the Romantic tradition of *Bildung*. Lewisham has devised a broad curriculum for himself that includes science, mathematics, literature, and languages. He reads Ralph Waldo Emerson and has a portrait of Thomas Carlyle on his wall: both writers are presumably responsible for inspiring his 'threats against the universe' – that is, his fantasies of Romantic genius and heroic self-overcoming.[43] Carlyle is also presumably a touchstone for Lewisham's feverish work ethic. Yet Lewisham's *Bildung* is clearly a form of discipline in the Foucauldian sense; he is perpetually acting as his own schoolteacher and exam invigilator, turning the 'stringent regulation' he practises as a pupil-teacher upon himself.[44] His meritocratic labour is an effort to be 'the same consistent intelligent human being' at all times and leave no 'region of his mind' 'undisciplined and unexplored'.[45] This entails the continuous monitoring and quantification of the self: Lewisham attempts to make his interior life conform to the structure of a school timetable and thereby to his larger plan, his 'Schema' of academic achievement; he even stands to do his work because 'sitting down is the beginning of laziness'.[46]

Lewisham's 'Schema' is suggestive of how Romantic *Bildung* has been sutured to disciplinary techniques for lower-class aspirants to the late Victorian scholarship ladder. Lewisham calls his own plans for success his 'Schema' rather than merely his 'scheme' because Latin has a scholarly glamour for him; and yet Lewisham's susceptibility to the romance of education is precisely what renders his mind 'schematic' in the negative sense of that word. The motivational quotations on Lewisham's wall promise that his academic ordeals will lead to a glorious expansion and empowerment of the self: 'Knowledge is power' and 'Who would control others must first control himself.'[47] Yet to the reader these maxims resonate ironically: it is clear that, for Lewisham, education is not a 'shining staircase to fame and power' but lonely self-subjugation, the 'greyness of a teacher's life'.[48] More precisely, Wells makes clear that Lewisham's Romantic plan for a 'brilliant career' is not truly a means of escaping his lowly status as a pupil-teacher but the encroachment of the school system into the depths of his psyche.[49] This is spelled out by the fact that Lewisham's commitment to solitary study duplicates the tyrannical rules – similarly rendered in pretentious Latin – of the headmaster, Mr Bonover, who is a 'typical representative of a social organisation which objects very strongly *inter alia* to promiscuous conversation on the part of the young unmarried junior master'.[50] When Lewisham tries to assert his independence to Mr Bonover by saying 'I am my own master out of school,' the phrase also recoils on Lewisham ironically: there is no 'out of school' for him because he is consumed by a fantasy of scholastic self-mastery.[51]

Lewisham's 'Schema' also underscores how intellectual aspirations have become yoked to a new logic of credentialism ushered in by the late Victorian expansion of education and the rise of a culture of professionalism that increasingly made paper qualifications the price of entry.[52] Although Lewisham wants to be a writer and a politician – two professions that even now do not strictly require educational qualifications – he imagines himself primarily as an accumulation of certificates and credentials, a walking curriculum vitae:

[At church] Lewisham [felt] painfully conspicuous, except in moods of exceptional vanity, [. . .] he used to imagine all these people were thinking how his forehead and his certificates accorded. He thought a lot, in those days, of his certificates and forehead, but little of his honest, healthy face beneath it. (To tell the truth there was nothing very wonderful about his forehead.)[53]

The joke here is not really Lewisham's vanity but his pitiable yearning for objective proof of his mental worth, whether in the form of certificates or according to the laws of physiognomy. This yearning is pitiable because of the alienation it betrays: Lewisham experiences himself primarily through the imagined judgements of strangers, and supposes that society at large shares his teacherly obsession with intellectual ability and professional credentials. In fact, the narrative as a whole makes clear that late Victorian society is much more preoccupied with surface signifiers of class – clothes and accent – and academic credentials do not confer social capital in the mechanical and transparent way that Lewisham supposes, especially not upon lower-class aspirants to the professions. When Lewisham later struggles to find a new teaching position, his faith in the value of his certified self begins to falter:

> He began to find out, too, how little the world feels the need of a young man of nineteen – he called himself nineteen, though he had several months of eighteen still to run – even though he adds prizes for good conduct, general improvement, and arithmetic, and advanced certificates signed by a distinguished engineer and headed with Royal Arms, guaranteeing his knowledge of geometrical drawing, nautical astronomy, animal psychology, physiography, inorganic chemistry, and building construction, to his youth and strength and energy.[54]

As Franklin aptly remarks, this list of qualifications 'proliferates so wildly as to leave the reader in doubt as to whether Lewisham is really qualified for anything'; 'Mr Lewisham has measured out his life in useless diplomas.'[55] However, it is important to be precise here: Lewisham's certificates are empty signifiers not because the education they document is useless or inferior in Wells's eyes. In fact, Lewisham pursues exactly the kind of practical and scientific training that Wells himself pursued and proselytised for, though – again like Wells – Lewisham gets distracted by his interests in literature and politics.[56] Wells is also not inviting us to despise Lewisham's autodidactic over-reaching or his efforts to become a Renaissance man in his spare time. Indeed, Wells thought that the hubris and haphazardness of lower-class autodidacticism often produced better minds than elite education could:

> There is something splendid and Titanic about [. . .] ambitious and self-taught men. They work in the dark and under tremendous disadvantage; [. . .] and yet withal they will often emerge at last with ideas cleverer, sounder and stronger than many student who had all the advantages – and relaxations – of university. There is a great future before these pilgrims from the proletariat to wisdom.[57]

Lewisham's credentials are farcical because he discovers that they lack market value and thus serve as consolation prizes for the professional future that they were supposed to guarantee. Not only does Lewisham's accumulation of certificates fail to advance him toward 'Greatness' as a scientist, writer, or politician, but it fails to secure him stable employment in his original profession, teaching. Instead, it leads him to what the novel repeatedly calls 'greyness': the petty indignities and economic precarity of lower-middle-class life.[58]

Wells's satirical portrait of Lewisham's aspirations is subtle and carries a strong undertow of pathos: its object is not to denigrate the aspirations themselves but to reveal how profoundly Lewisham misrecognises homogenising forms of self-discipline for the path to individual fulfilment and distinction. In other words, Wells aims to reveal how the limited and gruelling routes to social mobility opened up by the late Victorian expansion of education can ensnare lower-class men in the toils of cruel optimism. Like *Jude*, *Love and Mr. Lewisham* is an attack on the archetype of the bright scholarship boy, the heroic child whose exceptional virtues and talents make him fit for class transcendence. And like Hardy, Wells draws a veil over the question of whether Lewisham has genuine intellectual gifts, though – again like the case of *Jude* – this has not prevented readers from drawing conclusions about his mental ability and worthiness for meritocratic advancement. Reading him as a less fortunate avatar of Wells himself, Adam Roberts generously characterises Lewisham as a 'man of talents' with 'huge potential'; surveying Wells's lower-middle-class protagonists as though they were his students, Carey calls Lewisham 'the brightest of the bunch'.[59] By contrast, the novel's contemporary reviewer in *The Daily Telegraph* considered it self-evident that Wells had written a tragicomedy about a 'fifth-rate' young man whose 'vaulting ambition' outstrips his 'small capacities'.[60] In fact, it is crucial to the novel's critique of the cruel optimism of meritocracy that both interpretations are legitimate, and we cannot tell if Lewisham's abilities are 'huge' or 'small'.

As Wells makes clear, Lewisham's intelligence is indeterminable precisely because he is such a good scholarship boy. The deserving scholarship boy is always vulnerable to being slighted on the grounds of his deservingness: he can always be accused of being merely a 'mugger', a 'crammer', a 'swat', a 'prig', a 'grind', rather than the genuine article, the truly 'gifted' prodigy. In this way the lower-class boy's academic achievements can always be turned into proof of his true fitness for menial labour. Lewisham learns this lesson later in the novel when, as a scholarship boy at the Normal School of Science, he overhears a fellow student discussing his academic performance:

> [Lewisham] was pointed out to a raw hand, by the raw hand's experienced fellow-townsman, as 'that beast Lewisham – awful swat. He was second last year on the year's work. Frightful mugger. But all these swats have a touch of the beastly prig. Exams – Debating Society – more Exams. Don't seem to have ever heard of being alive. Never goes near a Music Hall from one year's end to the other.[61]

At the surface level of the plot, Lewisham's *Bildung* allegorises a shift from a liberal, mid-Victorian faith in hard work, individual agency, and meritocratic providence to what Beatrice Webb described as the 'new consciousness of sin' which seized many 'men of intellect' in the 1880s and drove them to embrace socialism (Wells himself being a representative example and surely one of the men Webb had in mind).[62] Lewisham's first significant progress toward his dream of a career in service to the 'Liberal cause' – he wins a scholarship to university – has the ironic effect of eroding his faith in the liberal precept that 'people [are] responsible for their own lives'.[63] The vast social inequality of London strikes Lewisham as a 'crime' and he becomes a socialist.[64] However, Lewisham's new socialist convictions do not produce any real transformation in his consciousness. His activism is confined to the adoption of a red tie and to honing his rhetorical skills in the university debating room. The fact his socialist dreams consist primarily of imagining himself as the 'Luther of socialism' also makes clear that he remains a liberal individualist and something of a puritan at the level of his fantasy life.[65] At its deepest level, the plot of *Love and Mr. Lewisham* does not allegorise the decline of liberalism and the rise of socialism in the 1880s so much as the process of attrition that compels people to adapt to what Wells calls 'the fraud of our social conditions' as they age. Wells attempted to theorise this process of attrition in his second sociological treatise, *Mankind in the Making* (1903):

> In ninety-nine cases out of a hundred [people] will accept the system [. . .] They will see that to repudiate the system by more than a chance word or deed is to become isolated, to become a discontented alien, to lose even the qualified permission to do something in the world. In

most cases they will take the oaths that come in their way and kiss the hands [. . .] And their reason for submission will not be absolutely despicable: they will know there is no employment worth speaking of without it. After all, one only has one life, and it is not pleasant to pass through it in a state of futile abstinence from the general scheme [. . .] The beginning of concessions is so entirely reasonable and easy! But the concessions go on [. . .] Many a man whose youth was a dream of noble things, who was all for splendid achievements and the service of mankind, peers today, by virtue of such acquiescences, from between preposterous lawn sleeves or under a titled coronet, sucked as dry of his essential honour as a spider sucks a fly.[66]

Lewisham illustrates Wells's thesis that individual disenchantment with the social order rarely translates into outward political dissent. Although Lewisham's socialist convictions distract him from his study and therefore seem to contribute to his ultimate failure at university, they do not really unsettle his faith in meritocratic social mobility. The socialist critique of meritocracy is instead articulated by Mr Chaffery, a huckster spiritualist who justifies his imposture on the grounds that the 'social contract is nothing more or less than a vast conspiracy of [. . .] lies'.[67] As Matthew Taunton has noted in a brilliant analysis of *Kipps*, Wells often embeds socialist arguments in his fiction through the use of unsavoury minor characters who deliver jeremiads against the social order. The function of these characters as spokesmen for Wells's own views is complicated by the fact that they seem designed to repel readerly sympathy or identification. Taunton calls these Wellesian spokesmen 'chorus characters' and suggests that they serve an 'agonistic' function, enabling Wells to articulate radical arguments that cannot be reconciled with the norms of liberal debate and its aspirations toward compromise and consensus.[68] Although such chorus characters typically engage in extended dialogue with the novel's protagonist, they are generally strident monologuists who are bent on expounding a thesis rather than being open to debate and exchange, and the novel's protagonist can neither assimilate nor entirely reject their worldview. In this way, the reader is forced to confront socialist arguments and weigh their value not against any counter-argument offered in the novel but against the 'lifeworld' of the novel's protagonist.[69]

Unlike *Kipps*, *Love and Mr. Lewisham* does not have an avowedly socialist chorus character. Instead, Chaffery is a Nietzschean provocateur whose tirade against the social order is only fitfully socialist in its substance. Yet Chaffery clearly appears in the novel in part to challenge Lewisham's assumption that his dream of meritocratic social mobility is compatible with his socialist convictions. Chaffery assails the moral legitimacy of Lewisham's personal ambition (which, at this point in the novel, is to become a scientist):

> 'Take a professor of science [. . .] Notice the smug suppression of his face. In his mouth are Lies in the shape of false teeth. Then on the earth somewhere poor devils are toiling to get meat and corn and wine. He is clothed in the lives of bent and thwarted weavers, his Way is lit by phossy jaw, he eats from lead-glazed crockery – all his ways are paved with the lives of men [. . .] He pretends that his blessed little researches are in some way a fair return to these remote beings for their toil, their suffering; pretends that he and his parasitic career are payment for their thwarted desires [. . .]'
>
> 'But this is Socialism!' said Lewisham. 'I – '
>
> 'No Ism', said Chaffery. 'Only the ghastly truth of things – the truth that the warp and woof of the world is Lying. Socialism is no remedy, no *ism* is a remedy; things are so'.
>
> 'I don't agree – ' began Lewisham.
>
> 'Not with the hopelessness, because you are young, but with the description you do'.
>
> 'Well – within limits'.
>
> 'You agree that most respectable positions in the world are tainted with the fraud of our social conditions. If they were not tainted with fraud they would not be respectable. Even your own positions – who gave you the right to marry and prosecute interesting scientific studies while other young men rot in mines?'[70]

Chaffery is the only charismatic teacher that Lewisham encounters in the course of his education, and the effects of his nihilistic pedagogy are hard to judge. At the end of the scene quoted above, Lewisham is disgusted by Chaffery's self-serving moral relativism. However, Lewisham later finds himself 'more and more in sympathy with Chaffery's bitterness against those who order the world'.[71] As Taunton observes, the socialist arguments put forward by the chorus character in *Kipps* primarily provide the protagonist with a 'consoling psychological compensation for social failure' rather than the basis of any kind of political action.[72] In the case of *Love and Mr Lewisman*, the effects of the chorus figure's provocations are more ambiguous: if Chaffery provides Lewisham with consolation for his ultimate failure, he arguably also contributes to that failure by implanting in Lewisham the idea that all professional success and the bourgeois dream of the good life are irredeemably 'tainted'.

Wells's effort to debunk the fin de siècle vogue for spiritualism through the character of Mr Chaffery can seem like something of a non sequitur in a novel about late Victorian education and meritocracy. Yet the underlying connection between Mr Chaffery's spiritualism scam and Lewisham's thwarted meritocratic progress is made clear when Lewisham discovers that he must falsely profess Anglican orthodoxy to get ahead on the teaching job market, thereby confirming Mr Chaffery's thesis about the necessity of hypocrisy to social survival. In this, *Love and Mr. Lewisham* recalls George Gissing's *Born in Exile* (1895), which similarly critiques the continuing influence of the Anglican Church over the late Victorian education system and pathways to meritocratic advancement.[73] Like Gissing's hero, Godwin Peak, and like Hill in 'Under the Microscope', Lewisham discovers that the puritan virtues of honesty and hard work are a form of slave morality rather than the royal road to meritocratic success (indeed, this is the real thrust of Chaffery's tirade). However, unlike Peak's or Hill's, Lewisham's loss of faith in the meritocratic efficacy of puritan virtues is framed as a liberation as a much as a process of disillusionment. This positions the reader in an interestingly perverse relation to Lewisham's meritocratic ambitions: we are incited to desire the complication, if not the complete unravelling, of his plans for success precisely *insofar* as we desire his flourishing.

From the start of the novel, Well's narrator is very clearly in favour of play, pleasure, and distraction from study. As readers, we are encouraged to desire the weakening of Lewisham's academic will: we want him to escape his timetable and his 'stuffy, enervating bedroom', go outside in the sunshine, and fall in love.[74] The narrator's ironic attitude toward Lewisham turns upon the fact that Lewisham's banal and thoroughly bourgeois desires for leisure, refined conversation, and marriage all assume the hyperbolic allure of transgressive hedonism in his mind because they jeopardise his plan to become bourgeois in an economic sense. When Lewisham succumbs to the temptation to marry, he experiences it by turns as an illicit affair and a heroic rebellion against society:

> For three indelible days Lewisham's existence was a fabric of fine emotions, life was too wonderful and beautiful for any doubts or forethought. To be with Ethel was a perpetual delight [. . .] Even to be away from her was a wonder and in its way delightful. He was no common Student, he was a man with a Secret Life. To part from her on Monday near South Kensington and go up Exhibition Road among all the fellows who lived in sordid, lonely lodgings and were boys to his day-old experience! To neglect one's work and sit back and dream of meeting again!
>
> [. . .] 'We are Fighting the World', [Lewisham] said, finding great satisfaction in the thought. 'All the world is against us – and we are fighting it all'.
>
> 'We will not be beaten', said Ethel.
>
> 'How could we beaten – together?' said Lewisham. 'For you I would fight a dozen worlds'.[75]

Lewisham's romantic illusions and grandiosity are only superficially the object of Wells's irony here; its real target is that the fact that early marriage has all the excitement of 'vice' for lower-class men who cannot afford it. And as the passage quoted above makes clear, marriage represents not just Lewisham's desire for erotic and romantic fulfilment, but his desire for a vivid and poetic inner life; Lewisham longs to have his 'whole being irradiated with emotion'.[76] Richard Higgins has observed that Wells's project in *Kipps, Love and Mr. Lewisham,* and *The History of Mr. Polly* is to make the interior lives of lower-middle-class clerks and scholarship boys 'seem much richer, more significant, and more complicated' than they were generally imagined to be in fin de siècle and Edwardian literature.[77] Yet, as Wells makes explicit in *Love and Mr. Lewisham,* a rich and complicated interior life is not a given but an upper-class privilege that lower-class men can seize only by putting themselves in economic peril. 'Only people who are well off can be – complex,' Lewisham laments at one point.[78] The novel is itself Wells's effort to redress this injustice: Lewisham is granted the luxury of inner complexity, if only by the narrator. Lewisham is also granted what the novel underscores is the upper-class privilege of having his youthful mistakes treated indulgently, if – again – only by the narrator and not diegetically. As the contemporary reviewer from *The Daily*

Telegraph commented, Wells's narrator has a 'tenderness almost maternal' for the novel's protagonist, and this tenderness throws into relief both the pitilessness of the Victorian class system and Lewisham's commensurate pitilessness toward himself.[79]

At the end of the novel, the narrator's light-hearted, ironising attitude toward Lewisham's self-discipline becomes jarring because Lewisham's perception of the high stakes of that discipline turns out to have been warranted: his desire to have rich emotional experiences leads him to under-perform in an exam and thus to the 'practical Destruction' of his 'Career'. To borrow Bourdieu and Passeron's frameworks, Lewisham's 'tense application' turns out to have been the 'educational realism' of the lower-class student who correctly grasps the 'improbability' of his success within the education system: Lewisham was right to perceive that he could not afford the distractions of romance or politics and that there are no second chances for lower-class scholarship boys.[80] Yet Lewisham's neglect of his studies and his exam failure are not moralised nor even mourned by the narrator. Indeed, they are not even framed as failure: the fact that Lewisham strays from the 'narrow' path of meritocratic virtue is celebrated, if ambivalently, as an assertion of Lewisham's right to a full humanity.[81] And by the end of the novel, Lewisham has come to share the narrator's more expansive view of what constitutes self-development and flourishing, and refuses to experience his failure *as* failure. When the pregnant Ethel discovers Lewisham's Schema – now abandoned and yellowing – he repudiates his youthful ambitions and affirms that he is 'glad' to be 'commonplace':

'You are not grieving?'
[. . .]
'No!'
'You are not – you are not even sorry?' she said.
'No – not even sorry'.
'I can't understand that. It's so much – '
'I'm glad', he proclaimed. '*Glad*'.
'But – the trouble – the expense – everything – and your work?'
[. . .]
'It was vanity', he said. 'A boy's vanity. For me – anyhow. I'm too two-sided . . . Two sided? Commonplace!'
'Dreams like mine – abilities like mine. Yes – any man! And yet . . .
—The things I meant to do!'

His thoughts went to his Socialism, to his red-hot ambition of world
mending. He marvelled at the vistas he had discovered since those
days.

[...]

'Come to think, it is all the Child. The future is the Child. What are
we – any of us – but servants or traitors to that? Natural Selection
– it follows . . . this way is happiness . . . must be. There can be no
other'.

[...]

Career! In itself it is a career – the most important career in the world.
Father! Why should I want more?[82]

As Franklin points out, Lewisham's embrace of the 'commonplace' conflates his social class with his new, more humble estimation of his own intellectual abilities.[83] There are telling ambiguities
in his conflation, however. When Lewisham says, 'dreams like
mine – abilities like mine' and 'yes – any man!', it is not clear
if he has lost faith in the exceptional nature of his abilities or
simply ceased to be invested in the notion of exceptional abilities.
Lewisham's suggestion that his 'dreams' and 'abilities' are those of
'any man' can be read as an admission of his own mediocrity or a
Rancièrean affirmation of the dreams and abilities of the common
man (the fact that Lewisham's thoughts turn to socialism imme-
diately after this utterance gives force to the latter interpretation).
Likewise, when Lewisham tears his Schema into fragments and
proclaims himself done with 'empty dreams', it is not clear if this
represents his liberation or his defeat. This is, of course, because
the Schema symbolises the meritocratic dream that the novel has
exposed as a punitive mirage; but Lewisham's rejection of that
dream can seem like 'conformist capitulation', as Franklin puts
it. The overreaching lower-middle-class boy has learnt his place,
accepted the justice of his class position, and so attained 'maturity'.[84] Lewisham suggests that his very ambivalence – his 'two
sided' nature – is the cause of his failure: if only he could have sustained his commitment to 'incessant unswerving work', he might
have been a success.[85] But this logic only stands as a further indictment of the meritocratic dream that required Lewisham to purge
himself of all 'affections and passions'.

It is Miss Heydinger, a fellow student at the Normal School,
who articulates the idea that 'to fail hopelessly' may be 'greater'
than success.[86] Miss Heydinger is Lewisham's female counterpart:

the late Victorian archetype of the 'exam girl' who renders herself neurotic through study and who secretly craves romantic love more than academic success. The anti-feminist dimensions of this archetype are softened in *Love and Mr. Lewisham* because Miss Heydinger's neurosis so precisely mirrors Lewisham's and thus does not seem to be a symptom of her gender. Miss Heydinger loves Lewisham unrequitedly, and her notion of failure is clearly literary and Romantic, as indicated by the capitalisation 'Great' receives in the text. Lewisham's effort to reconcile himself to a 'commonplace' life lacks this Romantic grandeur; even his melo-dramatic gesture of tearing up the Schema is undercut by his impulse to tidy the mess up 'carefully' afterwards. This conclud-ing line of the novel seems to hint that the 'commonplace' life of parenthood and domesticity will not be a haven of 'affections and passions' either – that Lewisham has traded one form of discipline and self-repression for another.

Wells's attempt to rewrite the tragedy of Hardy's *Jude* as comedy thus does not produce a happy ending so much as one in which happiness and despair, success and failure, cannot be distinguished. The rage and despair of Hardy's Jude surface inter-mittently in Lewisham: he is still wistful about 'things I meant to do' and bitter over the fact that 'Life [. . .] played me a trick – promised so much – given so little!'[87] But unlike Jude, Lewisham exalts in the idea of fatherhood, even if it spells the end of his dreams of upward mobility. Arguably, Lewisham's investment in fatherhood is itself born of his despair: the fact that his 'Child' now assumes the portentous capitalisation once reserved for his Schema and his Career suggests that he remains stuck in the same logic of cruel optimism, mortgaging the present to a redemptive but endlessly deferred future. As Berlant observes, 'the history of sentimentality around children which sees them as the reason to have optimism' bears a destabilising pessimism within it: it is possible to be optimistic about children only because 'their lives are not already ruined' (with the implication that they will be condemned to the same ruin and the same logic of deferral once they too are adults).[88] This logic is quite explicit at the end of *Love and Mr. Lewisham*: the just world Lewisham dreamed of may be possible for his child, or at least possible 'someday' and 'somewhen' for someone, but 'we' – meaning himself and his wife – 'must perish in the wilderness'.[89] Yet in the context of the novel as a whole, parenthood represents another conventional bourgeois privilege that Lewisham needed to sacrifice or at least postpone indefinitely to enable his meritocratic ascent. And for that reason, his rapture over his economically reckless fatherhood does not resonate simply as 'conformist capitulation' but as his minor act of rebellion against the puritanism of meritocracy. Whether that rebellion represents self-fulfilment or self-defeat is an open question for both Lewisham and the reader at the novel's end.

Simple souls: *Kipps* and *The History of Mr. Polly*

Wells's next realist-comic *Bildungsroman*, *Kipps*, is also a critique of the dream of upward mobility and meritocratic conceptions of intelligence and self-improvement. However, this time Wells constructs a protagonist who is manifestly undeserving of social mobility in meritocratic terms: Kipps is a 'simple little soul' who unexpectedly inherits a large fortune but turns out to be incapable of being educated or refined above his lower-middle-class origins.[90] In this case, Wells's primary intertext is not Hardy's *Jude* but Dickens's *Great Expectations* (1860): Kipps's name even rhymes with that of Dickens's protagonist, Pip, while the name of Kipps's cruel and socially superior love interest, Helen Walshingham, is a partial anagram of Estella Havisham. Wells's recycling of Dickens's plot is designed to underscore that an archaic obsession with aristocratic conventions of inheritance and gentlemanliness remains as virulent at the dawn of the twentieth century as it was in mid-Victorian England. However, unlike Pip, Kipps never manages to decipher and interiorise the aristocratic-cum-bourgeois code of gentlemanliness and so his money cannot buy him social elevation.

The few critics who have discussed this novel duly note the centrality of Kipps's naïveté and social ineptitude to the narrative without registering their full significance.[91] Kipps evokes the archetype of the wise fool or holy innocent, and in a way clearly indebted to Dickens's comic and sentimental handlings of this archetype across his *œuvre*.[92] Kipps's status as a holy fool is most obviously a satirical device, enabling Wells to expose the baroque cruelty of bourgeois manners and social distinctions. However, the object of Wells's critique is not simply the persistence of a traditional class hierarchy in Edwardian England but its entanglement with new categories and stratifications that emerged from the intersections between late Victorian medicine and psychiatry, the state education system, and the eugenics movement. Wells's construction of Kipps is designed both to evoke and to problematise the newly salient categories of the backward, the ineducable, and the feeble-minded: the nebulous class who occupied what the historian Mark Jackson has termed 'the borderland of imbecility'.[93]

In the late nineteenth and early twentieth centuries in England, intellectual disability –known as 'mental deficiency' – came to be classified more precisely and conceptualised as a continuum that stretched from idiocy (the severest form), through imbecility (the moderate form), to feeble-mindedness (the mildest form).[94] The national prevalence of mental deficiency was widely believed to be rising, though – as even some contemporary commentators pointed out – it is likely this perception was an artefact of the waves of legislative and institutional reform directed at schools, prisons, and asylums.[95] As discussed in the Introduction, the system of 'payment by results' established by the Revised Code of 1862 and the emergence of a system of universal elementary education from 1870 onwards highlighted that a large number of poor children did not meet expected academic standards or flourish in an ordinary classroom. From the 1880s onwards, Francis Warner's medical tests were deployed on a mass scale in schools to distinguish between 'ineducable' and 'defective' children, on the one hand, and the merely 'dull', 'backward', and 'slow', on the other.[96] There was a series of public inquiries into the problem of ineducable and backward children, culminating in the Defective Children's Education Act of 1899.[97] This Act tasked local authorities with determining which schoolchildren ought to be classified as defective and assigned to special classes or a special school.

Mental deficiency in general and feeble-mindedness in particular were central to the wide-ranging cultural panic over degeneration and national efficiency in the late Victorian and Edwardian years. In the mid-Victorian period, so-called idiots were commonly regarded in sentimental terms, as 'innocent and pitiable victims'.[98] Idiots were also believed to be amenable to education and to being 'integrated as useful, productive members of society', in Patrick McDonagh's words – a paradigm associated especially with the pioneering work of the French doctor and educationalist Édouard Séguin.[99] In the closing decades of the century, however, the intellectually disabled were much more decisively and conspicuously stigmatised by the intersecting discourses of degeneration and eugenics.[100] Both expert and lay commentators identified mental deficiency as a root cause of social ills, especially poverty and crime. The problem of mental deficiency was also now often met with what Jackson calls 'therapeutic pessimism': under the influence of thinkers such as Maudsley, the mentally deficient were increasingly understood as essentially and intractably tainted at the level of heredity.[101]

In the 1890s, burgeoning concern with the 'problem' of feeblemindedness – especially with its supposed hereditary nature and liability to spread out of control in the population – coalesced into a public campaign for a government inquiry and new legislative measures. This campaign was led by a coalition of politicians, medical professionals, educationalists, and charity workers, and it succeeded in prompting the Royal Commission on the Care and Control of the Feeble-minded in 1904.[102] As Stephen Byrne points out, the use of 'control' in the name of the commission is suggestive of the extent to which the perception of feeble-mindedness as a social menace had hardened into a presupposition. And as Byrne writes, 'the segregation, permanent detention and even the sterilisation of the feeble-minded in the national good formed a key component of the deliberations' of the Commission.[103] The recommendations of the Commission – which reported in 1908 – were heeded in the Mental Deficiency Act of 1913, which gave the state the power to institutionalise those deemed 'feeble-minded' against their will. Some eugenicists had also advocated for the sterilisation of the mentally deficient, but this measure was generally much less palatable than segregation to politicians and the general public in England; it was even reviled by some prominent eugenicists, such as Havelock Ellis.[104] The Act is nevertheless often identified by historians as the major victory of the eugenics movement in England, and at the time was celebrated as such by the Eugenics Education Society.[105]

Feeble-mindedness came to be regarded as the most troubling form of mental deficiency precisely because of its supposed mildness and its proximity to the intellectual norm: in many circumstances, the feeble-minded might be able to pass for normal. At the Commission, Crichton-Browne observed, 'You are constantly meeting feeble-minded people in life. There are supra-normal, infra-normal, and normal men and women; where to draw the line is extremely difficult.'[106] This logic rendered feeble-mindedness a particular focus of eugenicist scaremongering: the almost-normal status of the feeble-minded meant that their supposed tendencies to sexual promiscuity and hyper-fecundity flourished unchecked and could lead to the degeneration of the race.[107] Joseph Valente has remarked of the era's degeneration discourses generally that they 'stigmatised deviation' so floridly and in so many contexts that the 'norm itself was incriminated'.[108] This is especially true of feeble-mindedness, where the intimacy between the deviation and the norm was explicitly at issue. Mary Dendy, who was a eugenicist and one of the most prominent campaigners for the care and compulsory detention of the feeble-minded, remarked,

> It is not the severe cases [of mental deficiency] which are the most dangerous; it is the mild cases, which are capable of being well-veneered, so as to look, for a time at any rate, almost normal, against which there is the need to protect society.[109]

However, the amorphousness and novelty of the category of 'feeble-mindedness' could also provoke scepticism about its purchase on reality. G. K. Chesterton, perhaps the era's staunchest critic of eugenics, believed 'feeble-mindedness' was a eugenic concoction and a threat to everyone's freedom: 'feeble-mindedness is a new phrase under which you might segregate anybody'.[110] The Liberal MP Josiah Wedgwood, who waged an almost entirely lonely crusade against the Mental Deficiency Bill in parliament, highlighted that the bill's working definition of 'feeble-mindedness' (drawn from the Royal Commission) hinged on a logical fallacy that pathologised the intellect of half of the population:

> Feeble-minded persons – that is to say, persons who may be capable of earning their living under favourable circumstances, but are incapable, through mental defect existing from birth or from an early age,
>
> 1. (i) of competing on equal terms with their normal fellows or
> 2. (ii) of managing themselves and their affairs with ordinary prudence.
>
> Is it possible that there could be a more sweeping definition? There are a great number of Members in this House, and very nearly half the people of the country, because I presume their normal fellows must be the average, who are not capable of competing on equal terms with the average man, as otherwise he would not be an average man.[111]

Jackson has demonstrated that, by the start of the twentieth century, the 'feeble-minded' were commonly constructed as a natural biological kind, class, or type of persons – 'a totally distinct and pathological group', as the psychiatrist and eugenicist Dr Alfred Tredgold put it.[112] Yet it was evident, even at the time, that the category was freighted with contestable assumptions about race, gender, and class.[113] It is the last of these – the classist dimensions of the category – that are relevant to my reading of *Kipps*.

The perception that rates of feeble-mindedness were highest among the lower classes could pass for common sense. Writing in *The Westminster Review* in 1899, Isabel Foard wondered, 'Would not carefully tabulated statistics prove that [the feeble-minded child] predominates largely among the lower classes, who are not accustomed to place any control on their drink cravings?'[114] There was nevertheless considerable debate among scientists and medical experts about the class distribution of the phenomenon. Some prominent experts on the feeble-minded, such as Dendy and Tredgold, emphasised that the problem afflicted all classes.[115] Their insistence on the classlessness of mental deficiency was crucial to the logic of their eugenics: if feeble-mindedness were conflated too readily with poverty, then it might be construed in primarily environmental rather than hereditarian terms. Yet their arguments could create perplexity in other experts. In 1911, Dr James Niven, the Medical Officer of Health for Manchester, suggested that feeble-mindedness made little sense except as a problem besetting the lower classes. If a person is 'well-off' and able to 'occupy [a] good position in society', can he or she really be said to have a feeble mind?[116] And regardless of these debates, there was a pervasive rhetorical tendency in discussions of mental deficiency to conflate the feeble-minded with the urban working-class 'residuum', the unemployed, and the criminal classes, and to suggest that poverty and crime were effects of mental deficiency.[117] In 1901, the Liberal politician and member of the London School Board G. L. Bruce argued that special schools were not sufficient to address the problem of the feeble-minded. Mandatory detention was imperative:

> The 'worst third', who are now in the School Board's special schools [. . .] are only too likely to supply the ranks of the unfit and criminal classes; they are also apt, if left to themselves, to become parents at the earliest moment, and to bequeath to the next generation in an aggravated form the problem which we hesitate to deal with [. . .] The greater humanity of modern life has enabled such children to

be reared to adolescence and manhood instead of being eliminated in the struggle for existence before they were ever the subject for statistics.[118]

There is, of course, also the simple fact that lower-class children and adults were far more likely than anyone from the middle or upper classes to be classified as feeble-minded because their intellectual capacities came under the scrutiny of the state in the context of the state education system or in workhouses, prisons, and public asylums. For this reason, Wedgwood perceived the Mental Deficiency Bill as an attack on the dignity and liberty of the working classes. He denounced the bill as an expression of the 'spirit of the horrible Eugenic Society' and its desire to 'breed up the working classes as though they were cattle'.[119] Wedgwood also articulated his fear that the bill would lead to the pathologisation and detention of 'normal' working-class children who were simply 'a little bit lazy and backward' and who 'prefer life in the open streets to sitting at a desk and saying the ABC'.[120]

John Partington has argued that Wells was in a self-critical mood at the start of the twentieth century, having been surprised and stung by the hostility of some reviewers, as well as some of his friends, to the eugenicist pronouncements in *Anticipations*. Partington suggests that Wells was particularly chastened by a letter from his close friend Conrad, who had found the book elitist to the point of inhumanity. Partington also argues that Wells's follow-up work of sociology, *Mankind in the Making* (published two years later in 1903), represents something of a palinode to the eugenicist sections of *Anticipations*.[121] I want to suggest that *Kipps* is also infused with Wells's remorse over *Anticipations* and its hateful lamentation over 'the rapid multiplication of the unfit' and the fact there is nothing to 'prevent the birth of all the inadaptable, useless, or merely unnecessary creatures in each generation'.[122] Yet Partington's redemption narrative is too tidy: if Wells repented of his eugenicist attitudes in the wake of *Anticipations*, he also cycled back to those positions intermittently in the coming decades.[123] It was Chesterton, Wells's friend, who offered the most astute analysis of the intellectual restlessness that characterises Wells's engagements with eugenics:

An enormous number of newspaper readers seem to have it fixed firmly in their heads that Mr. HG Wells is a harsh and horrible Eugenist in great goblin spectacles, who wants to put us all into metallic microscopes and dissect us with metallic tools. As a matter of fact, of course, Mr Wells, so far from being too definite, is generally not definite enough [. . .] his answers are more agnostic than his questions. His books will do everything except shut. And so far from being the sort of man who would stop a man from propagating, he cannot even stop a full stop. He is not Eugenic enough to prevent the black dot at the end of a sentence from breeding a line of little dots.[124]

As Chesterton goes on to clarify, Wells's failure to be a dogmatic 'eugenist' was the product not of a vague agnosticism on the subject but rather of the incisiveness of his thinking on it. Chesterton believed that Wells had delivered a devastating blow to the eugenics movement in *Mankind in the Making* and lauded him as the 'eugenist who had destroyed Eugenics'.[125] For Chesterton, the most crucial part of Wells's critique was his recognition that eugenicists mistook their own social judgements about complex and unstable human states and attributes such as 'beauty', 'health', 'intelligence', and 'criminality' for unitary biological traits.[126] Tellingly, Wedgwood – also a friend of Wells's – found Wells's work imaginatively useful when articulating his moral objections to the eugenicist logic of the Mental Deficiency Bill in parliament. However, Wedgwood drew upon Wells's science fiction rather than his sociological writing:

> I think those people who are so anxious to improve the breed of the working classes had better remember that there is such a thing as a soul and that the mere desire to turn people into better money-making machines is merely some horrible nightmare of H. G. Wells. Hon. Members should remember how Mr. Wells in 'The Time Machine', figures a society thousands of years hence in which all disease is removed and a standard of a perfect type has been arrived at, but unfortunately the perfect type has no brain and the working classes become workers in the darkness below mere beasts of prey. In his book 'The Men in the Moon,' are to be bred some men with special hands, some with special eyesight, some with special brains, some with special bodily strength. In connection with that kind of thing, I am delighted to have a seat in this House in order to be able to put a spoke in its wheel, because I believe in such circumstances the whole of mankind would become mere brute beasts and would lose their intellectual development and spirituality.[127]

Wells's desire to interrogate the implications of eugenics may be most vivid in his science fiction, but it is also central to *Kipps*. This is a matter not simply of Wells's sentimental attachments to ordinary lower-middle-class life, as Carey's analysis sometimes implies, but of Wells's desire to probe the class-ridden nature of Edwardian distinctions between the educable and the ineducable mind.[128]

Like *Love and Mr. Lewisham*, *Kipps* is a transparently semi-autobiographical novel: in it, Wells draws upon many details of his own upbringing in Kent, his chaotic romantic life, and his apprenticeship as a draper.[129] But *Kipps* is a far more complex and unstable example of Wells's impulse to appear thinly veiled in his own fiction: where *Love and Mr. Lewisham* allowed Wells to write a counter-factual narrative of his own struggles as a scholarship boy – one in which those struggles culminated in failure rather than a successful literary career – *Kipps* is a novel in which Wells imagines himself as one of the 'inadaptable, useless, or merely unnecessary' people whose existence he deplored in *Anticipations*. Kipps is never identified in the novel as feeble-minded or as mentally deficient in any pathological sense. However, all of the novel's comedy and social critique hinges on the fact that Kipps can only 'maintain [. . .] the surface of ordinary intelligence with utmost difficulty'.[130] Kipps is conscious of a mysterious incapacity in himself: 'I know only there's such a lot of things I don't seem to be up to some'ow. That's where the trouble comes in.'[131] Kipps is perpetually found – and feels himself to be – 'muddled', 'futile', 'unfortunate', 'mute', 'perplexed', 'confused in his mind', 'clumsy in the uses of social life'.[132] Kipps's apprenticeship at a draper's is 'too much for his unfortunate brain', and his boss complains he has no more capacity for work than a 'bad potato'.[133] The narrator persistently invites us to regard the adult Kipps as an 'ignorant child', and uses imagery that encourages us to understand Kipps's agency and self-awareness as comparable to those of an animal or a plant: Kipps has a 'rabbit-like soul', looks 'out upon life in general as a very small nestling might peep out of its nest', and is 'only in a measure more aware of himself as a whole than is a tree'.[134]

As James has noted, Kipps's difficulties with negotiating the world seem to arise partly from the fact that he is only semi-literate: he is self-conscious about the fact that he reads 'slowlier' than his friend, Sid Pornick, despite the fact that Sid received a (putatively) inferior state education whereas Kipps attended a 'middle class academy'; he is 'not always clever enough' to keep his place in his prayerbook at church; and later, he despairs of searching for a job because he cannot spell well enough to write applications.[135] Yet Kipps's semi-literacy is, at least in part, a metaphor for his social illiteracy: he has a pervasive difficulty with interpreting social cues and with assessing the motives of others.[136] This double illiteracy comes to a climax toward the end of the novel when Kipps attends a society party called 'The Anagram Tea'. Kipps's struggle to understand the conversational sallies of other guests is mirrored by his struggle to play the game of anagrams (though it is not clear if this is because he does not understand the game or because he cannot spell), and his spiralling confusion prompts him to flee.[137] This is the pivotal moment when Kipps abandons his project of transforming himself into a gentleman and resolves to marry his childhood sweetheart rather than 'marrying above his breed-ing'.[138] It is significant that he makes this decision when his secret illiteracy, or at least semi-literacy, is on the brink of being publicly exposed. Nevertheless, Wells makes clear that Kipps's incapacities are not simply incapacities: they lead him to a critical insight and give him the courage to 'rebel'.[139] And if Kipps finds learning to pass as a gentleman an impossible form of 'intellectual toil', this does not expose his intellectual limitations so much as it does the 'meanly conceived' nature of his society.[140]

> These were a rotten lot of people, and the anagrams were rotten non-sense, and he (Kipps) had been a rotten fool to come [. . .] Here were all these chattering people, with money, with leisure, with every chance in the world, and all they could do was to crowd like this into a couple of rooms and jabber nonsense about anagrams [The anagram puzzle] floated like a dissolving wreath of mist across his mind. Abruptly resolution stood armed in his heart. He was going to get out of this![141]

Like *Love and Mr. Lewisham*, *Kipps* satirises the meritocratic dream of social mobility through intellectual distinction, though this time the satire is refracted through the perspective of a pro-tagonist with no particular intellectual interests, abilities, or work ethic. Kipps's consciousness of his own deficiencies does not, however, render him immune to the rhetoric of *Bildung* as it cir-culates within Edwardian culture: prior to his unexpected inherit-ance and while he is still working as a draper, he is seduced by the idea that he has unique 'potentialities' that he ought to cultivate.[142]

When he begins to take woodworking classes at a local technical college, several of his female fellow students develop a crush on him and decide he has an 'indefinable something in him' and that he 'owe[s] it to himself to develop his possibilities'.[143] The joke here is that Kipps is so intimidated by what he imagines to be the refined and intellectual atmosphere of the woodworking class that he has largely been 'mute' during his time there, and it is his mute-ness that inspires the girls' conviction that he is not 'common' but full of 'potentialities', 'sensitive[ness]', and 'natural delicacy'.[144] Having been identified by others as special and artistic on account of his muteness, Kipps begins to daydream that he might become a famous author in the pattern of Dickens. Since Kipps struggles to read books and regards literature as an 'occult' phenomenon, his literary aspiration is a naïve fantasy of class mobility: he imagines authors as 'essentially low' in class but able to enter upon 'levels of social superiority'.[145] Kipps has barely entertained his fantasy of literary fame before he has despaired of it because drapers and working men like himself 'd[on't] get a chance' to write.[146]

As James suggests, Wells's satire can seem to 'belittle' Kipps here, insofar as Kipps and his admirers are clearly deluded and he has no special 'potentialities' to develop; plainly, it is not only Kipps's 'painfully restricted' life as a draper that prevents him from becoming an 'Nawther'.[147] Yet the satire here is not directed at Kipps himself so much as at the debasement of the Romantic ideal of *Bildung*, which here circulates as a flowery language of false consciousness. The satire is also directed at the meritocratic fairy tale of the lower-class man of genius, here exemplified by Dickens and his childhood experience of working at a blacking factory.[148] The romantic girls who discover latent 'potentialities' in Kipps are proxies for the presumptively middle-class reader, and the patent absurdity of their projections on to him is intended to correct any readerly illusion that he is a meritocratic hero. The grounds of our sympathy with Kipps and our investment in his flourishing cannot be that he has natural talents or abilities that distinguish him from his humble origins. Indeed, the novel inverts meritocratic morality: we are asked to invest in Kipps's progress precisely insofar as he is apparently ineducable (at least in a world where education means the cultivation of class pretensions).

The plot of *Kipps* has more kinship with the picaresque tradi-tion than with the *Bildungsroman* form insofar as Kipps does not learn or develop over the course of the novel but is instead caught up in a chain of accidents, mishaps, and adventures. Kipps is also essentially passive: he is adopted and, to varying degrees, coerced, indoctrinated, or exploited by a series of would-be pedagogues, some relatively benign, some predatory, and all of whom Kipps signally fails to understand. Although these various informal pedagogues – Mr Coote, Mr Chitterlow, Helen Walshingsham, Mrs Walshingham, and Masterman – all attempt to 'enlarge and refine and expand the intelligence of Kipps', Kipps proves essentially ineducable: although a willing student, he cannot assimilate the lessons of his apparent intellectual and social superiors.[149] However, the narrator encourages us to perceive that the deficiency may lie in the lessons as much as in the student. Kipps's teachers are gripped by what the narrator calls

> that sinister passion for pedagoguery to which the Good Intentioned are so fatally liable, that passion for infinite presumption that permits one weak human being to arrogate the direction of another human being's affairs [. . .].[150]

Kipps's struggles to learn are clearly partly due to the fact that the underlying logic of the class system cannot be explicated as though it were rational and benign, and so his teachers can only offer him mystifying tutorials in hypocrisy. For example, Helen Walshingham's advice on how to dress – 'it's possible to be over-conventional, over-elaborate [and] look like a common well-off person [. . .] A real gentleman looks right, without looking as though he tried to be right' – leaves Kipps staring in perplexity at his silk hat and wondering "Ow *is* one to know?"[151] And over the course of the novel, Kipps comes to experience his education as unrelieved humiliation. The superior 'intelligence' of his teachers comes to feel like an intimate violence to him:

> [Helen] told him things about his bearing, about his costume, and his way of looking at things. She thrust the blade of her intelligence in the tenderest corners of Kipps's secret vanity, she slashed his most intimate pride to bleeding tatters. He sought very diligently to anticipate at least some of these informing thrusts [. . .] She found his simple willingness a very lovable thing.[152]

Kipps's status as a 'simple soul' is itself complex. He turns out to be only superficially pliable; although receptive and deferential to all of his teachers, he has a seemingly innate incapacity to master bourgeois manners and culture. The novel never explicitly explains why he is so unteachable. The presence of the two far more worldly-wise lower-class characters in the novel – Kipps's socialist childhood friend, Sid, and the socialist guru, Masterman – makes clear that Kipps's naïveté is not simply due to his class or his inadequate education. Crucially, however, Kipps's mysterious ineducability is never posited as a pathology or even as a deficiency; instead, we are asked to appreciate that it is central to his human worth. As Valente has written of a particular strain within modernist depictions of cognitive disability, Kipps is 'not portrayed [. . .] as simply inferior to the social norm in play, but also as [a] living critique of that norm. The difference [his] condition makes is given as something other or something more than merely privative.'[153]

Within the Christian tradition, the archetype of 'holy fool' has its origins in the epistles of St Paul, who opposes the wisdom of Christ to worldly wisdom and affirms that those who follow Christ will necessarily appear foolish in worldly terms: this is 'foolishness for Christ', or divine folly. As McDonagh observes, this identification of foolishness with holiness has often been deployed as a 'subversive strategy for social commentary' and the 'legal and moral innocence of people identified as fools' is a venerable 'means of social critique' in Western literature.[154] Kipps is Wells's distinctively socialist variation on the Christian archetype of the holy fool: his moral goodness manifests itself not through any special gift of compassion or self-sacrifice but in his natural egalitarianism. Kipps's incapacity to assume the status of a 'gentleman' stems from this apparently incorrigible egalitarianism: though he tries, he can never really enter into the spirit of competition, hierarchy, and invidious distinctions that makes bourgeois culture intelligible. While Kipps may attempt to emulate the speech, dress, and manners of a gentleman, his performance is ultimately a failure because he lacks the inward class consciousness that would make the act persuasive. This is partly because he has no capacity for subterfuge or hypocrisy: 'I don't like to do anything under'and. I *must* speak out!'[155] But it is also because, unlike most of the other characters in the novel, Kipps has a simple faith that he is as good as anyone. At the start of the novel, the narrator observes: 'It had not yet come to Kipps to acknowledge any man as his better in his heart of hearts. When one does that the game is played and one grows old indeed.'[156] This sentence leads us to expect that the narrative will trace Kipps's process of disillusionment and his awakening to a consciousness of his mental inferiority. But this never happens: although Kipps is susceptible to feeling an 'abysmal' sense of 'inferiority' to his social and intellectual superiors, he keeps stubbornly reverting to his underlying 'perception of human equality'.[157] At the end of the novel, Kipps asserts that his former teachers have no right to 'sneer' at him and Ann because 'I'm as good – we're as good [as anyone] – whatever's 'appened.'[158] Kipps also fails to sustain a sense of social distinctions in his relationships with others: he listens with equal receptivity to the counsel of his lower-class friend, Sid, and to the socialist preaching of the lower-class malcontent, Masterman, as he does to the refined pedagogy of Mr Coote and Mrs Walshingham. And he ultimately brings 'social discredit' upon himself by marrying the servant girl, Ann, rather than the genteel Helen Walshingham.[159]

As Benjamin Kohlmann has pointed out, *Kipps* is threaded through with contemporary political debates about the distinction between earned and unearned wealth. When Kipps inherits his grandfather's fortune, he becomes 'a rentier, that bête noir of turn-of-the-century socialists', in Kolhmann's words.[160] It is socialist Sid who articulates Wells's own position:

> 'It's jest damn foolishness. Who's going to work and care in a muddle like this? Here first you do – something anyhow – of the world's work, and it pays you hardly anything, and then it invites you to do nothing, nothing whatever, and pays you twelve hundred pounds a year.'[161]

Significantly, however, Kipps fully accepts Sid's point that his wealth is morally arbitrary, and Sid comes to the conclusion that it is 'better' that wealth should befall Kipps 'than most people' because Kipps is humble enough to understand that he is merely the beneficiary of dumb luck.[162] Tellingly, the real villains in this novel are not, in fact, aristocrats or *rentiers* of any kind but two middle-class professionals: Helen Walshingham, an art teacher from the technical college Kipps briefly attends, and her unnamed twin brother, who is a solicitor. The Walshingham twins have been raised by their mother to believe that they are exceptionally gifted 'jewels' and 'need opportunities, as other people need [. . .] air'.[163] This is Mrs Walshingham's catchphrase, and it resonates as the origin of her children's ruthlessness. Helen plainly regards

Kipps as her inferior but feels it is legitimate to make a mercenary marriage to him because her education and intelligence give her a moral right to his wealth. Her solicitor brother's crime – he steals Kipps's money and speculates with it under the pretence of managing Kipps's affairs – both shadows and literalises Helen's romantic defrauding of Kipps. Helen embodies what Sandel calls 'meritocratic hubris': the tendency of 'winners to inhale too deeply of their own success' and believe that it is a matter primarily of moral desert.[164] In Helen's case, this hubris consists not in an excessive pride in her success – indeed, she is resentful of the fact that her education has not brought her great wealth or social distinction – but rather in her belief that her credentials mean that she 'counts' and Kipps does not:

> 'I suppose I'm ambitious. [My brother and I] both are. And we hadn't much of a springboard'. [. . .]
> 'I should think you could do anything if you wanted to', said Kipps.
> 'As a matter of fact I can't do anything I want to'.
> 'You done a good deal'.
> 'What?'
> 'Well, didn't you pass one of these here University things?'
> 'Oh! I matriculated!'
> 'I should think I was no end of a swell if *I* did, I know that'.
> 'Mr. Kipps, do you know how many people matriculate into London University every year?'
> 'How many then?'
> 'Between two and three thousand'.
> 'Well, just think how many don't!'
> Her smile came again, and broke into a laugh. 'Oh, *they* don't count', she said, and then, realising that might penetrate Kipps if he was left with it, she hurried on to, 'The fact is, I'm a discontented person [. . .] One hasn't had opportunities'.[165]

Helen's lofty meritocratic rhetoric of 'ambition' and 'opportunities' here is a mask for gold-digging; she clearly regards Kipps as her 'opportunity' because he is an easy mark. In the figures of Helen and her brother, Wells drains the figure of the talented striver who has 'lacked opportunities' of its conventional pathos and moral appeal. Kipps's wealth may be unearned and 'just damn foolish', but the Walshinghams' meritocratic claims on wealth are made to seem worse: they are fraudsters who use their educational credentials to justify a predatory – and clearly quasi-aristocratic – sense of entitlement. (Helen's brother is a casual reader of Nietzsche and regards himself as a 'Non-Moral Overman'.[166]) It is possible to read the Walshinghams in terms of Wells's critique of *rentier* capitalism: they epitomise a social system which demoralises the meritocratic strivers and makes gold-digging and theft more enticing than professional work. Yet in the immediate context of Kipps's relationship with Helen, the moral logic of the novel is less concerned with the evils of unearned wealth than it is with the evils of the meritocratic sense of entitlement: Kipps may be Helen's inferior in intellect and education, but his dumb luck seems less pernicious than her narcissistic elitism.

Twice in the novel, the relatively unobtrusive narrator directly addresses the reader, and in a voice which both recalls and subverts Helen's Olympian judgements about the educated few who 'count' and the uneducated masses who do not. In the first of these moments, the narrator entertains the notion of what he would do on Judgement Day if he were God. He asserts that he would want to extend the most clemency to the Kippses of the world, but that this desire to make an exception for the Kippses would paralyse his capacity to pass judgement on humanity in general:

> For all human dignity, for all conscious human superiority, I should lack the beginnings of charity; for bishops, prosperous schoolmasters, judges, and all large respect-pampered souls [. . .] – all these people, I say, I should treat below their deserts; but on the other hand, for such as Kipps – there the exasperating indecisions would come in. The Judgment would be arrested at Kipps. Everyone and everything would wait. The balance would sway and sway, and whenever it heeled towards an adverse decision, my finger would set it swaying again. Kings, warriors, statesmen, brilliant women, [. . .] humanity in general would stand undamned, unheeded, [. . .] while my eye went about for anything possible that could be said on behalf of Kipps . . .[167]

As this passage makes clear, the narrator's confessedly exorbitant sense of sympathy with Kipps – itself clearly based upon Wells's sense of identification with him – is meant to trouble the reader's capacity to make absolute judgements about humanity in general. The example of Kipps would apparently confound even God's capacity to disentangle social, intellectual, and moral worth, and force him to suspend judgement indefinitely. This passage reads irresistibly as self-parody and self-critique: the narrator's fantasy of godlike powers of judgement calls to mind the prophetic conceit of *Anticipations* – Wells imagined he could predict the future direction of society – as well as that book's eugenicist deliberations on who does and does not have a 'claim upon the future'. Wells here at once mocks his own presumption of godlike authority in *Anticipations* and confesses himself, in fact, a hopelessly biased arbiter of human worth – if all the more merciful for that bias.

The second intrusion of the narrator is even more jarring in its rhetorical instability. Wells here attacks the novel's status as a comedy of manners, and attacks it because of the cruelly condescending attitude the genre apparently constrains him to adopt toward his 'stupid' and 'limited' lower-middle-class hero and heroine, Kipps and Ann:

> The stupid little tragedies of these clipped and limited lives! What is the good of keeping up the idyllic sham and pretending that ill-educated, misdirected people 'get along very well', and that all this is harmlessly funny and nothing more? You think I'm going to write fat, silly, grinning novels about half-educated, under-trained people, and keep it up all the time, that the whole thing's nothing but funny! [. . .] I have laughed, and I laugh at [Kipps and Ann]; I have sought to make you laugh. But I see through the darkness of the souls of my Kippses as they are, as little pink strips of quivering living stuff, as things like the bodies of little, ill-nourished, ailing, ignorant children – children who feel pain, who are naughty and muddled and suffer, and do not understand why. And the claw of this Beast is upon them![168]

Wells's pluralisation of 'Kipps' here is ostensibly because he is referring both to Kipps and to Ann, who is now Mrs Kipps and is as 'artless' as Kipps himself.[169] But as the rest of the sentence makes clear, the purpose is also to gesture at Kipps's representativeness as a victim of what the narrator calls 'Stupidity', 'the ruling power of this land'. The narrator asserts that 'Stupidity' is the 'anti-soul' which infests all of English society and 'all the ideas that have made Kipps what he is'.[170] That Wells's narrator intrudes to condemn social and economic inequality and the English education system in terms of 'Stupidity' suggests Wells's awareness of the instability of the novel's intervention in the contemporary politics of mental ability and disability: it is always possible that the reader will simply arrive at the conclusion that Kipps himself is 'stupid' and 'limited'. As I have been arguing, Kipps's stupidity is the wise and noble stupidity of the holy fool, and Wells is clearly anxious to ensure that we understand that the ultimate 'Stupidity' lies with society and not with Kipps, who is merely struggling to live under its 'shadow'. The narrator interpellates the reader as a complacent member of the intelligentsia: he writes sardonically of 'we favoured ones' who, unlike Kipps and Ann, have access to the 'thought of the world' and 'the quickening sunshine of litera- ture'.[171] At the same time, Wells inculpates himself for gratifying the educated reader's presumed desire to mock the Kippses of the world, and thereby casts doubt on the value of his own novel. In effect, Wells suggests that the comic form of the novel and the nature of literary culture mean that he can only flatter the class distinctions he means to excoriate.

It is significant that Wells likens the adult Kipps and Ann – who become parents themselves in the following chapter – to 'ignorant children'. This may seem simply like Wells relapsing into the very class condescension for which he has just rebuked himself and his imagined reader. 'This is not the way we talk about equals,' Carey notes.[172] Yet it also reflects the novel's preoccupation with the class dimensions of contemporary understandings of backward, ineducable, and feeble-minded children. The paternalistic voice of Wells's narrator may infantilise Kipps and Ann by characterising them as 'naughty and muddled' children, but this is also a sympa- thetic and non-pathologising characterisation at a moment when lower-class children were being imagined as vectors of social and biological contamination. Wells's emphasis upon Kipps's child- ishness reflects his thesis that the class-bound education system served to keep the lower classes in a condition of arrested devel- opment: Kipps and Ann remain 'naughty and muddled' children because they are 'half-educated' and 'under-trained'. However, their status as permanently innocent children also stems from the novel's reparative fairy-tale dimensions – its desire to protect Kipps and Ann from full knowledge of their class position and give them the happy ending that the narrator insists is implausible, an 'idyllic sham'. (Wells also protects them from an economic reck- oning with their class position: although Kipps loses most of his money to Walshingham's perfidy, he retains the portion of it he invested in a house and – in a fantastical Dickensian vein – recoups still more from his investment in Chitterlow's career as a playwright.) Although several of Kipps's pedagogues are 'sinister' and he is thoroughly humiliated and miserable under their tutelage, no serious harm comes to him. And the novel ends with pastoral: we leave Kipps and Ann floating on a rowboat, serene and pondering the 'beauty, the purposeless, inconsecutive beauty' of life.[173]

It is Masterman, the novel's socialist chorus character, who suffers the Jude-like class tragedy from which the narrator is determined to spare Kipps. Masterman also articulates the idea that the state education system does not provide opportunities so much as formalise their foreclosure for lower-class children:

> 'What have *I* had? I found myself at thirteen being forced into a factory like a rabbit into a chloroformed box. Thirteen! – when [the children of the rich] are babies. But even a child of that age could see what it meant, that Hell of a factory! Monotony and toil and contempt and dishonour! And then death. So I fought – at thirteen! [. . .] A'nd never once have I had a fair chance, never once!' His lean, clenched fist flew out in a gust of tremulous anger. 'These Skunks shut up all the university scholarships at nineteen for fear of men like me. And then – do *nothin* [. . .] We're wasted for nothing. By the time I'd learnt something the doors were locked.'[174]

Masterman means that by the time he had developed an adult political consciousness and might make serious – perhaps revolutionary – use of a university education, he had aged out of the scholarship ladder. The example of Masterman suggests that a perverse effect of the state provision of elementary education may be to make adults despair of their potential and count themselves 'wasted for nothing' (though Masterman implies that is by conservative design: by focusing on young children and not providing them with a 'fair chance', the state education system effectively protects society from adult working-class intellectuals like himself).

Wells's 1910 novel *The History of Mr. Polly* directly addresses the fact that the lower classes emerge from 'the valley of the shadow of education' with a sense of 'obscured and thwarted' potential.[175] The novel is also an attempt to compensate for this condition of arrested development: it confers the privileges of *Bildung* not upon a young man but a middle-aged shopkeeper and gives him the opportunities for self-discovery and self-fulfilment that the education system denied him as a child. Like Mr Lewisham and Kipps,

Mr. Polly can be read as a kind of Wells *manqué* – a projection of who Wells might have become if he had never managed to escape his lower-middle-class origins or the 'compression' of his 'body and soul' wrought by the education system.[176] And like Kipps, Mr Polly is a holy fool character who can neither interiorise the logic of the class system nor 'grasp what [is] wrong with him'.[177] However, unlike Kipps, Mr Polly has an exceptional gift: he has a linguistic flair and a heightened sensitivity to beauty that mark him out as a natural poet.

Mr Polly's passion for language is partly constructed as a comic eccentricity: he collects and invents words not with a view to writing poetry or even to impressing others with his eloquence, but simply for his own 'queer incommunicable joy'.[178] He is a man

> whose brain devotes its hinterland to making odd phrases out of ill-conceived words, whose conception of life is a lump of auriferous rock to which all the value is given by rare veins of unbusiness-like joy, who reads Boccaccio and Rabelais and Shakespeare with gusto.[179]

In other words, Mr Polly is an authentic aesthete: he rejoices in words and in literature for their own sake, not with a view to making money or accruing any kind of social capital. However, because Mr Polly is a lower-middle-class draper and later a shopkeeper, his aestheticism is ludicrous. His attempts to beautify everyday life through his speech mostly irritate or confound his interlocutors and leave him trapped in an innocent kind of solipsism:

> [Mr Polly] specialised in slang and the disuse of English [. . .] Words attracted him curiously, words rich in suggestion, and he loved a novel and striking phrase. His school training had given him little or no mastery of the mysterious pronunciation of English, and no confidence in himself. His schoolmaster indeed had been both unsound and variable. New words had a terror and fascination for him; he did not acquire them, he could not avoid them, and so he plunged into them. His only rule was not to be misled by spelling. That was no guide anyhow. He avoided every recognised phrase in the language, and mispronounced everything in order that he shouldn't be suspected of ignorance but whim.
> 'Sesquippledan', he would say. 'Sesquippledan verboojuice'.
> 'Eh?' said Platt.

'Eloquent Rapsodooce'.
'Where?' asked Platt.[180]

Mr Polly's bizarre flights of linguistic invention are central to the novel's social critique. Mr Polly is Wells's attempt to imagine what innate and spontaneous literary genius would actually look like – how it would manifest itself if it were entirely independent of educational privileges and social pretensions. The novel's answer is that it would be socially unintelligible: the born poet would seem merely 'eccentric', 'a queer little flower', if not a 'fool' or even an *idiot savant*.[181] However, like Kipps, Mr Polly is not merely a buffoon character: the narrator demands that we respect his 'insatiable hunger for bright and delightful experiences, for the gracious aspects of things, for beauty'.[182] And like *Kipps*, *The History of Mr. Polly* is, in essence, a comic romance that strives to fulfil Mr Polly's 'restless craving for joy and leisure' and protect him from the worst ravages of the social system in which he is entrapped.[183]

Wells's celebration of lower-middle-class failure, autodidacticism, and eccentricity in his comic-realist novels of the fin de siècle and Edwardian period is his queasy response to the age's preoccupation with differentiating the 'educable' from the 'ineducable' and policing the boundaries of 'normal' intelligence: a preoccupation that he fully internalised and propagated in his own work, particularly his sociological writings. Although more enamoured of the IQ model of intelligence and its eugenic possibilities than any other writer in this study, Wells also was driven to think through its implications more fully than any other – to the point of imagining himself being judged 'inadequate' and even 'unfit to live' by its standards. In *Love and Mr. Lewisham*, *Kipps*, and *The History of Mr. Polly*, Wells constructs semi-autobiographical counter-histories that allowed him to imagine himself failing in various ways to measure up to his own meritocratic ideals. If Wells often dreamed of a meritocratic elite, that dream just as often failed the tests of his imagination.

Notes

1 H. G. Wells, *The First Men in the Moon* (London: George Newnes, 1901), p. 323.
2 Stiles, p. 122 and p. 152.
3 Wells, *Men in the Moon*, pp. 332–3.

4 Letter from Sidney Webb to H. G. Wells, 8 December 1901, in Norman MacKenzie, ed., *The Letters of Sidney and Beatrice Webb*. Vol. 2. *Partnership 1892–1912* (Cambridge: Cambridge University Press, 2008), p. 144. For an analysis of the prominence of meritocratic elitism within Fabian thought, see Rosemary Jann, 'Fabian Socialism and the Rhetoric of Gentility', *Victorian Literature and Culture* 41.4 (2013), pp. 727–42; and Wooldridge, *Aristocracy of Talent*, pp. 169–72.

5 Wells, *Anticipations of the Reaction of Mechanical and Scientific Progress upon Human Life and Thought*, 4th edition (London: Chapman & Hall, 1901), p. 291.

6 John Carey, *The Intellectuals and the Masses: Pride and Prejudice Among the Literary Intelligentsia 1880–1839* (London: Faber & Faber, 1992), p. 118.

7 Ibid., pp. 118–34 and pp. 135–51.

8 H. G. Wells, *An Experiment in Autobiography: Discoveries and Conclusions of a Very Ordinary Brain (Since 1866)*, vol. 1 (London: Faber & Faber, 1984), pp. 29–31.

9 H. G. Wells, *H. G. Wells in Love: Postscript to an Experiment in Autobiography* (London: Faber & Faber, 1984), p. 202. Qtd in Richard Higgins, 'Feeling Like a Clerk', *Victorian Studies* 50.3 (2008), 457–75, p. 458.

10 Carey, pp. 118–34.

11 Wells, *Autobiography*, vol. 1, p. 291.

12 Wells, *Mankind in the Making*, 4th edition (London: Chapman & Hall, 1904), pp. 70–1.

13 Ibid.

14 Wells, *Autobiography*, vol. 1, p. 28.

15 Ibid., p. 36. Wells directly critiques Smiles's doctrine of self-help in *Kipps*. See *Kipps: The Story of a Simple Soul*, ed. Simon James (London: Penguin, 2005), p. 51.

16 Wells, *Autobiography*, vol. 1, pp. 76–82.

17 Wells, *Autobiography*, vol. 2, p. 620.

18 Ibid., p. 620.

19 Wells, *Mankind in the Making*, p. 40 and pp. 46–8.

20 Wells, *Autobiography*, vol. 1, p. 83.

21 Wells, *Experiment in Autobiography*, vol. 2 (London: Faber & Faber, 1984), pp. 619–21.

22 Wells, *Autobiography*, vol. 1, pp. 30–1.

23 Wells, *A Modern Utopia*, ed. Gregory Claeys and Patrick Parrinder (London: Penguin, 2005), p. 189.

24 Ibid., p. 180.

25 Ibid., p. 180.

26 Wells, *Autobiography*, vol. 1, p. 174.

27 Wells, *Autobiography*, vol. 2, p. 630.

28 Wells, *Autobiography*, vols 1 and 2, pp. 29–36, p. 174, and p. 630; and Carey, pp. 23–70.

29 Carey, p. 135.

30 For an analysis of the centrality of class-inflected feelings of shame and self-loathing to Wells's work, see Higgins, 'Feeling Like a Clerk'. For insightful analysis of Wells's relationships with Woolf, Conrad, and James and his status as an object of modernist critique and snobbery, see Sarah Cole, *Inventing Tomorrow: HG Wells and the Twentieth Century* (New York: Columbia University Press, 2019), pp. 18–29; Simon James, *Maps of Utopia: HG Wells, Modernity and the End of Culture* (Oxford: Oxford University Press, 2012), pp. 19–33; and Lynda Dryden, "The Difference Between Us: Conrad, Wells, and the English Novel', *Studies in the Novel* 45.2 (2013), pp. 214–33.

31 Wells, 'A Slip under the Microscope', in *The Plattner Story and Others* (London: Methuen & Co., 1897), pp. 274–301.

32 Ibid., p. 290.

33 Ibid., p. 289.

34 Ibid., p. 291.

35 Ibid., p. 288.

36 Qtd in Gillian Beer, 'Introduction', in H. G. Wells, *Love and Mr. Lewisham* (Penguin: London, 2005), p. xxv.

37 Simon James, p. 91.

38 Qtd in ibid., p. 91.

39 Wells also analyses this 'embittering' double-bind in *Mankind in the Making*. See Wells, *Mankind in the Making*, p. 69.

40 Wells, *Mr Lewisham*, p. 60.

41 Jonathan Franklin, 'Those Who Can't: A Cultural History of Teacher-Phobia, 1789–1915', PhD thesis, New York University, 2018, p. 227.

42 Wells, *Mr Lewisham*, p. 8.

43 Ibid., p. 8.

44 Ibid., p. 7. Foucault famously analyses the school as a site of modern disciplinary power and the examination as a prime disciplinary instrument in *Discipline and Punish*. See Michel Foucault, *Discipline and Punish: The Birth of the Prison*, trans. Alan Sheridan (London: Penguin, 1977), pp. 184–94.

45 Ibid., p. 11.

46 Ibid., p. 11.

47 Ibid., pp. 7–8.

48 Ibid., p. 97 and p. 12.

49 Ibid., p. 51.

50 Ibid., p. 27.

51 Ibid., p. 30.

52 For an analysis of the anxieties provoked by the professional ideal and the new culture of credentialism in the Edwardian period, as well as in relation to Wells's work, see David Trotter, *Paranoid Modernism: Literary Experiment, Psychosis, and the Professionalisation of English Society* (Oxford: Oxford University Press, 2001), pp. 6–14 and pp. 128–58.

53 Wells, *Mr. Lewisham*, p. 20.

54 Ibid., p. 46.

55 Franklin, 'p. 232.

56 On Wells's advocacy of scientific education, see Steven McLean, *The Early Fiction of HG Wells: Fantasies of Science Fiction* (Basingstoke: Palgrave Macmillan, 2009), pp. 67–8.

57 Wells, 'What is Cram?', *University Correspondent* (18 March 1893), p. 10. Qtd in Simon James, p. 91.

58 Wells, *Mr Lewisham*, p. 12, p. 46, p. 111, and p. 175.

59 Adam Roberts, *HG Wells: A Literary Life* (Basingstoke: Palgrave Macmillan, 2019), p. 89; and Carey, p. 142.

60 Unsigned review, *Daily Telegraph* (6 June 1900). Reprinted in Patrick Parrinder, ed., *HG Wells: The Critical Heritage* (London: Routledge, 1972), p. 21.

61 Wells, *Mr Lewisham*, p. 54.

62 Qtd in Ian Britain, *Fabianism and Culture: A Study in British Socialism and the Arts 1884–1918* (Cambridge: Cambridge University Press, 2005), p. 2.

63 Wells, *Mr Lewisham*, p.53.

64 Ibid., p. 53.

65 Ibid., p. 102.

66 Wells, *Mankind in the Making*, pp. 250–3.

67 Wells, *Kipps*, p. 134.

68 Matthew Taunton, 'Chorus and Agon in the Political Novel: Staging Left-wing Arguments in H. G. Wells, Iris Murdoch, and Doris Lessing', *Modern Fiction Studies* 67.2 (2021), pp. 248–54.

69 Ibid., p. 254.

70 Wells, *Mr Lewisham*, p. 137.

71 Ibid., p. 162.

72 Taunton, 'Chorus and Agon', p. 255.

73 See Sara Lyons, 'Secularism and Secularisation at the Fin de Siècle', in *Edinburgh Companion to Fin de Siècle Literature, Culture, and the Arts*, ed. Josephine Guy (Edinburgh: Edinburgh University Press, 2018), 212–50, pp. 132–8.

74 Wells, *Mr Lewisham*, p. 13.

75 Ibid., pp. 121–4.

76 Ibid., p. 24.

77 Higgins, p. 460.

78 Wells, *Mr Lewisham*, p. 203.

79 Qtd in Beer, 'Introduction', in Wells, *Mr Lewisham*, p. xxv.

80 Bourdieu and Passeron, p. 161.

81 Wells, *Mr Lewisham*, p. 179.

82 Ibid., pp. 207–8.

83 Franklin, p. 237.

84 Ibid., p. 228.

85 Wells, *Mr Lewisham*, p. 164.

86 Ibid., p. 60.

87 Ibid., p. 207.

88 Berlant, p. 171.

89 Wells, *Mr Lewisham*, p. 207.

90 Wells, *Kipps*, p. 155.

91 See Higgins, 'Feeling like a Clerk'; Simon James, pp. 97–10; Roberts, pp. 120–34; and Taunton, 'Chorus and Agon'.

92 For a discussion of Dickens's handlings of the holy fool archetype, see Robert M. McCarron, 'Folly and Wisdom: Three Dickensian Wise Fools', *Dickens Studies Annual* 6 (1977), pp. 40–56; and Patrick McDonagh, *Idiocy: A Cultural History* (Cambridge: Cambridge University Press, 2008), pp. 170–91.

93 Jackson, *The Borderland of Imbecility*.

94 Ibid., pp. 28–33.

95 Ibid., pp. 37–9.

96 See Introduction, pp. 34–5.

97 For an analysis of these public inquiries and the 1899 Education Act, see Sutherland, *Ability, Merit and Measurement*, pp. 8–24.

98 Ibid., p. 33.

99 McDonagh, p. 201.

100 Jackson, pp. 37–40. See also Greenslade, pp. 201–3.

101 Jackson, pp. 35–7.

102 Ibid., pp. 53–6.

103 Byrne, p. 257.

104 Kevles, p. 106.

105 See Searle, *Eugenics and Politics*, p. 111; and Matthew Thomson, 'Disability, Psychiatry and Eugenics', in *The Oxford Handbook of the History of Eugenics*, ed. Alison Bashford and Philippa Levine (Oxford: Oxford University Press, 2010), 116–33, p. 118, and Kevles, p. 99.

106 Qtd in Byrne, p. 264.

107 Jackson, pp. 139–42.

108 Joseph Valente, 'Modernism and Cognitive Disability: A Genealogy', in *A Handbook of Modernism Studies*, ed. Jean-Michel Rabaté (Oxford: John Wiley & Sons, 2013), 379–98, p. 385.

109 Qtd in Jackson, p. 67.

110 G. K. Chesterton, *Eugenics and Other Evils* (London: Cassell and Company, 1922), p. 61.

111 Wedgwood at the Debate on the Mental Deficiency Bill in the House of Commons, Friday, 19 July 1912. Available at: <https://hansard.parliament.uk/commons/1912-07-19/debates/7d188a6f-ca8a-4d9f-815c-8fdebde5a9a9/MentalDeficiencyBill> (accessed 29 November 2021).

112 Jackson, p. 129. Tredgold qtd in Jackson, p. 95.

113 For an analysis of the racist and sexist assumptions underpinning the construction of feeble-mindedness in the period, see Jackson, pp. 131–7 and pp. 144–8.

114 Isabel Foard, 'The Power of Heredity', *Westminster Review* 151.5 (May 1899), 538–53, p. 539.

115 See Jackson, pp. 138–41.

116 Qtd in Jackson, p. 143.

117 Jackson, pp. 138–44.

118 G. L. Bruce, 'The Future of our Feeble-Minded Children', *The Speaker* (6 June 1901), 380–1, p. 318.

119 Wedgwood at the second reading of the Feeble-Minded Persons (Control) Bill in the House of Commons, 17 May 1912. Hansard. Available at: <https://api.parliament.uk/historic-hansard/commons/1912/may/17/feeble-minded-persons-control-bill> (last accessed 30 November 2021).

120 Wedgwood debating the Mental Deficiency Bill, Monday, 28 July 1913. Hansard. Available at: <https://hansard.parliament.uk/commons/1913-07-28/debates/0e227576-1e34-4f79-be15-36b20d250265/Clause1—(DefinitionOfDefectives)> (last accessed 24 March 2022).

121 John Partington, 'The Death of the Static: HG Wells and the Kinetic Utopia', *Utopian Studies* 11.2 (2000), 96–111, pp. 101–2.

122 Wells, *Anticipations*, p. 89 and p. 80.

123 Roberts's comprehensive overview of Wells's published work makes this apparent. See Roberts's analysis of Wells's collection of essays *An Englishman Looks at the World* (1914), his novel *Men Like Gods* (1923), and his 'outline of biology' co-written with his son Gip and Julian Huxley, *The Science of Life* (1930), in Roberts, pp. 273–4, pp. 315–16, and p. 375.

124 Chesterton, pp. 69–70.

125 Ibid., pp. 70–2.

126 Wells, *Mankind in the Making*, pp. 40–50.

127 Wedgwood at the second reading of the Feeble-Minded Persons (Control) Bill in the House of Commons, 17 May 1912. Hansard. Available at: <https://api.parliament.uk/historic-hansard/commons/1912/may/17/feeble-minded-persons-control-bill> (last accessed 30 November 2021).

128 See Carey, pp. 140–1.

129 For discussion of the autobiographical dimensions of the novel, see Roberts, p. 123.

130 Wells, *Kipps*, p. 164.

131 Ibid., p. 134.

132 Ibid., p. 310, p. 62, p. 89, p. 30, and p. 199.

133 Ibid., pp. 40–1.

134 Ibid., p. 310, p. 237, and p. 210.

135 Simon James, p. 100; and Wells, *Kipps*, p. 22, p. 39, and p. 89.

136 I am conscious that some of my characterisation of Kipps aligns him with contemporary understandings of autism spectrum disorder. For a subtle exploration of the complexities of this kind of anachronistic reading of autism, see Joseph Valente's 'The Accidental Autist: Neurosensory Disorder in Conrad's *The Secret Agent*', *Journal of Modern Literature* 38.1 (2014), pp. 20–37. Interestingly, Conrad's epigraph gestures at a link between Wells's *Kipps* and his own novel: Conrad dedicates that novel to 'H.G. Wells: the chronicler of Mr Lewisham's love/the biographer of Kipps and the historian of the ages to come/this simple tale of the nineteenth century/is affectionately offered'. Conrad's echo of *Kipps*'s subtitle – 'the story of a simple soul' – perhaps suggests that Kipps was an imaginative source for his construction of Stevie, the character Valente identifies as the novel's 'accidental autist'.

137 Wells, *Kipps*, pp. 250–4.

138 Ibid., p. 174.

139 Ibid., p. 252.

140 Ibid., p. 135 and p. 280.

141 Ibid., p. 253.

142 Ibid., p. 62.

143 Ibid., pp. 62–3.

144 Ibid.

145 Ibid., p. 50 and p. 61.

146 Ibid., *Kipps*, p. 61.

147 Simon James, p. 99.

148 Wells, *Kipps*, p. 61.

149 Ibid., p. 192.

150 Ibid., p. 134.

151 Ibid., pp. 172–3.

152 Ibid., p. 185.

153 Valente, 'Cognitive Disability', p. 390.

154 McDonagh, p. 134.

155 Wells, *Kipps*, p. 134.

156 Ibid., p. 54.

157 Ibid., pp. 53–4.

158 Ibid., p. 296.

159 Ibid., p. 309.

160 Benjamin Kohlmann, '"The End of Laissez-Faire": Literature, Economics, and the Idea of the Welfare State', *Late Victorian into Modern*, ed. Laura Marcus, Michèle Mendelssohn, and Kirsten E. Shepherd-Barr (Oxford: Oxford University Press, 2016), 448–62, p. 456.

161 Wells, *Kipps*, p. 180.

162 Ibid., p. 180.

163 Ibid., p. 170.

164 Sandel, p. 25.

165 Wells, *Kipps*, p. 153.

166 Ibid., p. 158.

167 Ibid., p. 206.

168 Ibid., p. 310.

169 Ibid., p. 279.

170 Ibid., p. 310.

171 Ibid., p. 310.

172 Carey, p. 144.

173 Wells, *Kipps*, p. 334.

174 Ibid., p. 234.

175 H. G. Wells, *The History of Mr. Polly* (London: Penguin, 1946), p. 15.

176 Ibid., p. 16.

177 Ibid., p. 49.

178 Ibid., p. 133.

179 Ibid., p. 43.

180 Ibid., p. 27.

181 Ibid., p. 128, p. 145, and p. 92. 'Savant syndrome' was first described by the English doctor John Langdon Down in 1887. See David Henry Feldman and Martha J. Morelock, 'Prodigies and Savants', in *The Cambridge Handbook of Intelligence*, ed. Robert J. Sternberg and Scott Barry Kaufman (Cambridge: Cambridge University Press, 2011), 210–34, p. 219.

182 Ibid., p. 128.

183 Ibid., p. 75.

Coda

Virginia Woolf's Hereditary Genius

Virginia Woolf's second novel, *Night and Day* (1919), is probably her least loved and least esteemed. When considered at all, it is understood as a belatedly 'Victorian' novel, both because of its relatively conventional realist form and because it broods over the legacies of Victorian culture. Woolf's modernist contemporaries were rather disdainful even when claiming to admire it: Katherine Mansfield marvelled that it harkened back to the work of Jane Austen and failed to confront the trauma of the First World War; Ford Madox Ford thought it read as if it was written by a George Eliot who had lost the courage of her didacticism.[1] These damning judgements – often partially affirmed even in recent and more sympathetic appraisals – overlook the complexity of the novel's critique of Victorian ideas about professionalism, meritocracy, and intelligence.[2] This is in part because critics have overlooked the significance of the novel's opening reflections on Galton's *Hereditary Genius* – a work which actually traced Woolf's own family lineage as part of its effort to prove the heritability of intellectual gifts. The heroine of *Night and Day*, Katharine Hilbery, attempts to escape Galton's biological determinism by turning away from literary ideals of creativity and inspiration: her grandfather was a famous poet, and so by rejecting literature she makes a feminist bid for autonomy and self-determination. However, Katharine actually affirms the Galtonian model of intelligence in her very effort to escape it: she becomes a mathematician, the supreme type of Galtonian genius. I read *Night and Day* as Woolf's effort to confront the implications of the cultural shift from humanist and Romantic ideals of genius to posthuman intelligence. Perhaps

238

surprisingly, this is a shift that the novel tries to celebrate, or at least not simply to mourn. However, Woolf's underlying ambivalence toward it shapes the novel's melancholic representations of feminist and democratic politics, as well as its jaundiced view of the meritocratic ideal.

At the opening of *Night and Day*, Katharine feels suffocated by her illustrious family and by the weight of the Victorian past in general, particularly its cult of 'great men'.[3] Her grandfather was Richard Alardyce, a famous poet, and she and her mother are engaged in the barren and apparently unfinishable task of co-writing his biography. Woolf makes clear that Katharine's sense of paralysis is a condition peculiar to her class: like Woolf herself, Katharine is a daughter of the Victorian intellectual aristocracy, and Woolf's evocation of the Hilbery family is transparently semi-autobiographical. At the start of the novel, Katharine is beginning to feel that being to the manor born intellectually is more a burden than a blessing:

> The quality of her birth oozed into Katharine's consciousness from a dozen different sources as soon as she was able to perceive anything [. . .] From hearing constant talk of great men and their works, her earliest conceptions of the world included an august circle of beings to whom she gave the names Shakespeare, Milton, Shelley, and so on, who were, for some reason, much more nearly akin to the Hilberys than to other people. They made a kind of boundary to her vision of life [. . .] Her descent from one of those gods was no surprise to her, but matter of satisfaction, until, as the years wore on the privileges of her lot were taken for granted, and certain drawbacks made themselves very manifest. Perhaps it is a little depressing to inherit not lands but an example of intellectual and spiritual virtue [. . .] the glorious past [. . .] intruded too much upon the present, and dwarfed it too consistently, to be altogether encouraging to one forced to make her experiment in living when the great age was dead.[4]

Katharine finds the 'quality of her birth' depressing because intellectual virtue is not really supposed to be a matter of birth right, at least not within the liberal, proudly meritocratic terms of the upper-middle-class intelligentsia to which she belongs. But the meritocratic achievements of one generation become the patrimony of the next, and meritocracy thereby ossifies into a new, modern kind of aristocracy. Katharine is mired in this ideological contradiction: by dutifully revering her family inheritance, she is at the same time betraying its meritocratic spirit. For this reason, Katharine envies the novel's two lower-middle-class characters, Ralph Denham and Mary Datchet, their lack of privileges and family connections. Both Ralph and Mary are depicted as unglamorous strivers; they are defined by the 'infinite dreariness and sordidness' of their families and by their dogged commitment to hard work.[5] Where Katharine's intellectual life is quasi-aristocratic, dominated by the 'refinements' of literature and by her duties as a hostess in her family's salon, Ralph's and Mary's have been dominated by formal education, competitive exams, and office work.[6] Woolf underscores that both Ralph and Mary's educations have been a utilitarian grind, lacking the aesthetic and spiritual forms of *Bildung* that Katharine has had at her disposal in abundance.[7] Yet Katharine perceives their struggles to prove their merit – Ralph as a solicitor and a critic, Mary as a suffragist and political writer – as freedom: 'People like Ralph and Mary, [Katharine] thought, had it all their own way, and empty space before them.'[8] This is because Katharine recognises Ralph and Mary are the rightful heirs of her own meritocratic inheritance.

Early in the novel, Woolf suggests that Katharine's double-bind may not be purely psychological or ideological. The narrator wryly alludes to Galton's *Hereditary Genius* and suggests that the renown of the Alardyce family may be explained by it. Galton's *Hereditary Genius* thoroughly confounds meritocratic and aristocratic conceptions of human worth just as Katharine's family does *Night and Day*. This is no accident; Woolf descended from the same original network of influential dissenting families as Galton and Darwin. Galton was a friend of Woolf's father, Leslie Stephen, and he even cited Woolf's own family as one of his examples of hereditary genius, listing her father, paternal uncle, and paternal grandfather as 'eminent men'.[9]

At first glance, Woolf's narrator in *Night and Day* seems to dispose of Galton's ideas with a brief but trenchant critique:

Denham had accused Katharine Hilbery of belonging to one of the most distinguished families in England, and if anyone will take the trouble to consult Mr Galton's *Hereditary Genius*, he will find that this assertion is not far from the truth. The Alardyces, the Hilberys, the Millingtons and the Otways seem to prove that intellect is a possession which can be tossed from one member of a certain group to another almost indefinitely, and with apparent certainty that the brilliant gift will be safely caught and held by nine out of ten of the privileged race. They had been conspicuous judges and admirals, lawyers and servants of the state for some years before the richness of the soil culminated in the rarest flower any family can boast, a great writer [. . .]; and having produced him, they proved once more the amazing virtues of their race by proceeding unconcernedly again with their usual task of breeding distinguished men. They had sailed with Sir John Franklin to the North Pole, and ridden with Havelock to the Relief of Lucknow [. . .]

It may be said, indeed, that English society being what it is, no very great merit is required, once you bear a well-known name, to put you into a position where it is easier on the whole to be eminent than obscure. And if this is true of the sons, even the daughters, even in the nineteenth century, are apt to become people of importance [. . .] It is true that there were several lamentable exceptions to this rule in the Alardyce group, which seems to indicate that the cadets of such houses go more rapidly to the bad than the children of ordinary fathers and mothers, as if it were somehow a relief to them. But on the whole, in the first years of the twentieth century, the Alardyces were keeping their heads well above water. One finds them at the tops of professions, with letters after their names; they sit in luxurious public offices, with private secretaries [. . .]; they write solid books in dark covers, issued by the presses of the two great universities, and when one of them dies the chances are that another of them writes his biography.[10]

Woolf here coolly demystifies the Victorian intellectual aristocracy, revealing how it sustains itself not by virtue of natural superiority but through the class magic of a 'well-known name'.[11] Woolf also underscores the emphatically patrilineal nature of Galton's theory of intelligence. As noted in the Introduction, *Hereditary Genius* essentially treats the 'female line of descent' as 'noisy' data: mothers are obscure, probably meaningless information, dead branches in the patriarchal tree of genius. Nevertheless, the logic of Galton's genealogy means that women necessarily bask in the reflected glow of their illustrious male kin, as Katharine is expected to do. Throughout *Night and Day*, Woolf underscores how women in fact play an essential role in the social reproduction of an intellectual aristocracy: both Katharine and her mother are the high priestesses of the Alardyce family myth and legacy, not merely producing the biography of their famous forebear but devoting their lives to sanctifying the literary culture of the nineteenth century and thereby preserving the context in which Alardyce's 'genius' makes sense. Woolf suggests that literary genius is what really seals the mystique of an intellectual aristocracy: breeding 'judges and admirals, lawyers and servants of state' is the bread and butter of social reproduction, but it requires a famous poet to make inherited privilege seem truly spiritual and beautiful, a matter of poetic justice. At the same time, this intellectual aristocracy clearly has interests in political power: throughout the novel, Woolf calls attention to the critical role such intellectual elites play not just in management but also in the glamour of Britain's empire.[12] This glamour inheres partly in how such elites imbue their political and colonial positions with their sentimentality about literature. Later in the novel, we learn that Katharine's Uncle Aubrey 'ruled a large part of the Indian Empire, but was in the habit of saying that he had rather have written the works of Dickens'.[13] The novel's insistent references to the Civil Service, to competitive examinations, and even to Macaulay reveal Woolf's awareness of the origins of the modern, meritocratic ideal of intellectual ability in the mid-Victorian Civil Service reforms: at bottom, 'intellectual ability' is the ability to be a useful administrator of the empire and the state, even if those origins are partly mystified by the aesthetic sensibilities of the intellectual aristocracy.[14]

The narrator's arch analysis of the sociology of 'distinguished families' would seem to banish the spectre of Galton's *Hereditary Genius*. But it does not: Galton's biological determinism, as well as his posthumanist conception of 'genius', cast a long shadow over the novel. Galton's ideas lie at the core of Katharine's coldness and nihilism, her desire to disentangle herself from all human relationships and not be human herself. They are equally central to the novel's own formal impasse: while *Night and Day* continually expresses its disenchantment with Victorian plots and cultural paradigms, it is nevertheless doomed to repeat them.

The plot of *Night and Day* revolves around two overlapping love triangles, with Katharine as the nexus between them. Throughout the novel, Woolf makes clear that these love triangles have actually arisen from a deficit of passion. Love is this novel is chilly and abstract, driven by fantasies of professional success and class mobility. The various love plots keep stalling out because characters recognise that they are not, in fact, in love; they continually have to talk themselves into being in love, and they repeatedly lose faith in what seems a dishonest labour, much like the unwritable

biography of Katharine's grandfather. The chill emanates principally from Katharine, who is demoralised by the fact that her
two suitors – Ralph and William Rodney – fetishise her because
of her intellectual pedigree. Both ambitious *littérateurs* stifled by
their official careers (William is a clerk in a government office),
Ralph and William each hope that, by marrying Katharine, they
will be touched by the spirit of hereditary genius and become great
themselves. The upper-class mediocrity William fantasises that
Katharine is a kind of latter-day feminine incarnation of Matthew
Arnold: he thinks of her as a 'distinguished figure', 'an arbitress of
life [. . .] whose judgment was naturally right and steady'.[15] His
desire to marry her is a matter of both professional and eugenic
choice: he wants her to 'glorif[y] him and his doings' and be
'a perfect mother – a mother of sons'.[16] The lower-middle-class
Ralph's idealisation of Katharine is edged with class *ressentiment*,
but he also imagines Katharine as a kind of mystical judge of
male intellectual worth: he fantasises that her mind is 'exalted and
infallible' and that, 'though fastidious at first, she [will] swoop
[. . .] from her eminence to crown him with her approval'.[17] In
her evocations of both Ralph and William's fantasy lives, Woolf
highlights that women often bear the secret symbolic burdens of
the idea of an intellectual aristocracy despite the fact that they are
generally effaced from its official scrolls of achievement. Being
objectified as the symbol, 'arbitress', and potential vessel of literary genius has spoiled not just literature but romantic love (or at
least heterosexual love) for Katharine: she strives to avoid both
passion and introspection and 'hates' poetry and heterosexual
romance with equal vehemence.[18]

Like ideas of genius and literary creativity, romantic love has
been thoroughly secularised, naturalised, and disenchanted in
this novel. Woolf makes clear that her characters are unable to
experience strong romantic passion because a post-Darwinian,
post-Mendelian understanding of human relationships has robbed
them of the capacity for ennobling illusions. Woolf clarifies the
neo-Darwinian context of the novel's unromantic love triangles
somewhat heavy-handedly: lengthy courtship scenes take place at
Kew Gardens and at the London Zoo, and these become opportunities for characters to ponder the connections between human,
plant, and animal evolution. Cassandra Otway, Katharine's cousin
and technically her rival for William's hand in marriage, muses
over Mendelian genetics at the zoo: 'she had once trifled with the

psychology of animals, and still knew something about inherited characteristics [. . .] and the recurrence of blue eyes and brown'.[19] Katharine compares William to 'a wretched misanthropical ape' in the monkey cage, and the ensuing fight between them 'pull[s] Katharine down into some horrible swamp of her nature where the primeval struggle between man and woman still rages'.[20] Katharine also has a classically Victorian spasm of horror when contemplating Darwinian evolution: she imagines the human body 'reduced [. . .] to an apelike, furry form, crouching amid the brushwood of a barbarous clod of mud'. Yet the wider context of this moment of horror is pointedly un-Victorian, insofar as Katharine actually rejoices in the idea of humanity's displacement from the centre of the universe:

> the stars did their usual work upon the mind, froze to cinders the whole of our short human history, and reduced the human body to an ape-like, furry form, crouching amid the brushwood of a barbarous clod of mud. This stage was soon succeeded by another, in which there was nothing in the universe save stars and the light of stars; as she looked up the pupils of her eyes so dilated with starlight that the whole of her seemed dissolved in silver and spilt over the ledges of the stars for ever and ever indefinitely through space.[21]

Throughout *Night and Day*, Katharine's interests in astronomy and mathematics reflect her desire to escape not just the literary culture of her family, but all human intimacy and – as the above passage suggests – her own embodiment. 'I want to work something in figures – something that hasn't got to do with human beings. I don't want people particularly,' she says to William.[22] The narrator later tells us: 'Spiritually there was no human being with whom [Katharine] could claim comradeship; [. . .] nothing remained in whose reality she could believe, save [. . .] abstract ideas – figures, laws, stars, facts.'[23] And if a Darwinian understanding of the animality of human beings appals Katharine, Mendelian genetics appeals to her desire to dissolve into the 'star-like impersonality' of mathematics. Katharine is beguiled when Ralph tells her about modern efforts to understand plant evolution in terms of Mendelian genetics:

> She wished he would go on for ever talking of plants, and showing her how science felt not quite blindly for the law that ruled their endless

variations. A law that might be inscrutable but was certainly omnipotent appealed to her at the moment, because she could find nothing like it in possession of human lives. Circumstances had long forced her, as they force most women in the flower of youth, to consider, painfully and minutely, all that part of life which is conspicuously without order; she had had to consider moods and wishes, degrees of liking or disliking, and their effect upon the destiny of people dear to her; she had been forced to deny herself any contemplation of that other part of life where thought constructs a destiny which is independent of human beings.[24]

Throughout *Night and Day*, Katharine detaches herself from social interactions in favour of private contemplation of a posthuman sublime. While her family members and suitors struggle to command her attention, she secretly ruminates upon 'a vast external world which recks little of the happiness, of the marriages or deaths of individuals'.[25] Her desire to expunge her personality is so radical that she wishes she did not exist even in the consciousnesses of other people: 'She wished that no one in the whole world would think of her.'[26] If Katharine's desire to escape all social and fleshly entanglements registers at times as a rather abstract kind of suicide ideation, Woolf also underscores that it is a post-theological yearning for transcendence: Katharine likes to imagine she has a second body 'concentrated to a silver globe in the fine blue space above the scum of vapors that was covering the visible world'.[27]

Superficially, Katharine's preference for mathematics and astronomy over literature is an attempt to negate the determinism of Galton's *Hereditary Genius*. By rejecting her family's cult of poetic genius, she attempts to assert her existential freedom; by pursuing the 'unwomanly' disciplines of mathematics and science for herself, she attempts to resist her eugenic destiny as a mother of distinguished men.[28] Yet Katharine affirms the deeper logic of Galton's project in her very efforts to defy it. Katharine is markedly Galtonian in her preference for 'the exactitude, the starlike impersonality' of numbers to the 'confusion, agitation, and vagueness' of literature.[29] She is also markedly Galtonian in her desire to discard her individual, embodied subjectivity and live as a machine intelligence, apprehending abstract patterns without emotion. Another way to put this is to say that Katharine shares elements of Galton's posthumanism. As Robin

Durnford has argued, Galton ought to be recognised not simply as the father of eugenics but a proto-posthumanist. Durnford draws primarily upon N. Katherine Hayles's definition of posthumanism: 'the posthuman appears when computation rather than possessive individualism is taken as the ground of being, a move that allows the posthuman to be seamlessly articulated with intelligent machines'.[30] Durnford writes:

> By reducing the knowledge of Great Men to a measurable number, Galton effectively transforms intelligence into 'cognition', a more precisely technoscientific and posthuman term, as it is more directly related, in the twentieth and twenty-first centuries, with computation and information processing. The shift occurs at time when the term 'genius' was being popularly transferred from the arts, where it still retained its old relationship with 'spirit', to the then differentiating sciences, where it was increasingly associated with mathematical logic.[31]

Katharine's rejection of her family's quasi-religious obsession with literature in favour of what she thinks of as the 'impersonality' of science and mathematics allegorises this shift in the cultural significance of genius. That Katharine turns out to be a mathematician rather than a writer also seems to affirm Galton's claim that intelligence is a kind of genetic transferable skill: a hereditary genius may just as easily become a poet or a mathematician, since all intellectual achievement is the expression of an underlying, unidimensional 'ability'. Katharine also shares with Galton a desire to escape her material body and personal identity and exist on a plane of cosmic abstraction. Durnford points out Galton's eugenics is pervaded by a quasi-religious aspiration to transcend the chaos and mortality of Darwinian nature in favour of an ideal of a scientifically perfected intelligence. The fact that Katharine is disgusted by the animality implied by Darwinian nature but enchanted by the mathematical order implied by genetics suggests her underlying kinship with Galton. Durnford observes:

> Galton's eugenics – based on the data-regulated transmission of minds cleansed of bodies (inside a new mind–body dualism) formulated an antibody to Darwin's embodied disharmony. The study of heredity itself becomes a way of edulcorating Darwin's evolutionary theory, with all its labyrinthine materialism; Galton seeks to untangle the

tangled bank [. . .] While both evolution and eugenics question the integrity of the human subject, eugenics calls for new transcendent subjects to be built from any already evolving, and so fragmented and permeable species. Galton's desire to move away from the gross materiality at the heart of evolutionary theory is what connects him most to the posthumanists of the digital age.[32]

In highlighting how Katharine confirms Galton's thesis in *Hereditary Genius* in spite of herself, I do not mean to imply that Katharine or Woolf endorses Galton's eugenics.[33] Rather, I am highlighting that Galton's posthumanist conception of intelligence had implications beyond its explicit eugenicist aims. Both as the daughter of the intellectual aristocracy and as a novelist, Woolf could not fail to find these implications ironic: they seemed to make her own intellectual gifts a matter of scientific certainty and at the same time to announce the obsolescence of her chosen field of endeavour, literature. Woolf projects this double bind on to Katharine but attempts to purge it of her own investments in literature and literary culture – investments which seem, in the context of this novel, to lead only to the Victorian past and thus back to Galtonian 'eminent men'. Katharine is Woolf's effort to imagine a character who could embrace a posthumanist conception of intelligence without a backward glance. *Night and Day* as a whole is nevertheless suffused with Woolf's own ambivalence toward the displacement of literature and literary ideals of creativity and genius. Throughout the novel, Katharine's antipathy to literature and desire to disappear into 'figures, laws, stars, facts' are themselves thoroughly poeticised and romanticised, as though Woolf were attempting to reabsorb Katharine's posthumanism back into the traditions it leaves behind. Take, for example, this passage, where Woolf assigns 'tragic beauty' to Katharine's desire to appraise human relationships as if they were geometry:

> Her mind, passing from Mary to Denham, from William to Cassandra, and from Denham to herself [. . .] seemed to be tracing out the lines of some symmetrical pattern, some arrangement of life, which invested, if not herself, at least the others, not only with interest, but with a kind of tragic beauty. She had a fantastic picture of them upholding splendid palaces upon their bent backs. They were the lantern-bearers, whose lights, scattered among the crowd, wove a pattern, dissolving, joining, meeting again in combination.[34]

It is equally significant that Katharine's attraction to a posthumanist conception of intelligence seems to render her passive and ideologically rudderless, particularly by comparison to Mary. At the end of the novel, Katharine betrays her desire to 'maintain an absolute and fearless independence' and immerse herself in science and mathematics.[35] After evading both William's and Ralph's romantic suits and then contemplating a free union with Ralph, she finally agrees to a conventional marriage to Ralph. In other words, Katharine ultimately succumbs both to the Victorian marriage plot and to the plot of Galton's *Hereditary Genius*, which would cast her as a handmaiden to male greatness. That other plots – more interesting feminist futures – were open to Katharine is underscored in the final scene of the novel when she feels an impulse to walk past Mary's window. By the end of the novel, Mary represents not only a dawning feminist future, but also a more democratic, less class-bound, and perhaps even socialist future. This is underscored by Mary's involvement with the work of Mr Bassnett, a young socialist who has drawn up 'a scheme for the education of labour, for the amalgamation of the middle class and the working class, and for the joint assault of the two bodies [. . .] upon capital'.[36] Woolf initially leads us to expect a romance between Mary and Mr Bassnett, but instead Mary seems only to absorb Mr Bassnett's socialist politics, and she remains the figure of 'absolute and fearless independence' that Katharine wanted to be. Mary's solitude and devotion to her work make Katharine so wistful she is brought to tears, and this suggests that her engagement to Ralph spells the end of her own intellectual ambitions. It also seems to suggest that Katharine can only admire the more egalitarian future Mary is working toward from a distance; her own status as a daughter of the intellectual aristocracy apparently excludes her from it.

Woolf makes clear that Katharine's Victorian forebears were actually like Mary in their commitment to the 'good of a world that none of them were ever to know'.[37] Mrs Hilbery laments that she lacks the philanthropic and reformist zeal of her ancestors, even though she tries to pay homage to it: 'We're virtuous, we're earnest, we go to meetings, we pay the poor their wages, but we don't live as [the Victorians] lived.'[38] As Annan emphasised, the Victorian intellectual aristocracy was initially animated by a strong sense of moral and political purpose: its origins in Evangelical Christianity and the abolitionist movement evolved over the nineteenth century into a more secular sense of obligation to turn one's intellectual gifts to account and improve the world.[39] Woolf was herself highly conscious of her own familial connections to the Clapham Sect and the abolition of the slave trade.[40] In the figure of Mrs Hilbery, the moral and progressive *raison d'être* of the Victorian intellectual aristocracy has faded into a conservative and almost superstitious aestheticism; Shakespeare's grave seems more intensely meaningful to her than any living person or the modern world in general.[41] That Katharine can only appreciate Mary's political commitment from an aestheticised, if somewhat anguished, distance underscores that she is equally alienated from the spirit of moral reform and public service that galvanised her Victorian ancestors. Katharine's wistfulness about Mary's politically engaged life also seems to encode Woolf's own wistfulness about the fact that the novel she is writing is not a New Woman *Bildungsroman* or something more experimental still, but is instead an exhausted rendition of a Victorian realist novel, where the heroine must marry at the end.[42]

Why can Katharine only envy Mary's politically engaged life and not choose it for herself? Why can *Night and Day* only explain its entrapment within a conservative Victorian plot and gesture at other possibilities wistfully? Woolf is partly attempting to convey the extent to which Victorian culture, particularly Victorian literature, can stultify the imagination of even those who have no nostalgia for it: Victorian culture forms a 'boundary' to the 'vision' of this novel no less than it does to Katharine's capacity to plot her future. At the same time, the novel's network of allusions to Galton, Darwin, and Mendel seem to hint that Katharine may be the victim of biological determinism as much as of an overwhelming cultural inheritance. But the deeper logic behind Katharine's bleak *Bildungsroman* is that the idea of hereditary genius produces not more genius but fatalism and apathy. At the start of the novel, Woolf highlights that some members of eminent families find failure and disgrace tempting precisely because of the high achievements expected of them: for some, 'it is almost a relief' to 'go to the bad'.[43] As a woman, Katharine is, of course, generally exempt from such pressures; her desire to be a mathematician is a secret, and she is not expected to pursue a profession beyond the 'ceremony of ancestor worship'.[44] As the novel's satirical depiction of Cassandra's education makes clear, the daughters of the intellectual aristocracy are only expected to be charming dilettantes:

Cassandra was twenty-two, and had never passed an examination, and daily showed herself less capable of passing one. The more serious prediction that she could never possibly earn her living was also verified. But from all the short strands of different accomplishments Cassandra wove for herself an attitude, a cast of mind, which, if useless, was found by some people to have the not despicable virtues of vivacity and freshness.[45]

Yet Katharine's failure to commit to her own ambitions is not simply attributable to this culture of feminine dilettantism. Katharine herself considers Mary's dedication to her work 'infinitely preferable' to Cassandra's 'frivolous' enthusiasms.[46] Katharine betrays her ambitions and drifts into marriage not because she lacks intellectual passion or seriousness – Woolf everywhere indicates that Katharine only really cares about science and mathematics – but because she feels 'dwarfed' by her ancestors and demoralised by a sense of biological determinism.[47] In particular, she is made 'despondent' by the idea that the Alardyce family, having produced its genius, can now produce only a healthy crop of mediocrities: 'it seems as if, having flowered so splendidly nothing now remained possible but the steady growth of good, green stalk and leaf'.[48] Afflicted by both a sense of biological determinism and her bad conscience about the fact that she did not earn her own 'privileged position', Katharine feels little inspiration or energy to 'make her experiment in living'.[49] The tendency of aristocracies toward decadence was a key plank in the Victorian intellectual aristocracy's moral and political critique of the traditional landed aristocracy.[50] However, in the figure of Katharine, Woolf suggests that an intellectual aristocracy may be as prone to exhaustion and decadence as the landed aristocracy it meant to usurp.

Woolf largely affirms the wisdom of Katharine's apathy and lack of professional ambition by making meritocratic striving seem like limitation rather than self-realisation throughout the novel. The self-discipline required by Ralph in his work as a solicitor has led him to believe that 'life for most people compels the exercise of lower gifts and wastes the precious ones, until it forces us to agree that there is little virtue, as well as little profit, in what seemed to us the noblest part of our inheritance'.[51] The novel also persistently highlights the psychic and domestic toll of professional ambition. For example, we are given the brief case study of Katharine's uncle, Sir Francis Otway, who was in the Indian Civil

Service but whose 'career had not come up to his expectations' because his 'merits had been passed over in a disgraceful manner'. The narrator tells us that this career disappointment had 'poisoned' not only the life of Sir Francis, but the lives of his wife and children – despite the fact that the 'rights and wrongs' of his professional failure are obscure to them.[52] The novel's vignettes about the psychic and moral costs of professional ambition – particularly the costs borne by the wives and children of ambitious men – make the marriage between Ralph and Katharine seem ill-fated, at least for Katharine. Right up until the end of the novel, Woolf emphasises that Ralph desires Katharine because he thinks of her as a talisman which can protect him against professional failure. Ralph's impulse to pursue Katharine one last time, despite her obviously lukewarm feelings for him, is triggered by his encounter with a homeless drunk on a bench on the Embankment. The drunk is a kind of Ancient Mariner figure who undermines Ralph's faith in meritocratic success:

> It was a windy night, [the drunk] said; times were hard; some long story of bad luck and injustice followed, told so often that the man seemed to be talking to himself [. . .] When he began to speak Ralph had a wild desire to talk to him; to question him; to make him understand. He did, in fact, interrupt him at one point; but it was useless. The ancient story of failure, ill-luck, undeserved disaster, went down the wind, disconnected syllables flying past Ralph's ears with a queer alternation of loudness and faintness as if, at certain moments, the man's memory of his wrongs revived and then flagged, dying down at last into a grumble of resignation [. . .] And when the elderly man refused to listen and mumbled on, an odd image came to [Ralph's] mind of a lighthouse besieged by the flying bodies of lost birds, who were dashed senseless, by the gale, against the glass. He had a strange sensation that he was both lighthouse and bird; he was steadfast and brilliant; and at the same time he was whirled, with all other things, senseless against the glass. He got up, left his tribute of silver, and pressed on, with the wind against him. The image of the lighthouse and the storm full of birds persisted [. . .] but he never lost his sense of walking in the direction of Katharine's house.[53]

Ralph's surreal vision of himself as at once a steadfast, brilliant lighthouse – an unmistakably phallic image – and one of the birds 'dashed' 'senseless' against it encodes the novel's bleak sense of the arbitrariness of intellectual gifts and meritocratic success. Although *Night and Day* is ostensibly a novel about what it means to think of oneself as intellectually 'brilliant' and as destined to be one of the 'victors, masters of life', it is threaded through with an awareness of the tragic – 'the ancient story of failure, ill-luck, undeserved disaster'.[54] Ralph resolves once again to pursue Katharine as a way of warding off the truth of the drunk's story of injustice – and thereby clarifies once again the quasi-religious role of the intellectual aristocracy in rationalising an irrational social order. The Hilberys, the narrator informs us, possess 'an indefinable freedom and authority of manner' which makes clear they are 'well within the gates' of privilege and 'can smile indulgently at the vast mass of humanity which is forced to wait and struggle'.[55] By marrying Katharine, Ralph hopes that he too will be 'well within the gates'. But Woolf makes clear that Ralph's troubled sense of identification with the 'lost birds' – the masses condemned to failure and disaster – is inseparable from his preferred image of himself as a meritocratic success story, a 'brilliant' individual exception. For this reason, the image of the lost birds will 'persist' in Ralph's imagination – as it is meant to persist in ours.

Notes

1 Ford Madox Ford, 'Romance' (1919) and Katherine Mansfield, rev. of *Night and Day* (1919), reprinted in *Virginia Woolf: The Critical Heritage*, ed. Robin Majumdar and Allen McLaurin (London: Routledge and Kegan Paul, 1975), p. 82 and p. 74.

2 For sympathetic readings, see Mary Jean Corbett, 'Virginia Woolf and the "Third Generation"', *Twentieth Century Literature* 60.1 (2014), pp. 27–58; Jane de Gay, *Virginia Woolf's Novels and the Literary Past* (Edinburgh: Edinburgh University Press, 2006), pp. 44–66; Steve Ellis, *Virginia Woolf and the Victorians* (Cambridge: Cambridge University Press, 2007), pp. 12–42; and Elizabeth Outka, 'The Transitory Space of Night and Day', in *A Companion to Virginia Woolf*, ed. Jessica Berman (Oxford: Wiley Blackwell, 2019), pp. 55–66.

3 Virginia Woolf, *Night and Day* (Ware: Wordsworth Editions, 2012), p. 29.

4 Ibid., pp. 42–3.

5 Ibid., p. 39.

6 Ibid., p. 220.

7   Ibid., pp. 48–51 and pp. 106–7.

8   Ibid., p. 92.

9   See David Bradshaw, 'Eugenics: They Should Certainly be Killed', in *Concise Companion to Modernism*, ed. Bradshaw (Oxford: Wiley Blackwell, 2003), 49–54, p. 50; and Galton, *Hereditary Genius*, p. 185.

10 Woolf, pp. 40–1.

11 One detects the influence of Lytton Strachey here, whose iconoclastic evaluation of the Victorian age, *Eminent Victorians*, was published the year before *Night and Day*. Strachey was yet another self-conscious scion of the Victorian intellectual aristocracy, and his ironic use of 'eminent' is surely in part a gibe at Galton, who had attempted to turn 'eminence' into a biological trait and the basis of a eugenic utopia. For the influence of Strachey on *Night and Day*, see Steve Ellis, pp. 13–16.

12 As Michèle Barrett has pointed out, Woolf was conducting research for her husband, Leonard Woolf's, book *Empire and Commerce in Africa* (1920) while she was writing *Night and Day*. As Roberts writes, *Night and Day* is 'peppered throughout with references to imperial questions' and reflects the broadly anti-imperialist agenda of Woolf's fiction, despite its reputation for being an 'apolitical novel'. My own reading attempts to show that there is a logic to the novel's references to colonialism and empire: they insistently underscore the intimate relationship between the British empire and the meritocratic ideal. See Barrett, 'Virginia Woolf's Research for *Empire and Commerce in Africa* (Leonard Woolf, 1920)', *Woolf Studies Annual* 19 (2013), 83–122, p. 118.

13 Woolf, p. 268.

14 At one point in the novel, Katharine's cousin, Cassandra, is reading Macaulay's *History of England* (1848). Katharine asks her: 'Must you read Macaulay's history?' and stretches, indicating her boredom. The cousins have just been discussing the likelihood that their grandfather was 'a fraud like the rest of them' – that is, like other Victorian men venerated as 'great' – and Macaulay is included by implication in the women's general irreverence toward their familial legacy and the Victorian past. See Woolf, p. 327.

15 Ibid., p. 188.

16 Ibid., p. 193.

17 Ibid., p. 32.

18 Ibid., p. 120 and p. 46.

19 Ibid., p. 281.

20 Ibid., p. 284.

21 Ibid., p. 157.

22 Ibid., p. 156.

23 Ibid., p. 221.

24 Ibid., pp. 255–6.

25 Ibid., p. 256.

26 Ibid., p. 92.

27 Ibid., p. 233.

28 Ibid., p. 48.

29 Ibid., p. 48.

30 N. Katherine Hayles, *How We Became Posthuman: Virtual Bodies in Cybernetics, Literature and Informatics* (Chicago: University of Chicago Press, 1999), p. 34.

31 Durnford, p. 27.

32 Ibid., p. 110.

33 Donald Childs has argued that Woolf was herself a committed eugenicist. His argument rests on meagre evidence: a single diary entry and on the fact that Woolf numbered eugenicists among her acquaintances. His efforts to delineate eugenicist thinking in Woolf's published work are tendentious in the extreme and often perplexing: his own analysis persistently calls attention to the fact that Woolf, as a person who suffered from mental illness, had reason to feel stigmatised by eugenics rather than to champion it obliquely in her work. David Bradshaw provides a valuable critique of Child's reading and uses *Night and Day* as his primary evidence. Bradshaw's reading of *Night and Day* dovetails with my own, but he understands Woolf's engagement with Galton and ideas of hereditary genius as primarily satirical and so under-estimates the scope and complexity of their presence in the novel. See Childs, *Modernism and Eugenics: Woolf, Eliot, Yeats and the Culture of Degeneration* (Cambridge: Cambridge University Press, 2001), pp. 22–37; and Bradshaw, pp. 49–54.

34 Woolf, p. 243.

35 Ibid., p. 243.

36 Ibid., p. 273.

37 Ibid., p. 384.

38 Ibid., p. 101.

39 Annan, p. 245.

40 See Jane de Gay, *Virginia Woolf and Christian Culture* (Edinburgh: Edinburgh University Press, 2018), pp. 20–48.

41 Woolf, p. 326.

42 As de Gay notes, *Night and Day* is often considered a regressive step for Woolf because it is less experimental than her first novel, *The Voyage Out* (1915), and thus spoils any simple narrative of Woolf's journey toward modernism. As my own reading makes clear, I think the retrograde Victorianism of *Night and Day* is by design, not a failure of modernist courage: it embodies the novel's preoccupation with cultural and biological forms of determinism. See de Gay, *Woolf and the Literary Past*, p. 44.

43 Woolf, p. 41.

44 Ibid., p. 247.

45 Ibid., p. 263.

46 Ibid., p. 220.

47 Ibid., p. 43.

48 Ibid., p. 43.

49 Ibid., p. 43.

50 See Wooldridge, *Aristocracy of Talent*, pp. 156–60.

51 Ibid., p. 107.

52 Ibid., p. 164–164.

53 Ibid., p. 301.

54 Ibid., p. 383.

55 Ibid., p. 280.

Bibliography

Adams, James Eli, *Dandies and Desert Saints: Styles of Victorian Masculinity* (Ithaca, NY: Cornell University Press, 1995)

Alaya, Flavia, 'Victorian Science and the "Genius" of Woman', *Journal of the History of Ideas* 38.2 (1977), 261–80

Allen, Ansgar, *Benign Violence: Education In and Beyond the Age of Reason* (Basingstoke: Palgrave Macmillan, 2014)

Allen, Grant, 'Genius and Talent', *Popular Science Monthly* 34 (1889), 341–56

—. 'The Genesis of Genius', *Atlantic Monthly* 47 (1881), 371–81

—. 'Idiosyncrasy', *Popular Science Monthly* 24 (1884), 387–403

—. 'The Recipe for Genius', *Cornhill Magazine* 5 (1885), 406–15

—. Review of L. F. Ward's *Dynamic Sociology*, *Mind* 9 (1884), 305–31

Annan, Noel, 'The Intellectual Aristocracy', in *Studies in Social History*, ed. J. H. Plumb (London: Longmans, 1955), 256–83

Anonymous, 'Competitive Examination', *The Examiner* (5 April 1862), 211

Anonymous, 'Education à la Mode', *Journal of Education* (January–December 1883), 90–1

Armstrong, Isobel, 'Eliot, Hegel, and *Middlemarch*', *19: Interdisciplinary Studies in the Long Nineteenth Century* 29 (2020), <https://doi.org/10.16995/ntn.1992> (last accessed 24 November 2021)

—. *Novel Politics: Democratic Imaginations in Nineteenth Century Fiction* (Oxford: Oxford University Press, 2016)

Bain, Alexander, *Emotions and the Will*, 3rd edition (London: Longmans Green, 1880)

—. *Mental and Moral Science: Psychology and the History of Philosophy*, vol. 1 (London: Longmans Green, 1872)

—. *Mind and Body* (New York: D. Appleton & Co., 1873)

—. *On the Study of Character: Including an Estimate of Phrenology* (London: Parker, Son & Bourn, 1861)

Barrett, Michèle, 'Virginia Woolf's Research for *Empire and Commerce in Africa* (Leonard Woolf, 1920)', *Woolf Studies Annual* 19 (2013), 83–122

Beer, Gillian, *Darwin's Plots: Evolutionary Narrative in Darwin, George Eliot, and Thomas Hardy* (Cambridge: Cambridge University Press, 2000), xiii–xxv

—. 'Introduction', in H. G. Wells, *Love and Mr. Lewisham* (Penguin: London, 2005)

—. 'What's Not in Middlemarch?', in *Middlemarch in the Twenty First Century*, ed. Karen Chase (Oxford: Oxford University Press, 2006), 15–35

Berberich, Christine, *The Image of the English Gentleman in Twentieth-Century Literature* (Farnham: Ashgate, 2013)

Berlant, Lauren, *Cruel Optimism* (Durham, NC: Duke University Press, 2011)

Birch, Dinah, ed. *The Oxford Companion to English Literature*, 7th edition (Oxford: Oxford University Press, 2009)

Blair, Sara, *Henry James and the Writing of Race and Nation* (Cambridge: Cambridge University Press, 1996)

Bonaparte, Felicia, *Will and Destiny: Morality and Tragedy in George Eliot's Novels* (New York: New York University Press, 1975)

Bonea, Amelia, Dickson, Melissa, Shuttleworth, Sally, and Wallis, Jennifer, *Anxious Times: Medicine and Modernity in Nineteenth-century Britain* (Pittsburgh: University of Pittsburgh Press, 2019)

Boos, Florence S., 'The Education Act of 1870: Before and After' (2015), <https://www.branchcollective.org/?ps_articles=florence-s-boos-the-education-act-of-1870-before-and-after> (last accessed 20 November 2021)

Boswell, James, *Life of Johnson*, ed. George Birkbeck Hill (New York: Harper & Bros, 1891)

Boumelha, Penny, '"A Complicated Position for a Woman": *The Hand of Ethelberta*', in *The Sense of Sex: Feminist Perspectives on Hardy*, ed. Margaret R. Higonnet (Champaign: University of Illinois Press, 1993), 242–59

Bourdieu, Pierre, *Distinction: A Social Critique of the Judgment of Taste*, trans. Richard Nice (London: Routledge, 2000)

—. *Homo Academicus* (Stanford, CA: Stanford University Press, 1988)

—. and Jean-Claude Passeron, *Reproduction, Education, Society, and Culture*, 2nd edition, trans. Richard Nice (Los Angeles: Sage, 2000)

Bourrier, Karen, *Measure of Manliness: Disability and Masculinity in the Mid-Victorian Novel* (Ann Arbor: University of Michigan Press, 2015)

Bowler, Peter J., *The Mendelian Revolution: The Emergence of Hereditarian Concepts in Modern Science and Society* (London: The Athlone Press, 1989)

Bownas, Jane L., *Thomas Hardy and Empire: The Representation of Imperial Themes in the Work of Thomas Hardy* (London: Routledge, 2016)

Bradshaw, David, 'Eugenics: They Should Certainly be Killed', in *A Concise Companion to Modernism*, ed. Bradshaw (Oxford: Wiley Blackwell, 2003), 49–54

Brazier, M. A. B., 'Historical Introduction: The Discoverers of the Steady Potentials of the Brain', in *Brain Function*, ed. Mary A. B. Brazier (Berkeley: University of California Press, 1963), 1–14

Britain, Ian, *Fabianism and Culture: A Study in British Socialism and the Arts 1884–1918* (Cambridge: Cambridge University Press, 2005)

Brilmeyer, Pearl S., 'Plasticity, Form and the Matter of Character in *Middlemarch*', *Representations* 130.1 (2015), 60–83

Brooks, Peter, *Henry James Goes to Paris* (Princeton, NJ: Princeton University Press, 2008)

Bruce, G. L., 'The Future of our Feeble-Minded Children', *The Speaker* (6 June 1901), 380–1

Bryant, Sophie, 'Experiments in Testing the Character of School Children', *Journal of the Anthropological Institute of Great Britain and Ireland* 15 (1886), 338–51

Bryce Report: Report on the Royal Commission of Secondary Education (London: Eyre and Spottiswoode, 1895)

Bulmer, Michael, *Francis Galton: Pioneer of Heredity and Biometry* (Baltimore: Johns Hopkins University Press, 2003)

Burt, Cyril, 'Experimental Tests of General Intelligence', *British Journal of Psychology* 3.1–2 (1909), 94–117

—. 'Historical Sketch of the Development of Psychological Tests', *Hadow Report on Psychological Tests of Educable Capacity and their Possible Use in the Public System of Education* (London: Her Majesty's Stationery Office, 1924)

Byrne, Stephen, 'Classification, Variation, and Education: The Making and Remaking of the Normal Child in England, c. 1880–1914', PhD thesis, Oxford Brookes University, 2013

Carey, John, *The Intellectuals and the Masses: Pride and Prejudice Among the Literary Intelligentsia 1880–1839* (London: Faber & Faber, 1992)

Carson, John, *The Measure of Merit: Talents, Intelligence, and Inequality in the French and American Republics, 1750–1940* (Princeton, NJ: Princeton University Press, 2007)

Castle, Gregory, *Reading the Modernist Bildungsroman* (Gainesville: University Press of Florida, 2006)

Cattell, J. M., 'Mental Tests and Measurements', *Mind* 15 (1890), 373–80

Chesterton, G. K., *Eugenics and Other Evils* (London: Cassell and Company, 1922)

Childs, Donald J., *Modernism and Eugenics: Woolf, Eliot, Yeats and the Culture of Degeneration* (Cambridge: Cambridge University Press, 2001)

Christoff, Alicia Mireles, *Novel Relations: Victorian Fiction and British Psychoanalysis* (Princeton, NJ: Princeton University Press, 2019)

Clark, William, *Academic Charisma and the Origins of the Research University* (Chicago: University of Chicago Press, 2008)

Clarke, Edwin and Jacyna, L. S., *The Nineteenth-Century Origins of Neuroscientific Concepts* (Berkeley: University of California Press, 1987)

Clauzade, Laurent, 'From the Science of the Mind to Character Study: Alexander Bain and the Psychology of Individual Differences', *Revue d'histoire des sciences* 60.2 (2007), 281–301

Cohen, William, 'Arborealities: The Tactile Ecology of Hardy's *Woodlanders*', *19: Interdisciplinary Studies in the Long Nineteenth Century* 19 (2014), 1–22, <https://www.19.bbk.ac.uk/articles/10.169 95/ntn.690/> (last accessed 28 November 2022)

Cole, Sarah, *Inventing Tomorrow: HG Wells and the Twentieth Century* (New York: Columbia University Press, 2019)

Coleman, Dermot, *George Eliot and Money: Economics, Ethics, and Literature* (Cambridge: Cambridge University Press, 2014)

Collins, K. K., *George Eliot: Interviews and Recollections* (Basingstoke: Palgrave Macmillan, 2010)

—. 'G. H. Lewes Revised: George Eliot and the Moral Sense', *Victorian Studies* 21.4 (1978), 463–92

Compton, J. M., 'Indians and the Indian Civil Service, 1853–1879: A Study in National Agitation and Imperial Embarrassment', *Journal of the Asiatic Society of Great Britain and Ireland* 3/4 (1967), 99–113

—. 'Open Competition and the Indian Civil Service, 1854–1876', *English Historical Review* 83.327 (1968), 265–84

Cooper, Andrew, 'Voicing the Language of Literature: Jude's Obscured Labour', *Victorian Literature and Culture* 28.2 (2000), 391–410

Cooter, Roger, *The Cultural Meaning of a Popular Science: Phrenology and the Organisation of Consent in Nineteenth-Century Britain* (Cambridge: Cambridge University Press, 1984)

Corbett, Mary Jean, *Family Likeness: Sex, Marriage, and Incest from Jane Austen to Virginia Woolf* (New Haven, CT: Cornell University Press, 2008)

—. 'Virginia Woolf and the "Third Generation"', *Twentieth Century Literature* 60.1 (2014), 27–58

Cordner, Sheila, *Education in Nineteenth-century British Literature: Exclusion as Innovation* (London: Routledge, 2016)

Crichton-Browne, James, *Report of Dr. Crichton-Browne to the Education Department upon the Alleged Over-pressure of Work in Public Elementary Schools* (London: Henry Hansard & Son, 1884)

Danziger, Kurt, *Naming the Mind: How Psychology Found its Language* (London: Sage, 1997)

Darwin, Charles, *The Descent of Man, and Selection in Relation to Sex* (London: John Murray, 1871)

Daston, Lorraine, 'The Naturalised Female Intellect', *Science in Context* 5.2 (1992), 209–35

Davis, Michael, *George Eliot and Nineteenth-century Psychology: Exploring the Unmapped Country* (London: Routledge, 2016)

De Gay, Jane, *Virginia Woolf and Christian Culture* (Edinburgh: Edinburgh University Press, 2018)

—. *Virginia Woolf's Novels and the Literary Past* (Edinburgh: Edinburgh University Press, 2006)

Dell, Katherine Julia, *The Book of Job as Sceptical Literature* (Berlin: Walter de Gruyter, 1991)

Dellamora, Richard, *Friendship's Bonds: Democracy and the Novel in Victorian England* (Philadelphia: University of Pennsylvania Press, 2004)

Deslandes, Paul R., 'Competitive Examinations and the Culture of Masculinity in Oxbridge Undergraduate Life, 1850–1920', *History of Education Quarterly* 42. 4 (2002), 544–78

Dryden, Lynda, 'The Difference Between Us: Conrad, Wells, and the English Novel', *Studies in the Novel* 45.2 (2013), 214–33

Durnford, Robin, 'Posthumanous Victorians: Francis Galton's Eugenics and Fin de Siècle Science Fictions', PhD thesis, University of Alberta, 2013

Dutta, Shanta, *Ambivalence in Hardy: A Study of His Attitude to Women* (Basingstoke: Macmillan, 2000)

Dyson, Carol, *No Distinction of Sex? Women in British Universities 1870–1939* (London: UCL Press, 1995)

Eagleton, Terry, *Sweet Violence: The Idea of the Tragic* (Oxford: John Wiley & Sons, 2003)

Eliot, George, *Daniel Deronda*, ed. Terence Holt (London: Penguin, 1995)

—. *Impressions of Theophrastus Such* (New York: A. L. Burt, [1879] 1900)

—. *Middlemarch*, ed. Rosemary Ashton (Penguin: London, 2003)

—. *The Mill on the Floss*, ed. A. S. Byatt (London: Penguin, 1979)

—. 'Women in France', in *Selected Critical Writings*, ed. Rosemary Ashton (Oxford: Oxford University Press, 1992), 37–68

Ellis, Havelock, *Little Essays on Love and Virtue* (New York: George H. Doran Company, 1921)

Ellis, Heather, 'Efficiency and Counter-revolution: Connecting University and Civil Service Reform in the 1850s', *History of Education* 42.1 (2013), 23–44

Ellis, Steve, *Virginia Woolf and the Victorians* (Cambridge: Cambridge University Press, 2007)

Elwick, James, *Making a Grade: Victorian Examinations and the Rise of Standardised Testing* (Toronto: University of Toronto Press, 2021)

Etsy, Jed, *Unseasonable Youth: Modernism, Colonialism and the Fiction of Development* (Oxford: Oxford University Press, 2011)

Fancher, Raymond, 'Francis Galton's African Ethnography and its Role in the Development of Psychology', *The British Journal for the History of Science* 16.1 (1983), 67–79

—. *The Intelligence Men: Makers of the IQ Controversy* (New York: W. W. Norton, 1985)

Feldman, David Henry and Morelock, Martha J. 'Prodigies and Savants', in *The Cambridge Handbook of Intelligence*, ed. Robert J. Sternberg and Scott Barry Kaufman (Cambridge: Cambridge University Press, 2011), 210–34

Fisher, H. A. L., 'Heredity and Imitation', *The Speaker* (28 July 1900), 455–6

Fiske, John, 'Sociology and Hero-worship: An Evolutionist's Reply to Dr. James', *Atlantic Monthly* 47 (1881), 75–84

Flint, Kate, *The Woman Reader, 1837–1914* (Oxford: Clarendon Press, 1993)

Foard, Isabel, 'The Power of Heredity', *Westminster Review* 151.5 (May 1899), 538–53

Ford, Ford Madox, 'Romance' (1919), in *Virginia Woolf: the Critical Heritage*, ed. Robin Majumdar and Allen McLaurin (London: Routledge and Kegan Paul, 1975), 72–5

Foucault, Michel, *Discipline and Punish: The Birth of the Prison*, trans. Alan Sheridan (London: Penguin, 1977)

—. *The History of Sexuality, vol. 1: An Introduction*, trans. Robert Hurley (London: Penguin Books, 1976)

—. *Society Must be Defended: Lectures at the Collège de France, 1975–76*, trans. David Macey (London: Penguin, 1997)

Franklin, Jonathan, 'Those Who Can't: A Cultural History of Teacher-Phobia, 1789–1915', PhD thesis, New York University, 2018

Freedman, Jonathan, *Professions of Taste: Henry James, British Aestheticism and Commodity Culture* (Stanford, CA: Stanford University Press, 1993)

Fulton Committee, *The Civil Service: Volume I: Report of the Committee 1966–69* (London: Her Majesty's Stationery Office, 1969)

Galbraith, Gretchen R., *Reading Lives: Reconstructing Childhood, Books, and Schools in Britain, 1870–1920* (Basingstoke: Macmillan, 1997)

Galton, Francis, *Anthropometric Laboratory: Notes and Memoirs* (London: Richard Clay & Sons, 1890)

—. *English Men of Science: Their Nature and Nurture* (London: Palgrave Macmillan, 1874)

—. *The Eugenic College of Kantsaywhere*, University College London digital edition, <https://www.ucl.ac.uk/library/special-collections/kantsaywhere> (last accessed 21 March 2022).

—. *Hereditary Genius: An Inquiry into Its Laws and Consequences*. 2nd edition (London: Macmillan, [1869] 1892)

—. 'Hereditary Talent and Character', *Macmillan's Magazine* 12 (1865), 157–327

—. *Inquiries into Human Faculty and its Development* (London: Macmillan, 1883)

—. *Memories of My Life* (London: Methuen, 1908)

Gannon, Christine, 'Walter Besant's Democratic Bildungsroman', *Narrative* 22 (2014), 372–94

Garber, Marjorie, *Hardy's Fables of Integrity: Woman, Body, Text* (Oxford: Oxford University Press, 1991)

Gardner, Howard, *Frames of Mind: The Theory of Multiple Intelligences, Twentieth-Anniversary Edition* (New York: Basic Books, 2004)

Garratt, Peter, *Victorian Empiricism: Self, Knowledge, and Reality in Ruskin, Bain, Lewes, Spencer, and George Eliot* (Cranbury: Farleigh Dickinson University Press, 2010)

Garrett Izzo, David, 'A Pair of Afterwords', in *Henry James Against the Aesthetic Movement: Essays on the Middle and Late Fiction,* ed. Garrett Izzo and David T. O'Hara (Jefferson, North Carolina: McFarland, 2006), 229–38

Gigante, Denise, *Life: Organic Form and Romanticism* (New Haven, CT: Yale University Press, 2009)

Gilham, Nicholas Wright, *A Life of Sir Francis Galton: From African Exploration to the Birth of Eugenics* (Oxford: Oxford University Press, 2001)

Gilman, Sander L., *Smart Jews: The Construction of the Image of Jewish Superior Intelligence* (Lincoln: University of Nebraska Press, 1997)

Gökyiğit, Emel Aileen, 'The Reception of Francis Galton's *Hereditary Genius* in the late Victorian Periodical Press', *Journal of the History of Biology* 27 (1994), 215–40

Goleman, Daniel, *Emotional Intelligence: Why It Can Matter More Than IQ* (London: Bloomsbury, 1996)

Goodman, Lesley, 'Rebellious Identification, or, How I Learned to Stop Worrying and Love Arabella', *Narrative* 18.2 (2010), 163–77

Gosse, Edmund, 'Mr. Hardy's New Novel', *Cosmopolis* (1896), 60–9

Gould, Stephen Jay, *The Mismeasure of Man, Revised and Expanded Edition* (New York: W. W. Norton & Company, 2006)

Graver, Suzanne, *George Eliot and Community: A Study in Social Theory and Fictional Form* (Berkeley: University of California Press, 1984)

Greenslade, William, *Degeneration, Culture, and the Novel* (Oxford: Oxford University Press, 1994)

Hacking, Ian, *The Taming of Chance* (Cambridge: Cambridge University Press, 1995)

Hadjiafxendi, Kyriaki, 'Gender and the Woman Question', in *George Eliot in Context*, ed. Margaret Harris (Cambridge:Cambridge University Press, 2013), 137–44

Haralson, Eric, *Henry James and Queer Modernity* (Cambridge: Cambridge University Press, 2003)

Hardy, Thomas, 'Destiny and a Blue Cloak', in *An Indiscretion in the Life of an Heiress and Other Stories*, ed. Pamela Dalziel, Oxford World's Classics (Oxford: Oxford University Press, 1999), 11–35

—. *Jude the Obscure*, ed. Dennis Taylor (Oxford: Oxford University Press, 1998)

—. *A Pair of Blue Eyes*, ed. Alan Manford (Oxford: Oxford University Press, 1985)

—. *Tess of the d'Urbervilles*, ed. John Paul Riquelme (Boston: Bedford St. Martin's, 1998)

—. *The Woodlanders*, ed. Dale Kramer (Oxford: Oxford University Press, 1981)

Hayles, Katherine N., *How We Became Posthuman: Virtual Bodies in Cybernetics, Literature and Informatics* (Chicago: University of Chicago Press, 1999)

Hayward, F. H., *Education and the Spectre of Heredity* (London: Watts & Company, 1908)

Heaney, John, 'Arthur Schopenhauer, Evolution, and Ecology in Thomas Hardy's *The Woodlanders*', *Nineteenth Century Literature* 71.4 (2017), 516–45

Hegel, G. W. F., *Phenomenology of Spirit*, trans. A. V. Miller (Oxford: Oxford University Press, 1977)

Higgins, Richard, 'Feeling Like a Clerk', *Victorian Studies* 50.3 (2008), 457–75

House of Commons, *Clause 1 – Definition of Defectives*, vol. 56, Monday, 28 July 1913, <https://hansard.parliament.uk/commons/1913-07-28/debates/0e227576-1e34-4f79-be15-36b20d250265/Clause1—(DefinitionOfDefectives)> (last accessed 30 November 2021)

—. *Feeble-Minded Persons (Control) Bill* (17 May 1912, vol. 38 cc1443–519), <https://api.parliament.uk/historic-hansard/commons/1912/may/17/feeble-minded-persons control-bill> (last accessed 30 November 2021)

—. *Hansard's Parliamentary Debates: The Government of India Bill* (24 June 1853, vol. 128 cc734–78), <https://api.parliament.uk/historic-hansard/commons/1853/jun/24/government-of-india-bill-adjourned> (last accessed 11 November 2021)

—. *The Mental Deficiency Bill*, vol. 41, Friday, 19 July 1912, <https://hansard.parliament.uk/commons/1912-07-19/debates/7d188a6f-ca8a-4d9f-815c-8fdebde5a9a9/MentalDeficiencyBill> (last accessed 29 November 2021)

Howell, Charles, 'Education as Positional Good Reconsidered', *Journal of the Philosophical Study of Education* 1 (2011), 19–36

Humes, Walter H., 'Alexander Bain and the Development of Educational Theory', in *The Meritocratic Intellect: Studies in the History of Educational Research*, ed. James V. Smith and David Hamilton (Aberdeen: Aberdeen University Press, 1980), 15–25

Hunter, Ian S., *Rethinking the School: Subjectivity, Bureaucracy, Criticism* (Sydney: Allen and Unwin, 1994)

Huxley, T. H., 'On the Natural Inequality of Men', *The Nineteenth Century* 27 (1890), 1–23

Imre, Merve, 'The Politics of Feeling', *New Yorker* (19 April 2021), 64–8

Ingham, Patricia, *The Language of Gender and Class: Transformation in the Victorian Novel* (London: Routledge, 1996)

Irwin, Jane, *George Eliot's Daniel Deronda Notebooks* (Cambridge: Cambridge University Press, 1996)

Jackson, Mark, *The Borderland of Imbecility: Medicine, Society, and the Fabrication of the Feeble Mind in Late Victorian and Edwardian England* (Manchester: Manchester University Press, 2000)

Jacobs, Joseph, 'The Comparative Distribution of Jewish Ability', *Journal of the Anthropological Institute of Great Britain and Ireland* 15 (1886), 351–79

—. 'Experiments on "Prehension"', *Mind* 45.1 (1887), 75–19

Jacobus, Mary, 'Tree and Machine: *The Woodlanders*', in *Critical Approaches to the Fiction of Thomas Hardy*, ed. Dale Kramer (Basingstoke: Palgrave Macmillan, 1979), 116–34

James, Henry, *Autobiography: A Small Boy and Others, Notes of a Son and Brother, and The Middle Years*, ed. Frederick W. Dupee (London: W. H. Allen, 1956)

—. *Roderick Hudson* (Oxford: Oxford University Press, 1980)

—. *The Spoils of Poynton* (London: Penguin, 1963)

—. *The Tragic Muse*, ed. Philip Horne (London: Penguin, 1995)

James, Simon, *Maps of Utopia: HG Wells, Modernity and the End of Culture* (Oxford: Oxford University Press, 2012)

James, William, 'Great Men, Great Thoughts, and the Environment', *Atlantic Monthly* 46 (1880), 441–59

Jann, Rosemary, 'Fabian Socialism and the Rhetoric of Gentility', *Victorian Literature and Culture* 41.4 (2013), 727–42

Kearns, Michael S., *Metaphors of Mind in Fiction and Psychology* (University of Kentucky Press, 1987)

Keen, Suzanne, *Thomas Hardy's Brains: Psychology, Neurology, and Hardy's Imagination* (Athens: University of Ohio Press, 2014)

Kevles, Daniel J., *In the Name of Eugenics: Genetics and the Uses of Human Heredity* (Berkeley: University of California Press, 1985)

Ketabgian, Tamara, *Lives of Machines: The Industrial Imaginary in Victorian Literature and Culture* (Ann Arbor: University of Michigan Press, 2011)

Kidd, Benjamin, *Social Evolution* (London: Macmillan, 1894)

Knight, Frances, *The Nineteenth-Century Church and English Society* (Cambridge: Cambridge University Press, 1995)

Koditschek, Theodore, *Class Formation and Urban Industrial Society: Bradford, 1750–1850* (Cambridge: Cambridge University Press, 1990)

Kohlmann, Benjamin, '"The End of Laissez-Faire": Literature, Economics, and the Idea of the Welfare State', *Late Victorian into Modern*, ed.

Laura Marcus, Michèle Mendelssohn, and Kirsten E. Shepherd-Barr (Oxford: Oxford University Press, 2016), 448–62

Kornbluh, Anna, 'Obscure Forms: The Letter, the Law, and the Line in Hardy's Social Geometry', *Novel: A Forum on Fiction* 48.1 (2015), 1–17

Kramer, Dale, *Hardy: Tess of the d'Urbervilles* (Cambridge: Cambridge University Press, 1991)

Kurnick, David, 'Erotics of Detachment: "Middlemarch" and Novel-reading as Critical Practice', *ELH* 74.3 (2007), 583–608

La Vopa, Anthony, *The Labour of the Mind: Intellect and Gender in Enlightenment Cultures* (Philadelphia: University of Pennsylvania Press, 2017)

Lewes, George Henry, 'Hereditary Influence, Animal and Human', *Westminster Review* 66 (1856), 135–62

—. 'The Lady Novelists', *Westminster Review* 58 (1852), 129–41

—. 'Mr. Darwin's Hypothesis', *Fortnightly Review* no.16 (1868), 354–509

—. *Physiology of Common Life* (Edinburgh: William Blackwood & Sons, 1859)

—. *Problems of Life and Mind. First Series: The Foundations of a Creed*, vol. 1, 3rd edition (London: Trübner & Co., 1874)

—. *Problems of Life and Mind. Third Series. The Study of Psychology* (London: Trübner & Co., 1879)

—. *Problems of Life and Mind. Third Series, Part 2* (Boston: Houghton, Osgood & Co., 1880)

—. *Problems of Life and Mind. Third Series. Mind as a Function of the Organism* (Boston: Houghton, Osgood & Co., 1880)

Lilly, W. S., 'Darwinism and Democracy', *Fortnightly Review* (1886), 34–50

Littler, Jo, *Against Meritocracy: Culture, Power, and Myths of Mobility* (Abingdon: Routledge, 2018)

Lombroso, Cesare, *Man of Genius* (London: Walter Scott, 1891)

Lukács, Georg, *Theory of the Novel* (London: Merlin Press, 1971)

Lyons, Sara, 'Recent Work in Victorian Studies and the Bildungsroman', *Literature Compass* 15.4 (2018), <https://doi.org/10.1111/lic3.12460> (last accessed 25 March 2022)

—. 'Secularism and Secularisation at the Fin de Siècle', in *Edinburgh Companion to Fin de Siècle Literature, Culture, and the Arts*, ed. Josephine Guy (Edinburgh: Edinburgh University Press, 2018), 212–50

MacCabe, Frederick, 'On Mental Strain and Overwork', *Journal of Mental Science* 21 (October 1875), 388–403

McCarron, Robert M., 'Folly and Wisdom: Three Dickensian Wise Fools', *Dickens Studies Annual* 6 (1977), 40–56

McDonagh, Patrick, *Idiocy: A Cultural History* (Cambridge: Cambridge University Press, 2008)

McGurl, Mark, *The Novel Art: Elevations of American Fiction after Henry James* (Princeton, NJ: Princeton University Press, 2001)

MacKenzie, Norman, ed., *The Letters of Sidney and Beatrice Webb*. Vol. 2. *Partnership 1892–1912* (Cambridge: Cambridge University Press, 2008)

Mackintosh, N. J., ed. *Cyril Burt: Fraud or Framed?* (Oxford: Oxford University Press, 1995)

McLean, Steven, *The Early Fiction of HG Wells: Fantasies of Science Fiction* (Basingstoke: Palgrave Macmillan, 2009)

Malabou, Catherine, *Morphing Intelligence: From IQ Measurement to Artificial Brains*, trans. Carolyn Shread (New York: Columbia University Press, 2019)

Malane, Rachel, *Sex in Mind: The Gendered Brain in Nineteenth-century Literature and Mental Sciences* (Oxford: Peter Lang, 2005)

Mansfield, Katherine, review of *Night and Day*, in *Virginia Woolf: The Critical Heritage*, ed. Robin Majumdar and Allen McLaurin (London: Routledge and Kegan Paul, 1975), 79–82

Markovitz, Daniel, *The Meritocracy Trap* (London: Penguin Random House, 2019)

Marroni, Francesco, *Victorian Disharmonies: A Reconsideration of Nineteenth-century English Fiction* (Newark: University of Delaware Press, 2010)

Mattisson, Jane, *Knowledge and Survival in the Novels of Thomas Hardy* (Lund: Lund University Press, 2002)

Matus, Jill, *Shock, Memory, and the Unconscious in Victorian Fiction* (Cambridge: Cambridge University Press, 2009)

Matz, Aaron, 'Hardy and the Vanity of Procreation', *Victorian Studies* 57.1 (2014), 7–29

Matz, Jesse, *Literary Impressionism and Modernist Aesthetics* (Cambridge: Cambridge University Press, 2004)

Maudsley, Henry, *Body and Mind* (New York: D. Appleton & Co., 1871)

Mazumdar, Pauline, *Eugenics, Human Genetics, and Human Failings: The Eugenics Society, Its Sources and Its Critics in Britain* (London: Routledge, 1991)

Meloni, Maurizio, *Political Biology: Science and Social Values in*

Human Heredity from Eugenics to Epigenetics (Basingstoke: Palgrave Macmillan, 2016)

Memel, Jonathan, '"Making the University Less Exclusive": The Legacy of *Jude the Obscure*', *Neo-Victorian Studies* 10.1 (2017), 64–82

Merivale, Herman, 'Galton on Hereditary Genius', *Edinburgh Review* 132 (1870), 100–25

Miles, Andrew, *Social Mobility in Nineteenth- and Early Twentieth-century England* (Basingstoke: Macmillan, 1999)

Mill, John Stuart, *On Liberty and Other Essays*, ed. John Gray (Oxford: Oxford University Press, 1991)

—. *Three Essays on Religion* (New York: Henry Holt, 1874)

Miller, J. Hillis, *Literature as Conduct: Speech Acts in Henry James* (New York: Fordham University Press, 2005)

Moretti, Franco, *The Way of the World: The Bildungsroman in European Culture* (London: Verso, 1987)

Morton, Peter, *The Vital Science: Biology and the Literary Imagination 1860–1900* (London: George Allen & Unwin, 1984)

Murray, Penelope, *Genius: The History of an Idea* (Oxford: Basil Blackwell, 1989)

Neve, Michael and Turner, Trevor, 'What the Doctor Thought and Did: Sir James Crichton-Browne (1840–1938), *Medical History* 39 (1995), 399–432

Newman, Daniel Aureliano, *Modernist Life Histories: Biological Theory and the Experimental Bildungsroman* (Edinburgh: Edinburgh University Press, 2019)

Newton, K. M., *George Eliot for the Twenty-First Century: Literature, Philosophy, Politics* (Basingstoke: Palgrave Macmillan, 2018)

—. *Modern Literature and the Tragic* (Edinburgh: Edinburgh University Press, 2008)

Nisbet, J. F., *The Insanity of Genius and the General Inequality of Human Faculty: Physiologically Considered*, 2nd edition (London: Ward & Downey, 1891)

Nussbaum, Martha, *Upheavals of Thought: the Intelligence of the Emotions* (Cambridge: Cambridge University Press, 2001)

Orel, Harold, ed., *Thomas Hardy's Personal Writings* (London: Macmillan, 1967)

Outka, Elizabeth, 'The Transitory Space of Night and Day', in *A Companion to Virginia Woolf*, ed. Jessica Berman (Oxford: Wiley Blackwell, 2019), 55–66

Parrinder, Patrick, ed., *HG Wells: The Critical Heritage* (London: Routledge, 1972)

Partington, John, 'The Death of the Static: HG Wells and the Kinetic Utopia', *Utopian Studies* 11.2 (2000), 96–111

Pater, Walter, *Appreciations* (London: Macmillan, 1889)

—. *Studies in the History of the Renaissance*, ed. Matthew Beaumont (Oxford: Oxford University Press, 2010)

Paton, J. L., 'The Secondary Education of the Working Classes', in *The Higher Education of Boys in England*, ed. C. Norwood and A. H. Hope (London: John Murray, 1909), 544–54

Pauk, Barbara, 'Evolution of Woman: George Eliot's Woman in France: Madame de Sablé', *Cahiers Victoriens & Edouardiens* 73 (2011), 37–50

Paul, Diane and Day, Benjamin, 'John Stuart Mill, Innate Differences, and the Regulation of Reproduction', *Studies in History and Philosophy of Biological and Biomedical Sciences* 39 (2008), 222–31

Paxton, Nancy, *George Eliot and Herbert Spencer: Feminism, Evolutionism, and the Reconstruction of Gender* (Princeton, NJ: Princeton University Press, 1991)

Pearson, Karl, *The Life, Letters and Labours of Francis Galton* (Cambridge: Cambridge University Press, 2011)

—. 'On the Inheritance of the Mental and Moral Characters in Man, and its Comparison with the Inheritance of Physical Characters', *Journal of the Anthropological Institute of Great Britain and Ireland* 33 (July–December 1903), 179–237

—. 'Socialism and Natural Selection'. *Fortnightly Review* 56 (1894), 1–21

Pecora, Vincent, *Secularisation and Cultural Criticism: Religion, Nation & Modernity* (Chicago: Chicago University Press, 2006)

Perkin, Harold, *The Rise of Professional Society: England Since 1880* (London: Routledge, 1989)

Philpott, Hugh B., 'The Educational Ladder', *The English Illustrated Magazine* (February 1904), 513–22

Plett, Heinrich F., *Rhetoric and Renaissance Culture* (Berlin: Walter de Gruyter, 2004)

Prewitt-Browne, Julia, 'The Moral Scope of the English *bildungsroman*', in *Oxford Handbook of the Victorian Novel*, ed. Lisa Rodensky (Oxford: Oxford University Press, 2013), 664–77

Privateer, Michael Paul, *Inventing Intelligence: A Social History of Smart* (Oxford: Blackwell, 2006)

Rancière, Jacques, *Aesthetics and its Discontents,* trans. Stephen Corcoran (Cambridge: Polity Press, 2009)

—. *Chronicles of Consensual Times*, trans. Stephen Corcoran (London: Continuum, 2010)

—. *Dissensus: On Politics and Aesthetics*, trans. Stephen Corcoran (London: Bloomsbury, 2015)

—. *The Flesh of Words: The Politics of Writing*, trans. Charlotte Mandell (Stanford University Press, 2004)

—. *The Ignorant Schoolmaster: Five Lessons in Intellectual Emancipation*, trans. Kristin Ross. (Stanford, CA: Stanford University Press, 1991)

—. *The Lost Thread: The Democracy of Modern Fiction*, trans. Steven Corcoran (London: Bloomsbury, 2017)

—. *Mute Speech: Literature, Critical Theory, and Politics*, trans. James Swenson (Columbia: New York University Press, 1998)

—. *The Politics of Literature*, trans. Julie Rose (Cambridge: Polity Press, 2011)

Reed, Edward S., *From Soul to Mind: the Emergence of Psychology from Erasmus Darwin to William James* (New Haven, CT: Yale University Press, 1997)

Reid, Fred, *Thomas Hardy and History* (Basingstoke: Palgrave Macmillan, 2017)

Richards, Robert J., *Darwin and the Emergence of Evolutionary Theories of Mind and Behaviour* (Chicago: Chicago University Press, 1987)

Richardson, Angelique, 'Darwin and Reductionisms: Victorian, Neo-Darwinian and Postgenomic Biologies', *19: Interdisciplinary Studies in the Long Nineteenth Century* 11 (2010), <https://doi.org/10.16995/ntn.583> (last accessed 24 November 2021)

—. 'George Eliot, G. H. Lewes, and Darwin: Animals, Emotions, and Morals', in *After Darwin: Animals, Emotions and the Mind*, ed. Richardson (Amsterdam: Rodopi, 2013), 136–71

—. 'Hardy and Biology', in *Thomas Hardy: Texts and Contexts*, ed. Philip Mallet (Basingstoke: Palgrave Macmillan, 2002), 156–79

—. 'Heredity', in *Thomas Hardy in Context*, ed. Philip Mallet (Cambridge: Cambridge University Press, 2013), 328–38

—. *Love and Eugenics in the Late Nineteenth Century: Rational Reproduction and the New Woman* (Oxford: Oxford University Press, 2003)

Ritchie D. G, 'Equality', *Contemporary Review* 62 (1892), 563–8

Roach, John, *Public Examinations in England 1850–1900* (Cambridge: Cambridge University Press, 1971)

Roberts, Adam, *HG Wells: A Literary Life* (Basingstoke: Palgrave Macmillan, 2019)

Romano, Serena, *Moralising Poverty: The 'Undeserving' Poor in the Public Gaze* (London: Routledge, 2017)

Ronnell, Avital, *Stupidity* (Urbana and Chicago: University of Illinois Press, 2002)

Rose, Nikolas, *Inventing our Selves: Psychology, Power and Personhood* (Cambridge: Cambridge University Press, 1998)

Rothblatt, Sheldon, *Education's Abiding Moral Dilemma: Merit and Worth in the Cross-Atlantic Democracies* (Oxford: Symposium Books, 2006)

Rowe, John Carlos, *The Other Henry James* (Durham, NC: Duke University Press, 1998)

Russett, Cynthia Eagle, *Sexual Science: The Victorian Constitution of Womanhood* (Cambridge, MA: Harvard University Press, 1989)

Ruth, Jennifer, *Novel Professions: Interested Disinterest and the Making of the Professional in the Victorian Novel* (Columbus: Ohio State University Press, 2006)

Rylance, Rick, *Victorian Psychology and British Culture 1850–1880* (Oxford: Oxford University Press, 2000)

Sabiston, Elizabeth, *Private Sphere to World Stage from Austen to Eliot* (London: Routledge, 2008)

Salamensky, Shelley, 'Henry James, Oscar Wilde, and "*Fin de Siècle* Talk": A Brief Reading', *Henry James Review* 20 (1999), 275–81

Salmon, Richard, 'Aestheticism in Translation: Henry James, Walter Pater, and Theodor Adorno', *Translating Life: Studies in Transpositional Aesthetics*, ed. Shirley Chew and Alistair Stead (Liverpool: Liverpool University Press, 1999), 277–98

Sandel, Michael J., *The Tyranny of Merit: What's Become of the Common Good?* (New York: Farrar, Straus and Giroux, 2020)

Searle, Geoffrey, *Eugenics and Politics in Britain 1900–1914* (Leyden: Noordhoff International Publishing, 1976)

—. *The Quest for National Efficiency: A Study in British Politics and Political Thought, 1889–1914* (London: The Ashfield Press, 1971)

Sedgwick, Eve Kosofsky, and Miller, Andrew, eds, 'Introduction', in *Performativity and Performance* (London: Routledge, 1995), 35–66

—. *Touching Feeling: Affect, Pedagogy, Performativity* (Durham, NC: Duke University Press, 2002)

Semmel, Bernard, *George Eliot and the Politics of National Inheritance* (Oxford: Oxford University Press, 1994)

Shih, Margaret, Pittinsky, Todd L., and Ambady, Nalini, 'Stereotype Susceptibility: Identity Salience and Shifts in Quantitative Performance', *Psychological Science* 10.1 (1999), 80–3

Shuman, Cathy, *Pedagogical Economies: The Examination and the*

Victorian Literary Man (Stanford, CA: Stanford University of Press, 2000)

Shuttleworth, Sally, *Charlotte Brontë and Victorian Psychology* (Cambridge: Cambridge University Press, 1996)

—. *George Eliot and Nineteenth-century Science: The Make-Believe of a Beginning* (Cambridge: Cambridge University Press, 1984)

—. *The Mind of the Child: Child Development in Literature, Science, and Medicine 1840–1900* (Oxford: Oxford University Press, 2013)

Silverman, Kaja, 'History, Figuration, and Female Subjectivity in *Tess of the d'Urbervilles*', *Novel: A Forum on Fiction* 18.1 (1984), 5–28

Skrupskelis, Ignas K. and Berkeley, Elizabeth B., eds, *William and Henry James: Selected Letters* (Charlottesville: University Press of Virginia, 1997)

Small, Helen, 'Artificial Intelligence: George Eliot, Ernst Kapp, and the Projections of Character', *19 Interdisciplinary Studies in the Long Nineteenth Century* 29 (2020), <https://19.bbk.ac.uk/article/id/1993/> (last accessed 24 November 2021)

Smiles, Samuel, *Self-Help with Illustrations of Character and Conduct* (London: John Murray, 1859).

Spearman, Charles, *The Abilities of Man: Their Nature and Measurement* (London: Macmillan, 1927)

—. 'General Intelligence: Objectively Determined and Measured', 15.2 (1904), 201–92

Spencer, Herbert, *An Autobiography*, vol 2. (London: Williams and Norgate, 1904)

—. *Education: Intellectual, Moral, and Physical* (New York: D. Appleton & Co., 1896)

—. *Essays: Scientific, Political, and Speculative*, vol. 1 (London: Williams and Norgate, 1868)

—. *First Principles* (London: Williams and Northgate, 1863)

—. *A New Theory of Population, Deduced from the General Law of Animal Fertility* (London: John Chapman, 1852)

—. *The Principles of Psychology* (London: Longmans, 1855)

—. *The Principles of Psychology*, vol. 2 (New York: D. Appleton & Co., 1873)

—. *Social Statics, or the Conditions Essential to Human Happiness Specified* (London: John Chapman, 1851)

—. *The Study of Sociology* (New York: D. Appleton & Co.), 1874

Steele, C. M. and Aronson, J., 'Stereotype Threat and the Intellectual Test Performance of African Americans', *Journal of Personality and Social Psychology* 69 (1995), 797–811

Steinlight, Emily, 'Hardy's Unnecessary Lives: The Novel as Surplus', *Novel: A Forum on Fiction* 47.2 (2014), 224–41

—. *Populating the Novel: Literary Form and the Politics of Surplus Life* (Ithaca, NY: Cornell University Press, 2018)

Stiles, Anne, *Popular Fiction and Brain Science in the Late Nineteenth Century* (Cambridge: Cambridge University Press, 2011)

Sumpter, Caroline, 'On Suffering and Sympathy: *Jude the Obscure*, Evolution and Ethics', *Victorian Studies* 53.4 (2011), 665–87

Sussman, Matthew, 'Henry James and Stupidity', *Novel* 48 (2015), 45–62

Sutherland, Gillian, *Ability, Merit, and Measurement: Mental Testing and English Education 1880–1940* (Oxford: Clarendon Press, 1984)

—. 'Measuring Intelligence: English Local Education Authorities and Mental Testing, 1919–1939', *The Meritocratic Intellect: Studies in the History of Educational Research*, ed. James V. Smith and David Hamilton (Aberdeen: Aberdeen University Press, 1980), 79–95

Sysling, Fenneke, 'Phrenology and the Average Person 1840–1940', *History of the Human Sciences* 34.2 (2021), 27–45

Szreter, Simon, *Fertility, Class, and Gender in Britain, 1860–1940* (Cambridge: Cambridge University Press, 1996)

Taunton, Matthew, 'Chorus and Agon in the Political Novel: Staging Left-wing Arguments in H.G. Wells, Iris Murdoch, and Doris Lessing', *Modern Fiction Studies* 67.2 (2021), 248–54

Taunton Report: Report of the Schools Inquiry Commission (London: George E. Eyre and William Spottiswoode, 1868)

Teale, Pridgin T., 'Address on Health', *Transactions of the National Association for the Promotion of Social Science* (London: Longmans, Green, & Co., 1884)

Thomson, Matthew, 'Disability, Psychiatry and Eugenics', in *The Oxford Handbook of the History of Eugenics*, ed. Alison Bashford and Philippa Levine (Oxford: Oxford University Press, 2010), 116–33

Travers, Tim, *Samuel Smiles and the Victorian Work Ethic* (London: Routledge, 2017)

Treagus, Mandy, *Empire Girls: The Colonial Heroine Comes of Age* (Adelaide: University of Adelaide Press, 2014)

Trotter, David, *Paranoid Modernism: Literary Experiment, Psychosis and the Professionalisation of English Society* (Oxford: Oxford University Press, 2001)

Valente, Joseph, 'The Accidental Autist: Neurosensory Disorder in Conrad's *The Secret Agent*', *Journal of Modern Literature* 38.1 (2014), 20–37

—. 'Modernism and Cognitive Disability: A Genealogy', in *A Handbook of Modernism Studies*, ed. Jean-Michel Rabaté (Oxford: John Wiley & Sons, 2013), 379–98

Van Whye, John, *Phrenology and the Origins of Victorian Scientific Naturalism* (London: Routledge, 2004)

Vargish, Thomas, *The Providential Aesthetic in Victorian Fiction* (Charlottesville: University Press of Virginia, 1985)

Venn, John, 'Cambridge Anthropometry', *Journal of the Anthropological Institute* 18 (1889), 140–54

Vrettos, Athena, 'Victorian Psychology', in *A Companion to the Victorian Novel*, ed. Patrick Brantlinger and William B. Thesing (Oxford: Blackwell, 2005), 68–74

Wakana, Maya Higashi, *Performing the Everyday in Henry James's Late Novels* (Farnham: Ashgate, 2013)

Walker-Gore, Clare, *Plotting Disability in the Nineteenth-century Novel* (Edinburgh: Edinburgh University Press, 2019)

Wallace, Alfred Russel, 'Hereditary Genius', *Nature* 1 (March 1870), 501–3

Warner, Francis, 'Mental and Physical Conditions among Fifty Thousand Children seen 1892–94 and the Methods of Studying Recorded Observations, with Special Reference to the Determination of the Causes of Mental Dullness and other Defects', *Journal of the Royal Statistical Society* 59.1 (1896), 71–100

—. *Report on the Physical and Mental Condition of 50,000 Children Seen in 106 Schools in London* (London: Committee on the Mental and Physical Condition of Children, 1891)

Warwick, Frances, 'The Cause of the Children', *Nineteenth-Century and After* 50.293 (1901), 67–76

Weale, Sally, '"An Education Arms Race": Inside the Ultra-competitive World of Private Tutoring', *The Guardian* (5 December 2018), <https://www.theguardian.com/education/2018/dec/05/an-education-arms-race-inside-the-ultra-competitive-world-of-private-tutoring> (last accessed 12 November 2021)

Weber, Max, *The Protestant Work Ethic and the Spirit of Capitalism*, trans. Talcott Parsons (Oxford: Taylor and Francis, 2001)

Weir, David, *Decadence and the Making of Modernism* (Amherst: University of Massachusetts Press, 1995)

Wells, H. G. *Anticipations of the Reaction of Mechanical and Scientific Progress upon Human Life and Thought* (London: Chapman & Hill, 1901)

—. *An Experiment in Autobiography: Discoveries and Conclusions of a*

Very Ordinary Brain (Since 1866), 2 vols. (London: Faber & Faber, 1984)

—. *The First Men in the Moon* (London: George Newnes, 1901)

—. *H. G. Wells in Love: Postscript to an Experiment in Autobiography* (London: Faber & Faber, 1984)

—. *The History of Mr. Polly* (Penguin: London, 1946)

—. *Kipps: The Story of a Simple Soul*, ed. Simon James (London: Penguin, 2005)

—. *Love and Mr. Lewisham*, ed. Gillian Beer (Penguin: London, 2005)

—. *Mankind in the Making*, 4th edition (London: Chapman & Hall, 1904)

—. *A Modern Utopia*, ed. Gregory Claeys and Patrick Parrinder (London: Penguin, 2005)

—. 'A Slip under the Microscope', in *The Plattner Story and Others* (London: Methuen & Co., 1897), 274–301

West, Anna, *Thomas Hardy and Animals* (Cambridge: Cambridge University Press, 2017)

White, John, *The Child's Mind* (Abingdon: Taylor & Francis, 2002)

—. *Intelligence, Destiny and Education: The Ideological Roots of Intelligence Testing* (London: Routledge, 2006)

White, Paul, 'Acquired Character: The Hereditary Material of the Self-Made Man', in *Heredity Produced: At the Crossroads of Biology, Politics, and Culture 1500–1870*, ed. Staffan Müller-Wille and Hans-Jörg Rheinberger (Cambridge, MA: MIT Press, 2007), 375–98

Wilson, Andrew, 'The Old Phrenology and the New', *The Gentleman's Magazine* 244 (1879), 68–85

Wolf, Lucien, 'What is Judaism?: A Question of Today', *Fortnightly Review* (1884), 237–56

Woloch, Alex, *The One Versus the Many: Minor Characters and the Space of the Protagonist in the Novel* (Princeton, NJ: Princeton University Press, 2003)

Wooldridge, Adrian, *The Aristocracy of Talent: How Meritocracy Made the Modern World* (London: Allen Lane, 2021)

—. *Measuring the Mind: Education and Psychology in England c.1860–1990* (Cambridge: Cambridge University Press, 2006)

Woolf, Virginia, *Night and Day* (Ware: Wordsworth Editions, 2012)

Young, Michael, *The Rise of the Meritocracy* (Abingdon: Routledge, 1958)

Young, Robert M., *Mind, Brain, and Adaptation: Cerebral Localisation and its Biological Context from Gall to Ferrier* (Oxford: Oxford University Press, 1990)

Zenderland, Leila, *Measuring Minds: Henry Herbert Goddard and the Origins of American Intelligence Testing* (Cambridge: Cambridge University Press, 2001)

Index